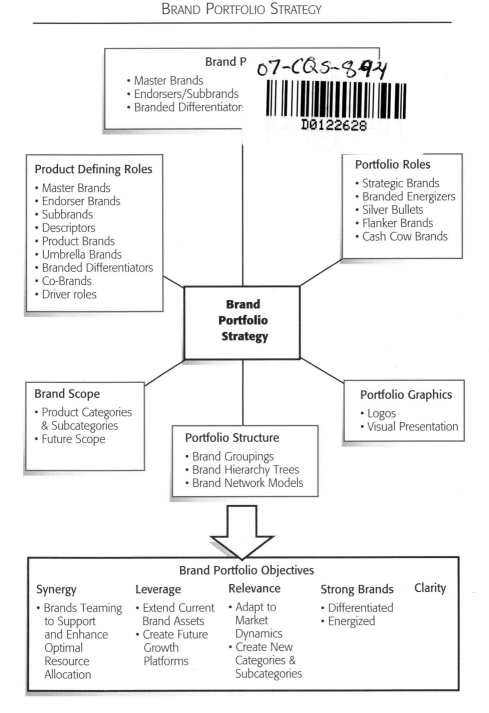

Brand P
- Master Brands
- Endorsers/Subbrands
- Branded Differentiator

Product Defining Roles
- Master Brands
- Endorser Brands
- Subbrands
- Descriptors
- Product Brands
- Umbrella Brands
- Branded Differentiators
- Co-Brands
- Driver roles

Portfolio Roles
- Strategic Brands
- Branded Energizers
- Silver Bullets
- Flanker Brands
- Cash Cow Brands

Brand Portfolio Strategy

Brand Scope
- Product Categories & Subcategories
- Future Scope

Portfolio Structure
- Brand Groupings
- Brand Hierarchy Trees
- Brand Network Models

Portfolio Graphics
- Logos
- Visual Presentation

Brand Portfolio Objectives

Synergy	Leverage	Relevance	Strong Brands	Clarity
• Brands Teaming to Support and Enhance Optimal Resource Allocation	• Extend Current Brand Assets • Create Future Growth Platforms	• Adapt to Market Dynamics • Create New Categories & Subcategories	• Differentiated • Energized	

*f*P

BRAND PORTFOLIO STRATEGY

Creating Relevance, Differentiation, Energy, Leverage, and Clarity

---

DAVID A. AAKER

Free Press

New York   London   Toronto   Sydney

FREE PRESS
A Division of Simon & Schuster, Inc.
1230 Avenue of the Americas
New York, NY 10020

For information about special discounts for bulk purchases,
please contact Simon & Schuster Special Sales:
1-800-456-6798 or business@simonandschuster.com

Designed by Karolina Harris

Manufactured in the United States of America

10   9   8   7   6   5   4   3   2   1

Library of Congress Cataloging-in-Publication Data

Aaker, David A.
    Brand portfolio strategy : creating relevance, differentiation, energy,
leverage, and clarity / David A. Aaker.
        p. cm.
    Includes bibliographical references and index.
    1. Brand name products—Planning.   2. Brand name products—Marketing.
    3. Brand name products—Management.   4. Brand name products—Valuation—
Management.   I. Title.

HD69.B7.A2154   2004
658.8'27—dc22   2003063055

ISBN 0-7432-4938-0

*To Tom DeJonghe, a real friend who enhances my life
with his remarkable ability to be stimulating,
adventurous, enthusiastic, humorous, and fun.*

Contents

Always design a thing by considering it in its next larger context—a chair in a room, a room in a house, a house in an environment, an environment in a city plan.

—FRANK LLOYD WRIGHT

PREFACE

Firms are motivated to be concerned with brand portfolio strategy because it provides the structure and discipline needed to have a successful business strategy. A brand portfolio strategy that is confused and incoherent can handicap and sometimes doom a business strategy. One that fosters organizational and market synergies, creates relevant, differentiated and energized brand assets, and leverages those brand assets, on the other hand, will support and enable business strategies.

The need to review brand portfolio strategy tends to become acute when the business becomes stressed because of scenarios such as the following:

- A business needs growth to achieve organizational vitality and to realize the objectives of investors. Most growth directions involve either leveraging an existing brand asset and/or creating new brand assets. In either, tools and methods need to be employed to develop and support the strategy.

- A business needs to stay relevant in a dynamic market. Subbrands and endorsed brands can help reduce the risk and difficulty of pursuing a new direction.

- A business is drifting toward being (or has basically become) a commodity, with very few points of differentiation and an emphasis on price. The challenge is to create a brand or brands that can drive differentiation and fit that brand or brands into the brand team.

- A brand has lost energy, perhaps because it is in a mature category. There is a need for a branded program, product, sponsorship, or something to create interest and energy.

- An acquisition or the emergence of several strong brands forces a firm to make tough choices to avoid confusion and waste.

- A firm's long-standing pride in being decentralized and entrepreneurial has led to a proliferation of brands and subbrands and, as a result, total confusion. Customers and employees alike become frustrated trying to determine not only what the firm stands for in the various product-market settings, but even how to order a product or service. Serious pruning, restructuring, and prioritizing are needed.

• Brand management simply cannot cope with the complexities of the marketplace with the reality of multiple products, segments, geographies, and distribution channels. In one sense, brand portfolio strategy is part of the problem, because the explosion of brands, subbrands, and endorsed brands in organizations spanning a variety of product-markets has inhibited the ability of firms to articulate coherent strategies, much less implement them. It is also part of the solution, though, because a reasoned, articulated brand structure can support a business strategy by replacing waste with synergy, confusion with clarity, and missed opportunities with leveraged assets.

This book will be the first to explicitly define the scope and structure of brand portfolio strategy. It will identify underlying concepts and tools and structure them into meaningful and related groupings. It will also illustrate how brand portfolio strategy can solve very relevant problems facing business strategists, including the following:

- How to grow by expanding the product-market scope through brand extensions.
- How to participate in value and premium niches with vertical brand extensions.
- How to keep your brand relevant while facing a dynamic market where "what is being purchased" is changing.
- How to energize and differentiate your brand using brand portfolio tools.
- How to make brand alliances work.
- How to leverage the corporate brand.
- How to manage the brand issues surrounding corporate restructuring.
- How to improve the clarity of the offerings and provide focus to the brand-building activities.

Developing brand portfolio strategy is complex and situation specific. There are no cookbook-style rules that are guaranteed to produce perfect strategies. The purpose of this book is to introduce options and issues, rather than easy answers.

This is my fourth book on brands and brand strategy. The initial book, *Managing Brand Equity*, was the first effort to define and structure the concept of brand equity. The second book, *Building Strong Brands*, introduced brand identity, the brand's aspirational associations, and encouraged managers to look beyond product attributes to brand personality, organizational associations, and brand symbols. The third book, *Brand Leadership* (written with Erich Joachimsthaler), extended the brand identity concept, discussed global brand management, and showed how to break out of media clutter by developing brand-building programs that extend beyond media advertising.

This book draws on the material relevant to brand portfolio strategy from the other three books. Most notably, Chapters 1 and 2 draw from *Brand Leadership*, and Chapters 7 and 8 draw from *Building Strong Brands* and *Managing Brand Equity*—but even these four chapters are updated with added case studies, new concepts, and new or extended conceptual models. Providing an integrated treatment of brand portfolio strategy has been a major reason for me to write this book. The remaining chapters contain largely new material; in total, there is about a 20 percent overlap with the other three books.

As both a confession and apology, I should note that the topic label has changed. In *Building Strong Brands*, I wrote of "brand systems" to emphasize that the portfolio brands must work together to form a coherent whole. However, systems seemed to become an overused engineering term. In *Brand Leadership*, we changed to "brand architecture," a nice metaphor that suggested foundations, structures, roles, relationships, and even the concept of upgrading and refurbishing. Brand architecture was an opaque concept for some, though, and for others suggested the more limited problem of naming brands and developing logos. Thus, in this book a new label, *brand portfolio strategy*, is used. It is more holistic, strategic, and compatible with the book's thrust—how to optimize and leverage a brand portfolio to enhance and enable business strategy.

The book includes ten chapters and an epilogue. Chapters 1 and 2 provide a description of the scope of brand portfolio strategy. Chapter 3 examines some inputs that will identify options and issues facing a brand portfolio. How to stay relevant in increasingly dynamic markets is treated in Chapter 4. The tools of branded differentiators and branded energizers are presented for the first time in Chapter 5. Ways to harness the power of brand alliances are discussed in Chapter 6. Growing by leveraging brand assets horizontally and vertically is explored in Chapters 7 and 8. Chapter 9 discusses why and how to leverage the corporate brand. Avoiding complexity and confusion is presented in Chapter 10. The epilogue provides a set of 20 takeaways.

ACKNOWLEDGMENTS

I am in debt to a host of people. In particular, my colleague at Prophet, Valerie Wilson, was a huge help throughout. She managed the process of getting illustrative material, reviewed all the chapters, helped get others to assist us, and provided incredible support. Her greatest contribution, however, was to challenge ideas, organization, flow, concepts, cases—pretty much everything. Her insight was always productive and, on not a few occasions, resulted in some breakthrough changes.

The Prophet team was extremely helpful. Their consistently brilliant brand portfolio work for many dozens of clients over three continents was both inspirational and informative. Cindy Levine comprehensively reviewed the manuscript several times and provided great insight. She was never shy about pointing out weaknesses and pushed me again and again to rethink and rewrite. Kevin O'Donnell, with whom I have worked for four years and I know firsthand to be a world-class brand strategist, will see his ideas sprinkled throughout the book. I also received help and suggestions from many others, including Matt Reback, Claudia Fisher-Buttinger, Mike Leiser, Ben Machtiger, Jill Steele, Andy Flynn, Kristiane Blomqvest, Jenni Chang, and Trevor Wade. And I owe a final word of acknowledgment for Prophet CEO Michael Dunn—a friend, gifted brand strategist, and brilliant organization builder who provided encouragement and resources for this project.

I also benefited from interacting with several strategists from Japan. The team at Dentsu's Brand Creation Center have been wonderful, stimulating colleagues. They are making progress in elevating brand management in Japan and elsewhere in Asia. I owe a debt to the insight of Hotaka Katahira, Japan's brand guru, and Toshi Akutsu, the future brand guru of Japan, and the translator of *Brand Leadership*. Hiro Takeuchi, the dean of Hitotsubashi, has supported me in many ways through the years.

Several people from a variety of firms helped me with ideas and illustrative figures. Among that group was Susan Rockrise (a good friend and graphics expert), Rhonda Walker and Todd Peters from Intel, Paul Kein from GE, Matt Ryan from Disney, Tricia Higgins from P&G, Anne Mac-Donald from Citigroup, Joanne Cuthbertson from Schwab, Akio Asada from Sony, Fiona Rouch from Unilever, Lisa O'Connor and Dee Lu Jackson from Ford, Mike Dwyer from Unilever, Duhe Leslie from UPS, and Al Steffle and Daniel Hachard from Nestlé. A special word of thanks to Matt Ryan of Disney, David Webster from Microsoft, Mary Ann Villanueva from Citigroup, Cindy Vallar from PowerBar, and Scott Helberg from Dell, all of whom generously helped polish the brand stories of their firms.

I have had the pleasure to work with a host of insightful brand strategists over the years who have stimulated and expanded my thinking. Scott Talgo, who is as good as it gets on branding, gave me some help on this book as he had on the others. Kevin Keller, my research colleague and the author of a superb brand strategy book, helped get me started on branding in the first place. Roberto Alvarez, one of the top brand experts in Europe and the translator of many of my books, has supported me through the years. My friend, colleague, and daughter, Jennifer Aaker, an authority on brand personality and cross-cultural marketing, pushed me to be rigorous in my thinking. My friend and colleague Erich Joachimsthaler, the CEO of Vivaldi Partners (a management consultancy with offices in New York and Germany), helped me develop many of the ideas in the book during the time when we were a consulting team and we created the *Brand Leadership* book. He is an insightful brand strategist who shares my passion for brands and is a delight to be around. There are many others as well.

Finally, my thanks to my wife, who allowed me time for yet another writing project, and the rest of my family—Jan, Jolyn, Jennifer, Semantha, Mylee, Devon, and Cooper—who inspire.

PART I

What Is Brand Portfolio Strategy?

CHAPTER 1

BRAND PORTFOLIO STRATEGY

We hire eagles and teach them to fly in formation.
—D. WAYNE CALLOWAY, FORMER CEO OF PEPSICO

You don't get harmony when everyone sings the same note.
—DOUG FLOYD

Nobody has ever bet enough on a winning horse.
—RICHARD SASULY

THE INTEL CASE

During the 1990s, Intel achieved remarkable success in terms of increase in sales, stock return, and market capitalization.* Sales of its microprocessors went from $1.2 billion in 1989 to more than $33 billion in 2000. Its market capitalization grew to more than $400 billion in just over thirty years. Intel's ability and willingness to reinvent its product line again and again—making obsolete business areas in which it had big investments—certainly played a key role in its success. Its operational excellence in creating complex new products with breathtaking speed and operating microprocessor fabrication plants efficiently and effectively was also critical.

Intel's brand portfolio strategy, however, played a critical role as well. And this brand portfolio strategy could not have emerged without the brilliance of Dennis Carter, Intel's marketing guru during the 1990s, and the support of Andy Grove at the very top of the organization. Few or-

---

* This section is based in part on "The Intel Case" by David A. Aaker, published in Jim Prost's Teacher's Manual for David Aaker, Strategic Market Management, New York, John Wiley & Sons, 2000; on Intel annual reports for 2000, 2001, and 2002; and on the Intel website. Thanks to Susan Rockrise, a gifted visual strategist, and Todd Peters and Rhonda Walker of Intel for comments—they are not responsible for the final product.

ganizations, particularly in the high-tech sector, are blessed with such assets.

Intel's brand story really starts in 1978, when it created the 8086 microprocessor chip, which won IBM's approval to power its first personal computer. The Intel chip and its subsequent generations (the 286 in 1982, the 386 in 1985, and the 486 in 1989) defined the industry standard and was the dominant brand.

In early 1991, Intel was facing pressure from competitors exploiting the fact that Intel failed to obtain trademark protection on the X86 series. These firms created confusion by calling their "clone" products names like the AMD386, implying that they were as effective as any other 386-powered PC.

To respond to this business challenge, Intel in the spring of 1991 began a remarkable ingredient-branding program ("Intel Inside"), with an initial budget of around $100 million. This decision was very controversial within Intel—such a large sum of money could have been used for R&D, and many argued that brand building was irrelevant for a firm that only sold its products to a handful of computer manufacturers. Within a relatively short time, however, the Intel Inside logo became ubiquitous, and the program became an incredible success. The logo, shown in Figure 1-1, has a light, personal touch, as if someone wrote it on an informal note—a sharp departure from the formal corporate logo (Intel with a dropped *e*).

The Intel Inside program involved a tightly controlled partnership between Intel and computer manufacturers. Each partner received a 6 percent rebate on its purchases of Intel microprocessors, which was deposited into a market development fund that paid for up to 50 percent of the partner's advertising. (To qualify, the advertising needed to pass certain tests, the main one being to present the Intel Inside logo correctly on product and in the ad.) Computer partners were required to create subbrands for products using a competing microprocessor so buyers would realize that they were buying a computer without Intel Inside. Although the program became expensive—its structure caused the budget to grow to well over $1 billion per year as sales rose—it also created a huge differential advantage over competitors trying to make inroads with computer manufacturers.

The bottom line was that for many years, "Intel Inside" meant a roughly 10 percent premium on the sales price of a computer featuring the logo. Because of the exposure of the branding program, Intel was given credit for creating products that were reliable, compatible with software products, and innovative, and for being an organization of substance and leadership. All this happened even though most computer users had no idea what a microprocessor was or why Intel's were better.

There were important secondary benefits. The Intel Inside program caused advertising for computers to explode. Ironically, advertising agencies, at first unhappy having their artistry compromised by foreign logos, became creatively flexible when they realized that advertising billings were going to skyrocket. In addition, the computer partner firms became attached to the advertising allowance; in fact, with margins squeezed, they had a hard time competing without it. The program thus became a significant loyalty incentive for Intel. "Intel Inside" became one of the most important brands in their portfolio.

In the fall of 1992, Intel was ready to announce the successor to the 486 chip in the face of increasing competitor confusion, even given the Intel Inside campaign. A huge decision loomed. Should the successor be called Intel 586, thereby leveraging the Intel Inside brand and providing a familiar and logical roadmap to customers who had adapted the X86 progression? Or should it be given a new name, such as Pentium? It was a very difficult decision.

Four key issues guided the decision to develop the Pentium brand. First, despite the success of the Intel Inside program, the basic confusion issue would remain if the product was named Intel 586, thanks to market entries such as AMD586. Second, the cost of creating a new brand and transitioning customers to it, although huge, was within the capacity and will of Intel—few new products in any industry are so blessed. The fact that a new brand had news value would make the job easier. Third, the Intel Inside equity and program, rather than being wasted, could be leveraged by linking the two brands. A visual presentation of the Pentium brand was integrated into the Intel Inside logo, as shown in Figure 1-1; in essence the Intel Inside brand became an endorser for the Pentium brand. Finally, the new product was judged to be substantive enough to justify a new name, even though a new name for every future generation would ultimately be costly and confusing. Because a costly new fabrication plant needed healthy initial demand to pay off, one motivation for the new brand was to signal to customers that the new generation was worth an upgrade.

Intel subsequently developed an improvement to the Pentium that provided superior graphic capability. Rather than naming the chip a Pentium II, or giving it an entirely new name, the branded technology name MMX was added to the Pentium brand (the graphical representation is shown in Figure 1-1). The Pentium brand would thus have more time to repay its investment, and a new-generation impact could be reserved for a time in which the advance was more substantial. Later generations did emerge, leveraging the Pentium brand and equity with names like Pentium Pro (1995), Pentium II (1997), Pentium III (1999), and Pentium 4 (2000). The advent of the Pentium 4 ushered in a new visual design (shown in Figure 1-1) to emphasize its newness and to provide a look that suggested substance, reliability, and quality.

Clearly, a crucial, ongoing brand portfolio strategy issue is how to use branding to identify product improvements. When the improvements are minor or involve corrections of prior mistakes, then it is not appropriate or worthwhile to signal a change. When the improvements are significant, the choice lies between a branded feature (like MMX), a new generation (like Pentium III), or a totally new brand (like the replacement of the X86 series with Pentium). The communication cost, the risk of freezing sales of the existing brand, and the degree of preempting the news value of future technological developments will all depend on which of the three brand signals is used.

In 1998 Intel decided that it needed to participate in the market for mid-range and higher servers and workstations. To address this market, Intel developed features that allowed four or eight processors to be linked to supply the power needed for these higher-end machines. A branding issue then arose. On one hand, the Pentium brand was strongly associated with lower-end personal computers for homes as well as businesses, and as such it would not be regarded as suitable for servers and workstations. On the other hand, the market would not support developing yet another standalone brand alongside Intel Inside and Pentium. The solution was to introduce a subbrand, the Pentium II Xeon. The subbrand distanced the new microprocessor enough from Pentium to make it palatable for the higher-end users. It had the secondary advantage of enhancing the Pentium brand. Another practical consideration was that the use of the Xeon name by itself had some trademark complications that disappeared when it was merged with the Pentium II name.

In 1999 another problem—or opportunity—emerged. As the PC market matured, a value segment emerged, led by some Intel competitors eager to find a niche and willing to undercut the price points of the premium microprocessor business. Intel needed to compete in this market, if only defensively, but using the Pentium brand (even with a subbrand) would have been extremely risky. The solution was a stand-alone brand, Celeron, that was not directly linked to Pentium (as Figure 1-1 shows). The brand-building budget, like that of many value brands, was minimal: the target market found the brand, rather than the other way around.

A decision was made to link the Celeron to Intel Inside, so there was an indirect link to Pentium. The trade-off was the need for the Intel endorsement to provide credibility to Celeron, versus the need to protect the Pentium brand from the image tarnishment of the lower-end entry.

In 2001, the Intel Xeon processor was introduced with the logo shown in Figure 1-1. Several factors combined to allow the subbrand to step out from behind the Pentium brand. Technological advances such as NetBurst architecture rather dramatically improved the processor's power, and now that the Xeon brand had been established it was thus more feasible to support it as a stand-alone brand (the initial trademark issues over the use of the brand name had been resolved). Finally, the target market became even more important to Intel, and having a brand devoted to it became a strategic imperative.

That same year, the Itanium processor was introduced as a successor to the Pentium series. Why not call it the Pentium 5? The processor had been built from the ground up with an entirely new architecture, with 64-bit power (as opposed to the 32-bit Pentiums) based on a branded design termed Explicitly Parallel Instruction Computing (EPIC). Capable of delivering a new level of performance for high-end enterprise-class servers, a new name was needed to signal that this processor was qualitatively different than the Pentium. The logo for the second generation of Itanium is shown in Figure 1-1.

In 2003, Intel introduced the Intel Centrino mobile technology, which provided laptops with enhanced performance, extended battery life, integrated wireless connectivity, and thinner, lighter designs. Its promise is to fundamentally affect personal lifestyles and business productively by enabling people to unconnect, to "Unwire Your Life." The new Centrino logo (shown in Figure 1-1) reflects the Intel vision of the convergence of communication and computing, and it also represented a new approach to product development. Rather than simply pushing the performance envelope, for this product Intel responded to real customer needs as determined by market research.

The most dramatic element of the Centrino logo is its shape, a sharp departure from the rectangular design family that preceded it. The two wings suggest a merger of technology and lifestyle, a forward-looking perspective, and the freedom to go where you will. The magenta color used for the Centrino wings balances the Intel blue and visually provides energy and excitement while suggesting a connection between technology and passion, logic and emotions. The Intel Inside logo has evolved as well. More precise, sophisticated, and confident, it now provides a link to the classic dropped-*e* Intel corporate logo and reflects a world in which the positives of the corporate connection and the loyalty program can be dialed up.

Intel used its brand name to enter other business areas. One of the most important was in the communications sector. A branding problem common to any firm with a strong well-defined brand is that it is confining; Intel is so closely associated with microprocessors and Pentium that creating credibility in other areas can be a challenge. Subbrands and branded components can help combat this problem. Intel operates an important segment of its business under the brand Intel Network Processor, with the Intel Inside brand nowhere to be found. In addition branded components such as the Intel Xscale microarchitecture processor (which provides the ability to tailor a general-purpose processor to specific tasks, avoiding the need for special-purpose processors) are developed.

Intel over the years has purchased many firms, and in each case it has had to make judgments about what to do with the brands that accompanied those firms. Retaining the brands in their present roles would capitalize on their equity and the customer relationships that they represented, while dropping them would allow for transferring the business areas to the Intel brand or one of the brands in the Intel portfolio. Finally, another role could be found for the brands, perhaps as a subbrand for a defined segment or as a value brand.

For example, in 1999 Intel bought Dialogic, a company providing

FIGURE 1-1
INTEL'S BRAND ROLES EXPRESSED VISUALLY

building blocks relevant to the converging Internet and telecommunication markets. The new organization was initially "Dialogic, an Intel company," but then changed to become a product brand within the Intel Communication Systems Products organization (for example, Intel Dialogic Boards).

It is clear that a host of critical brand portfolio decisions were made at Intel. New brands enabled the firm to address competitive threats and enter new markets. The relationships between brands were particularly important in defining new and transitioning business arenas, while the umbrella Intel Inside brand provided an essential synergetic force in the portfolio. Many of the branding decisions were difficult and internally controversial. But again and again, the portfolio structure reflected and enabled the business strategy, thereby enhancing the firm's chance to succeed. At times, it influenced the market environment and actually defined product categories. In doing so, Intel's effort to position itself as a differentiated leader brand was enhanced.

Too often, the implicit assumption is made that brand strategy involves the creation and management of a strong brand like HP, Viao, 3M, Ford, or Tide. Yet virtually all firms face the portfolio challenges created by multiple brands. Intel, for example, has a host of important brands, including Intel Inside, Pentium, Xeon, Centrino, Xscale, and Dialogic. For too many firms, the management of their portfolio is often deficient or nonexistent, despite the fact that there is often a huge competitive upside to getting it done better.

There are at least five reasons why understanding and managing the brand portfolio can be a key to both the development of a winning business strategy and its successful implementation. First, a portfolio in which each brand executes a clear role can create competitively decisive synergies. A key element of brand portfolio management is to make sure that each brand has a well-defined scope and role(s) to play in each context in which it is expected to contribute. Another is to make sure that the brands, acting within their roles, actively reinforce and support each other to provide a consistent synergistic team. Looking at brands as stand-alone silos is a recipe for suboptimization and inefficiency.

It is like an American football team with dozens of people playing different positions, each with its own role. On the defensive line, there are pass rushers and run stoppers. The strong safety has a different role to play than the free safety. The outside linebacker's role differs from that of the middle linebacker. One of the coach's jobs is to place each player in the right position. The very best offensive lineman may fail as a defensive lineman, just as a great endorser brand may make a weak master brand in a particular context. Another coaching task is to teach technique and create drills to make sure that each player plays up to his capabilities. On successful teams, every player is assigned to a role in which he can succeed, understands the role, and is well prepared to execute that role. Brands similarly need to be placed in roles to which they are suited, and given the resources needed to succeed.

The football team also needs to work together, with players executing in tandem to achieve success. The defensive line needs to work with the linebackers, and the linebackers with the defensive backs, to reflect the strategy that is in the game plan. Often the team that best works together wins, rather than the most talented team. The successful coaches strive to make teamwork a priority and make sure that individuals do not focus on their statistics to the detriment of the team. Similarly, strategic brand leadership requires that brand team goals be optimized as well as those of the individual brand players.

Second, a portfolio view can ensure that the brands of the future get the resources they need to succeed. In a silo organization, high-potential brands are often starved of resources, in part because their business is still small. The assignment of clear brand roles will help guide brand-building resources in the most productive directions to create future brand assets.

On any successful football team, coaches will devote the most re-sources to impact players and potential future impact players. The 320-pound freshman tackle, for example, may be a weak performer now, but could be a star if given extra coaching and opportunities to play. A sophomore who already plays well may have the potential to become a dominant force on the field if properly trained and motivated. The star player can, with work, become even better. High-potential brands need similar attention and resources; all brands and all brand roles are not created equal.

Third, understanding the perspectives, tools, and methods of brand portfolios can enable organizations to address competitive challenges by adjusting strategies. One branding challenge is to maintain or recapture points of differentiation and energy, without which a branded offering will be vulnerable. Portfolio tools such as subbrands and branded fea-tures can provide avenues to achieving this goal. Responsive strategies to create or maintain relevance within a market that is changing (per-haps at a rapid rate) can be enabled by the use of subbrands, endorsed brands, or co-brands, or by the development of new brand platforms. Chapters 4, 5, and 6 will detail the portfolio approach to these chal-lenges.

A football team may need to adapt when it senses a deficiency. If, for example, a weakness is found among the offensive linemen, a team re-sponse might address the problem. A new player might be acquired from another team, or perhaps a strong defensive lineman might be shifted to offense. An adjacent lineman could be called on to compensate by playing a different role, or the offensive strategy could be changed to make the point of vulnerability less visible. The brand portfolio needs to be similarly flexible and dynamic to respond to dynamic markets.

Fourth, strategic growth challenges can be addressed through portfolio tools. Virtually all organizations eventually run into a wall and need to find new sources of growth. Strategically, this usually means entering new markets, offering new products, or moving into upscale or value arenas. Any such strategy will need to be enabled with brand assets, however, whether by leveraging existing brands (perhaps with the use of subbrands or endorsed brands) or acquiring or developing new brands. Chapters 7 and 8 will discuss the brand portfolio as a device to enable growth.

A football coach needs to have a vision of the team's style, character, and strategy. Will it be a finesse or power team? Will it emphasize passing, running, or defense? Has it assembled the right set of players to execute the strategy? It is not enough to have the best players; a team must have the players that fit its strategy. A brand portfolio likewise will need to develop brands that will enable the business strategy.

Winning football coaches will fully exploit the talents of their players. If a team has an outstanding linebacker, the defense might be designed so that opposing running backs are funneled to that linebacker. If a defensive back is extremely fast, he might be asked to also play wide receiver at times, to get him on the field so that he can make plays. An offensive tackle might add size to the defensive front in goal-line situations. Similarly, a key of portfolio management is to identify key facets of strong brands and leverage them through brand extensions and added role responsibilities.

Fifth, an offering can get too complex, confusing customers and even employees. The result can be damaging to the customer relationship. More visibly, it can cause waste in brand-building efforts because the message is too cluttered to be retained. Chapters 9 and 10 will discuss ways to gain focus and clarity in the brand portfolio.

A football team can easily create an offensive strategy that provides so many options, and counters so many competitor actions, that it ends up confusing the team. The players end up thinking so much about the complexity that they do a poor job of their more basic tasks of running, blocking, and passing. Simplifying the offense—reducing it to a few basic plays that are well executed—can result in dramatic performance improvements.

Brand portfolio strategy becomes especially critical as brand contexts are complicated by multiple segments, multiple products, varied competitor types, complex distribution channels, multiple brand extensions, and the wider use of endorsed brands and subbrands. Brands such as Coca-Cola, Bank of America, Procter & Gamble, HP, Sony, Visa, Textron, and Volvo all operate in diverse markets and over multiple (sometimes disparate) products and channels. The resulting complexity often creates customer confusion, inefficiencies, and a brand strategy that seems muddled and unmotivated in the eyes of employees and brand-building partners. In the face of competitive pressure, a cohesive, well-defined brand portfolio becomes imperative.

Brand portfolio strategy is defined in the next section, after which its five components and the portfolio objectives are described. In the process, concepts will be defined and illustrated, some of which, like branded differentiators and branded energizers, are introduced for the first time. In the chapter that follows, key building blocks of brand portfolio strategy (master brands, subbrands, and endorsed brands) will be described, and their relationship will be modeled with the brand relationship spectrum. In Chapter 3, four types of inputs to the development of a brand portfolio strategy (market forces and dynamics, business strategy, brand equities and identities, and the brand portfolio audit) will be presented, along with a discussion of the portfolio management process itself.

In Part II of the book, the use of brand portfolios to help create relevance, differentiation, and energy is presented. Part III looks at growth avenues: horizontal and vertical brand extensions. Part IV discusses how to achieve clarity and focus in a portfolio.

WHAT IS A BRAND PORTFOLIO STRATEGY?

The brand portfolio strategy specifies the structure of the brand portfolio and the scope, roles, and interrelationships of the portfolio brands. The goals are to create synergy, leverage, and clarity within the portfolio and relevant, differentiated, and energized brands. The portfolio brands, both owned brands and brands linked through alliances, should be considered a team of brands working together, each with assigned roles to enable and support business strategies.

The development and management of a brand portfolio strategy involves making brand decisions such as whether to:

- Add, delete, or prioritize brands or subbrands
- Extend a brand into another product category with a descriptor or a subbrand, or as an endorser
- Extend a brand into the superpremium or value space
- Use the corporate brand on an offering, or expand its use as an endorser
- Develop a brand alliance
- Define or associate with a new product category or subcategory
- Create and/or dial up a branded differentiator, a branded feature, ingredient or technology, service, or program that differentiates
- Develop a branded energizer, a branded sponsorship, product, promotion, or other entity that is linked to the target brand adding associations, interest, and energy

Brand portfolio strategy can be further elaborated in terms of six dimensions: the brand portfolio, product-defining roles, portfolio roles, brand scope, portfolio structure, and portfolio graphics. Each of these, in which the tools and concepts of brand portfolio strategy reside, will be illustrated and discussed in the next section. A baker's dozen indicators of the existence of brand portfolio problems or opportunities, listed in the insert, also provide a perspective on brand portfolio strategy.

The brand portfolio strategy should not have an internal perspective that aims to reflect an organizational chart. While the internal organizational structure may change frequently as the firm adapts to its changing environment, the customer-facing brand architecture should be more stable. Customers will not be motivated to learn new organizational labels. In developing a sound brand portfolio strategy, the business-card concern (in other words, what will the organizational unit be on my business card) should not influence portfolio design decisions. The only concern should be making the offering clear and appealing from the customer perspective.

Figure 1-2 summarizes the six dimensions and five objectives of brand architecture. The following section will define each of the dimensions, followed by a presentation of the portfolio objectives.

Indicators of Brand Portfolio Problems
(and Opportunities)

1. Brands that potentially could drive future profits have inadequate brand-building resources, while mature brands are overfunded.

2. Business and marketing strategy is paralyzed because there is uncertainty as to the role of key master brands going forward.

3. Brand assets are not now in place to support the business strategy going forward, and a viable plan to remedy the situation is not in place.

4. Market share is eroding because of a decline in relevance of the offering caused by the emergence of new categories and subcategories.

5. Differentiation is harder to achieve, resulting in margin erosion. Branded differentiators are needed.

6. Key brands are bland and tired and/or need an image change. Branded energizers could help.

7. The organization lacks capabilities, resources, or brand power to respond to market dynamics. A brand alliance could be the answer.

8. Some brand assets are not leveraged enough in the face of unsatisfactory growth.

9. The corporate (organizational) brand has potential points of differentiation because of its heritage, values, citizenship programs, and assets/capabilities, and because it is underleveraged.

10. There is a growing superpremium subcategory with high margins and product vitality in which the firm is not participating, while the core market is turning hostile.

11. It is strategically important to find a way to participate in a healthy value market in order to remain economically viable.

12. The offering is so confused that customers and sometimes employees cannot figure out how to buy what they need.

13. There are too many brands and offerings diffusing the scarce brand-building resources.

DIMENSIONS OF THE BRAND PORTFOLIO STRATEGY

The development of a brand portfolio strategy involves six dimensions. The first of these is the *brand portfolio* itself, which provides the set of brands to be drawn upon to achieve the portfolio objectives. Two others, *product-defining roles* and *portfolio roles,* specify the varied set of roles that each brand could potentially play. The *brand scope* reflects the product categories or subcategories for which each brand will be relevant (both at present and in the future) and the relationships between brand contexts. The *portfolio structure* formalizes the relationships between the brands, and *portfolio graphics* indicate how they are to be presented by themselves and relative to other brands.

Brand Portfolio

The brand portfolio includes all of the brands managed by the organization, including the master brands, endorsers, subbrands, branded differentiators, co-brands, branded energizers, and corporate brands, even if they seem dormant. Branded differentiators and branded energizers will be illustrated in more detail later in this section. A corporate brand is a brand that represents a corporation—or, more generally, an organization—and reflects its heritage, values, culture, people, and strategy. As already noted, portfolio brands also include brands external to the organization whose link to internal brands are actively managed, such as branded sponsorships, symbols, celebrity endorsers, and countries or regions.

A basic portfolio issue is the composition of the brand portfolio. Should one or more brands be added? There are certainly situations in which a portfolio can be strengthened by the addition of brands. However, brand additions should always have a well-defined role. Further, the decision to add a brand should be made or approved by a person or group with a portfolio perspective. Too often, such decisions are left to decentralized groups that have little feel for (or incentive to care about) the total brand portfolio, which creates a bias toward brand proliferation. The goal should be to have the fewest relevant brands needed to meet business goals.

FIGURE 1-2
BRAND PORTFOLIO STRATEGY

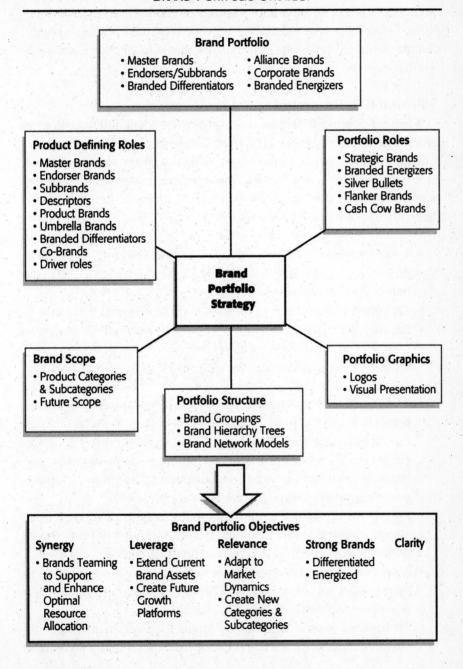

Brand Portfolio
- Master Brands
- Endorsers/Subbrands
- Branded Differentiators
- Alliance Brands
- Corporate Brands
- Branded Energizers

Product Defining Roles
- Master Brands
- Endorser Brands
- Subbrands
- Descriptors
- Product Brands
- Umbrella Brands
- Branded Differentiators
- Co-Brands
- Driver roles

Portfolio Roles
- Strategic Brands
- Branded Energizers
- Silver Bullets
- Flanker Brands
- Cash Cow Brands

Brand Portfolio Strategy

Brand Scope
- Product Categories & Subcategories
- Future Scope

Portfolio Structure
- Brand Groupings
- Brand Hierarchy Trees
- Brand Network Models

Portfolio Graphics
- Logos
- Visual Presentation

Brand Portfolio Objectives

Synergy	Leverage	Relevance	Strong Brands	Clarity
• Brands Teaming to Support and Enhance Optimal Resource Allocation	• Extend Current Brand Assets • Create Future Growth Platforms	• Adapt to Market Dynamics • Create New Categories & Subcategories	• Differentiated • Energized	

Or perhaps the question is, should brands be deleted? If the number of brands is excessive, there may not be adequate resources to support them. Perhaps worse, superfluous brands can contribute confusion simply by being there. The solution is to prune the brand portfolio, painful though that might be. Chapter 10 pursues this issue and suggests methods that help the process.

Product-Defining Roles

When an offering is proposed, it needs to be identified to customers by a brand or set of brands. The brand set with product-defining roles reflects an external view of the brands from the customer's perspective. Each brand will be in one of the following roles: master brand, endorser brand, subbrand, descriptor, product brand, umbrella brand, branded differentiator, or brand alliance.

- A *master brand* is the primary indicator of the offering, the point of reference. Visually, it will usually take top billing, such as 3M in the brand 3M Accuribbon.
- An *endorser brand* serves to provide credibility and substance to the offering (e.g., General Mills endorses Cheerios). Its role is to represent an organization and its credibility and substance is based on the strategy, resources, values, and heritage of that organization.
- A *subbrand* augments or modifies the associations of a master brand in a specific product-market context (e.g., Porsche includes the subbrand Carrera). Its role is to create a brand that will be significantly different from the master brand, perhaps by adding an attribute dimension or a personality element, and thus be appropriate for a particular product or segment.
- *Descriptors* describe the offering, usually in functional terms (e.g., aircraft engines, appliances, light bulbs). Although not brands per se, descriptors play key roles in any portfolio strategy.
- A *product brand* defines a product offering consisting of a master brand and a subbrand (Toyota Corolla), or a master brand plus a descriptor (Apple-Cinnamon Cheerios).
- An *umbrella brand* defines a grouping of product offerings (Microsoft Office Word, Microsoft Office Excel, etc.) under a common

brand (Microsoft Office). The umbrella brand such as FedEx eBusiness Tools, can be a more appropriate and effective vehicle to gain relevance, visibility, and differentiation than individual product brands, such as eShipping Tools, eCommerce Solutions, and eCommerce Builder.

- A *driver role* reflects the degree to which a brand drives the purchase decision and defines the use experience. While master brands usually have the dominant driver role, endorsers, subbrands, or even descriptors or second-level subbrands (that is, subbrands to subbrands) can also play driver roles that can vary in intensity. Toyota plays more of the driver role than Corolla, but both have influence.

Chapter 2 describes these brand roles in more detail and provides insights into how their power can be channeled into the creation of strong, flexible brands. The remaining roles—branded differentiators, covered in Chapter 4, and brand alliances, the subject of Chapter 6—are worth introducing here in order to complete this overview of brand portfolio strategy.

BRANDED DIFFERENTIATORS

A branded differentiator is a brand or subbrand that defines a feature, ingredient, service, or program. The customer-facing offering could be Lipton Tea, with a Flo-Thru bag as a branded differentiator. Creating a point of differentiation for a master brand makes the branded offering appear superior, or it augments the offering so that it provides more functions and benefits. Some examples of the various types of branded differentiators are as follows:

A *branded feature* is an owned attribute of the offering that creates a benefit for the customer:

Ziploc Sandwich Bags—ColorLoc Zipper
Whirlpool Electric Range—Whirlpool CleanTop, AccuSimmer Element
Reebok—3D UltraLite-sole design

A *branded ingredient (or technology)* is built into the offering and implies a benefit and/or feeling of confidence:

Cisco Aironet Access Point—LEAP technology
North Face parkas—Gore-Tex
Cheer—Advanced Color-Guard Power

A *branded service* augments the offering by providing a service:

American Express—Round Trip (a package of services for the corpo-
    rate travel office)
Ford/Mercury/Lincoln—Quality Care
United Airlines—Arrivals by United, United Red Carpet Club, United
    Mileage Plus, Ground Link, Business One

A *branded program* augments the offering and thus expands the
brand by providing a program that is linked to the offering and brand:

Hilton Honors
Kraft Kitchens
GM BuyPower

The value of a branded differentiator has been demonstrated in a variety of contexts. A consistent finding is that it provides a boost, particularly to a new or less established brand.

BRAND ALLIANCES—CO-BRANDING

Brand alliances involve brands from different firms that combine to
engage in effective strategic or tactical brand building programs or to
create co-branded market offerings. Thus, a sponsorship such as NFL
football or a personality such as Tiger Woods that has a long-term role in
building the equity of a portfolio brand would become part of the portfolio to be actively managed.

Co-branding occurs when brands from different organizations (or dis-
tinctly different businesses within the same organization) combine to
create an offering in which brands from each play a driver role. One of
the co-brands can be an ingredient brand, such as Pillsbury Brownies
with Nestlé syrup, or an endorser such as Healthy Choice cereal from
Kellogg's. It can also be a co-master brand, such as the credit card that
has three master brands (Citibank, American Airlines, and Visa). Or it

can be a joint brand-building effort, such as a cross-promotion involving a Universal movie and Burger King.

Co-branding has significant rewards, as the discussion in Chapter 6 will explore. The offering can capture two sources of brand equity and thereby enhance the value proposition and point of differentiation. It can also enhance not only the co-branded offering but the associations of both brands. And it can allow a firm to respond quickly and strategically to a dynamic market.

THE NATURE OF PRODUCT-DEFINING ROLES

The specification of a set of product-defining brands for an offering is where the rubber meets the road from a brand perspective. What should an offering be called? What is the customer-facing brand? A Bose Quiet-Comfort stereo headset with TriPort headphone technology is one such brand set. It has a master brand (Bose), a subbrand (QuietComfort), and a branded differentiator (TriPort headphone technology). Each of the brands that come together to identify an offering will have a well-defined role that will influence how that brand is managed. Three more examples are as follows:

- Cadillac Seville, with a Bose CD player and a Northstar engine endorsed by GM
- HP Color LaserJet 5500, with HP ImageREt technology
- Venus Shaving System from Gillette for Women, with aloe and the DLC Blade Edge

In the first, there is a master brand (Cadillac), a subbrand (Seville), a co-brand (Bose), an endorser brand (GM), and two branded differentiators (Bose and Northstar). In the second, we see a master brand (HP), a subbrand (Color LaserJet 5500), and a branded differentiator (HP ImageREt technology). In the third, there is a master brand (Venus), a product brand (Venus Shaving System), an endorser (Gillette for Women), and two branded differentiators (aloe and DLC Blade Edge).

Brand Scope

Every brand has a scope dimension that reflects the extent to which the brand spans product categories, subcategories, and markets.

Although all portfolio brands need to manage scope, master brands have the most critical scope judgments to make. Some master brands (like A-1 Steak Sauce) are very focused, often because they are tied to a product category and expansion would dilute the brand. Others, like 3M, GE, and Toshiba, cover a wide variety of product and market settings. For example, the GE master brand appears in financial services, aircraft engines, appliances, and other product settings, and within appliances serves such diverse segments as consumers, designers, and builders. Others, like Audi, have a wide umbrella under a single product category.

One objective of a brand portfolio is to leverage brand assets by extending strong brands whose associations will travel across product categories. When feasible, this approach can lead to more visible, stronger brands with more efficient and effective brand-building programs. It follows a central business strategy dictum—fully employ your strongest assets. However, there are limits as to how far any brand, especially a master brand, can go. Stretching the brand too far can cause it to lose differentiation and relevance in some contexts. Worse, some extensions may weaken or damage the brand because of the associations created.

The scope of the master brand can be extended by the use of sub-brands and co-brands. The brand can range even further as an endorser, since an endorser brand is asked to do less and risks less. So firms have a variety of tools and options in terms of leveraging a master brand.

Brand portfolio management must consider not only the current scope of the brand but the scope it will have going forward. Brands are best leveraged as part of a long-term plan that sets forth the ultimate product scope, what sequence will take them there, and what associations are needed to be successful. Chapter 7 elaborates on this concept.

When the brand scope spans product categories and markets, the brand portfolio strategy needs to be involved in deciding the nature of those relationships. For example, what is the relationship between the Cadillac Escalade SUV and the Cadillac Seville sedan? Or the Cadillac Escalade sold to fleets versus that sold to consumers? Is the Cadillac brand the same in each context, or is it modified? Meanwhile, Gillette offers the Gillette Mach3Turbo for men and the Gillette Satin Care Crystal Essence shave gel from Gillette for Women. Both products are sold in Europe and elsewhere, as well as in the United States. Is the Gillette brand the same in all contexts?

Portfolio Roles

Portfolio roles reflect an internal, managerial perspective on ‸‸ brand portfolio. When managing a brand portfolio as a whole, each brand is not a silo, nor is each brand manager an island. Treating brands as silos "owned" by individuals or organizational units can lead to a misallocation of resources and a failure to create and exploit synergy across brands. Portfolio roles in part serve the function of creating more optimal allocation of brand-building and brand management resources.

The portfolio roles include a strategic brand, a branded energizer, a silver bullet brand, a flanker brand, and a cash cow brand. These roles are not mutually exclusive. A brand could be simultaneously a strategic brand and a silver bullet brand, for example. Further, the same brand could at one point be a strategic brand and evolve into a cash cow brand.

The portfolio roles can differ by market context. A brand that is a strategic brand in one market, such as the United States, may not be one in the Far East. Similarly, a brand that is a silver bullet in the business market may not necessarily serve that role in the home market.

STRATEGIC BRAND

A strategic brand is one with strategic importance to the organization. It is a brand that needs to succeed and therefore should receive whatever resources are needed. The identification of strategic brands is a huge step toward ensuring that brand-building resources are allocated to the strategically most important business arenas.

There are, in general, three types of strategic brands:

- A *current power brand (or megabrand)* now generates significant sales and profits and is not a candidate for cash cow status. Perhaps it is already a large, dominant brand and is projected to maintain or grow its position. Microsoft Windows is in this category.
- A *future power brand* is projected to generate significant sales and profit in the future, even though it now is a small or emerging brand. Centrino would qualify for Intel.
- A *linchpin brand* will indirectly influence (as opposed to generate) significant sales and market position in the future, serving as the "linchpin" or leverage point of a major business area or of a future vision of the firm. Hilton Rewards is such a brand for Hilton Ho-

tels, because it represents the future ability to control a substantial and critical segment in the hotel industry—frequent travelers. If a competitor's rewards program for these travelers became dominant for any reason, Hilton would be at a strategic disadvantage. Yet the Hilton Rewards brand does not directly control significant sales and profits.

The classic problem is that if future power brands and linchpin brands have no current sales base, they get starved of resources. The ethic in a decentralized organization is that you earn your right to invest behind the brand—the business unit that earns the money should be able to invest it. Further, such investment is not painful to the firm because the earnings can support it. When there is no organizational mechanism to take a total portfolio view, the default strategy is to let each decentralized unit set its own budget. As a result, not only are future power brands and linchpin brands inadequately funded, but also there is overinvestment behind large power brands. The identification of strategic brands provides a vehicle to allocate brand-building resources with more wisdom and strategic perspective.

The other side of the coin is when emerging areas and the linchpins of the future organizational vision get too much attention, and the existing power brands get neglected. Procter & Gamble struggled during the 1990s in part because of an excessive investment in new brands. A new CEO in early 2000 turned around the firm by redirecting the focus to P&G's top billion-dollar brands: Tide, Crest, Charmin, Downy, Pampers, Folgers, Bounty, Ariel, Pringle's, Always, Pantene, and Iams.[1] The idea was simple—instead of finding new products, just sell more Tide and other established brands. Growth in major brands represents big numbers and avoids the costs and risk inherent in establishing new products.

Discipline must be used in identifying and prioritizing strategic brands based on future prospects. Wishful thinking from optimistic brand managers may result in an excessive number of strategic brand nominees. The solution is solid analyses of the nominees. Will the market area really develop in a reasonable time—or is it like the checkless society that took a half-century to get traction, or much of the dot.com world that was a mirage? Will there be profits for survivors—or will it be like the wireless space, with too many competitors destroying the market? Will the brand be able to create a sustainable point of differentiation that will result in a profitable market position? Tough questions like these need to be asked.

The identification of strategic brands should be guided by the business strategy. For example, AAA Insurance is a strategic brand for the American Automobile Association because the future of the organization is to move beyond roadside services. Nike All Conditions Gear (ACG) is a strategic brand for Nike, as it provides the basis for a position in the outdoor-adventure arena. Slates is a strategic brand for Levi Strauss, as it is one of the foundations for a position in men's slacks for business or casual settings.

BRANDED ENERGIZER

A branded energizer, as discussed in detail in Chapter 5, is any branded product, promotion, sponsorship, symbol, program, or other entity that by association significantly enhances and energizes a target brand. The association of the branded energizer with the target brand should be actively managed over an extended time period. Unlike a branded differentiator (which supports the offering by making it better or by augmenting it so that it does more), the branded energizer is an entity that can live beyond the product and its use. It can be owned and managed by the firm, as in the following examples:

- The Pillsbury Doughboy is a branded symbol that adds fun and energy to Pillsbury.
- Budweiser has a host of branded energizers (including the Clydesdales, the "Whassup!" commercials, and the Miss Budweiser racing team) that serve to add interest and energy to the Budweiser brand.
- The Chrysler PT Cruiser provides energy to the Chrysler brand.

A branded energizer also can be owned and managed by another firm, although the link to the target brand still needs to be actively managed. For example:

- The Mercedes Open golf tournament creates energy for Mercedes.
- The San Jose Sharks major league hockey team has changed the image of the city of San Jose, which had been stuck in the shadow of San Francisco.
- Serena Williams provides energy and a face to Puma.

SILVER BULLET BRANDS

Branded energizers and differentiators can be sorted into high, medium, and low priorities in terms of their impact on the target brand and the cost involved. The most important are considered silver bullet brands—the brands that can play a strategically significant role to positively change or support the image of another brand.

The specification of a silver bullet role creates some rather fundamental changes in how a brand should be funded and managed. When a brand or subbrand such as IBM's ThinkPad is identified as a silver bullet, the communication strategy and budget would logically no longer rest solely with the brand-level business manager. The parent brand group (IBM corporate communications, in this case) should also be involved, perhaps by augmenting the silver bullet's communication budget or featuring its brand in corporate communications.

FLANKER BRANDS

If a brand is attacked by a competitor with a value offer or unique position, any response can risk its image and brand equity. The solution is to use a flanker or fighting brand to fight a competitor, thereby insulating the original brand from the fray. For example, when Pepsi launched a clear cola, Coke did not want to risk its namesake franchise to compete, and yet it also could not leave Pepsi to distort the cola marketplace. The solution was to come out with a flanker brand, Tab Clear, which positioned the new subcategory as being in the Tab world, perceived by most to have inferior taste. In fact, Tab (itself a diet cola that preceded Diet Coke) lives not only because of a small hard-core loyal customer group, but because it is convenient to use as a flanker brand.

A flanker brand gets its label from a war metaphor. When an army advances to meet another army head-on, it keeps a small portion of its forces facing outward to protect its flanks. A flanker brand analogously protects the brand from a competitor that is not competing head-on with attributes and benefits the brand has cultivated. The concept of a flanker brand is to undercut the competitor brand where it is positioned without forcing the main brand to change its focus.

A flanker brand is often used when a competitor comes in with a low price position, intending to undercut a price premium. If a brand were to respond with price cuts to protect its market share, the profitability of the brand (if not the category) would be threatened. A flanker brand—in this case, a price brand—would seek to neutralize the competitor's position, preventing the latter from occupying an attractive niche without any resistance.

CASH COW BRANDS

Strategic, silver bullet, and flanker brands require investment and active management so that they can fulfill their strategic mission. The point of labeling a brand as belonging to one of these categories is to create additional corporate resources, as the involved brands may not be able to justify appropriate programs based on their current profit streams.

A cash cow brand, conversely, is a brand that does not require as much investment as other portfolio brands. The sales may be stagnant or slowly declining, but there is a hard-core loyal customer base that is unlikely to leave the brand. Campbell's Red & White label is such a brand—it is the heart of the Campbell's equity, but the company's real vitality is elsewhere. Other cash cows could be large brands that simply need less support because they are so established or hold a strong market position because of patent protection or market power. Microsoft Office and Sony Walkman are both probably in this position. The role of a cash cow brand is to generate margin resources that can be invested in strategic, silver bullet, or flanker brands that will be the bases for the future growth and vitality of the brand portfolio.

Brand Portfolio Structure

The brands in the portfolio have a relationship with each other. What is the logic of that structure? Does it provide clarity to the customer, rather than complexity and confusion? Does the logic support synergy and leverage? Does it provide a sense of order, purpose, and direction to the organization? Or does it suggest ad hoc decision making, leading to strategic drift and an incoherent jumble of brands?

The brand portfolio structure can be best understood and analyzed if there is a way to present its logic clearly and concisely. Several approaches can be useful, including brand groupings, brand hierarchical trees, and brand network models. The key is to use or adapt the one that fits the best.

BRAND GROUPINGS

A brand grouping or configuration is a logical grouping of brands that have a meaningful characteristic in common. Polo Ralph Lauren, for example, has a brand portfolio structure that is in part driven by brands grouped with respect to four characteristics:

- *Segment.* Polo (with the polo-player symbol) is a men's wear brand, and Ralph Lauren a women's fashion brand.
- *Design.* Polo Sport for men and Ralph Lauren Polo Sport for women are more contemporary and youth oriented than Polo and Ralph Lauren.
- *Quality.* Chaps by Ralph Lauren is the moderately priced version of Polo. In the women's arena, Ralph and Lauren are more affordable than the Ralph Lauren brand, and the Ralph Lauren Collection is more exclusive.
- *Product.* Ralph Lauren Home Collection, Ralph Lauren White Linen, and Ralph Lauren Paint Collection all signal product types.

The groups provide logic to the brand portfolio and help guide its growth over time. Three groupings used by Polo Ralph Lauren—segment, product, and quality—often play a role in many portfolios in creating logical groupings, since they are dimensions that define the structure of many product markets. In the hotel industry, for example, Marriott is structured according to segment (Courtyard Inn for business travelers versus Fairfield Inn for the leisure traveler), product (Marriott Residence Inns for extended stays versus Marriott for single nights), and quality level (Marriott for luxury versus Fairfield Inn by Marriott for economy). Portfolio brands grouped along such basic product-market segmentations tend to be more easily understood by consumers.

Other useful categorical variables are benefits, application, technologies, and distribution channels. Prince tennis rackets include the benefit-defined Thunder (for power), and Precision (for shot placement) models. Nike has a set of brands for individual sports and activities, creating an application logic to their branding strategy. HP has the Jet series that includes LaserJet, InkJet, and ScanJet to denote technology. L'Oréal uses the Lancôme and Biotherm brands for department and specialty stores, while the L'Oréal and Maybelline brands are used for drug and discount stores, and another set (including Redken) is for beauty salons.

BRAND HIERARCHY TREES

The logic of the brand structure can sometimes be captured by a brand hierarchy or family tree, as illustrated in Figures 1-3 and 1-4. The tree structure looks like an organizational chart, with both horizontal and vertical dimensions. The horizontal dimension reflects the scope of the brand in terms of the subbrands or endorsed brands that reside under the brand umbrella. The vertical dimension captures the number of brands and subbrands that are needed for an individual product-market entry, reflecting a key brand portfolio dimension. The hierarchy tree for Colgate oral care, for example, shows that the Colgate name covers toothpaste, toothbrushes, dental floss, and other oral hygiene products.

A firm with multiple brands will require trees for each; in effect, a forest may be needed. Colgate has three toothpaste brands (Colgate, Ultra Brite, and Viadent) and dozens of other major brands, including Mennen, Softsoap, Palmolive, Irish Spring, and Skin Bracer. In addition, some trees may be too extensive to present on a single page and thus will need to be broken into major trunks. Since the Colgate oral care products will be difficult to display in one tree structure, it may be useful to consider the toothbrush trunk separately.

FIGURE 1-3
BRAND HIERARCHY TREE—COLGATE ORAL CARE

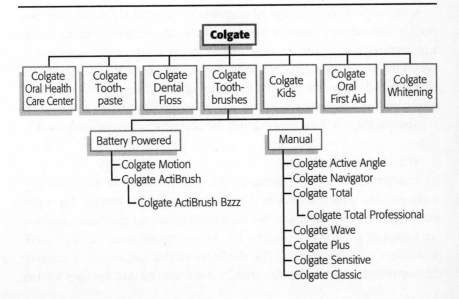

FIGURE 1-4
BRAND HIERARCHY TREE—TOYOTA

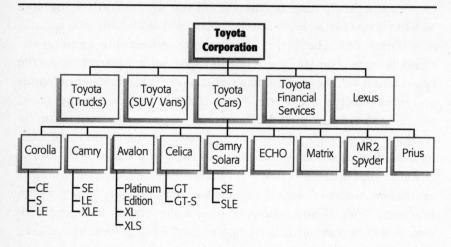

The tree presentation provides perspective to help evaluate the brand portfolio. First, are there too many or too few brands, given the market environment and the practical realities of supporting brands? Where might brands be consolidated? Where might a new brand add market impact? Second, is the brand system clear and logical, or confused and ad hoc? If logic and clarity are inadequate, what changes would be appropriate, cost-effective, and helpful?

A brand portfolio strategy objective is to achieve clarity of offerings, both to the customer and to those inside the organization. Having a logical hierarchy structure among subbrands helps generate that clarity. When the subbrands are each indicators of the same characteristic, the structure will appear logical. When one subbrand represents a technology, another a segment, and still another a product type, however, an organizing logic will be missing and the clarity may be compromised.

Network Model

Another approach to representing brand portfolio strategy is a network model, which shows graphically the portfolio brands that influence each master brand and the associated customer purchase decision. An example is shown in Figure 1-5. In the figure, some major brands that affect Nike are shown. The thickness of the link shows the impact of one brand on another; thus, the Niketown, Nike Air, Michael Jordan,

LeBron James, and Tiger Woods are denoted as being important drivers of the Nike brand. One advantage of such an approach is that it includes portfolio brands that are not product brands. Another is that it portrays indirect relationships as well as direct ones.

The approach could be expanded. Hill and Lederer proposed a three-dimension "molecule" model that gives meaning to the size of the circles, the distance to the master brand and the color of the circles (white is positive, black is negative, and gray neutral).[2] The problem with pushing this presentation approach, however, is that it quickly gets complex and hard to interpret.

A closely related alternative is the universe model, which visually represents the portfolio as a set of stars orbited by planets of various sizes, each themselves surrounded by moons. A very informative exercise is to create small disks for each brand and ask managers relevant to the brand (or customers) to arrange them using a universe model. Have

FIGURE 1-5
A PARTIAL NIKE BRAND NETWORK

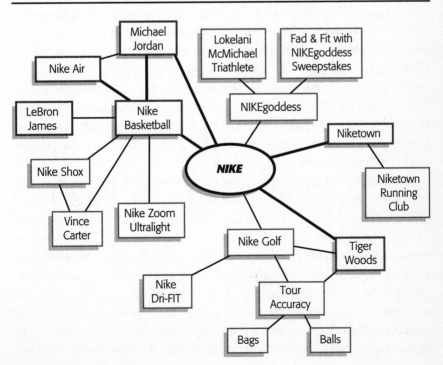

them identify the various "suns" and their respective planets and moons, then ask them to explain the logic. Compare the resulting structures and logic. How are the major brands linked? How do the brands cluster? There are usually some interesting commonalities and differences across participants that shed light on the existing portfolio structure and its problems. There are also some brands that turn out to be unclear, in that some people locate them in different places in the universe and others cannot place them at all.

Portfolio Graphics

Portfolio graphics are the pattern of brand visual representations across brands and across brand contexts. Often the most visible and central brand graphic is the logo, which represents the brand in nearly all roles and contexts. The primary logo dimensions, color, layout, and typeface, however, can be varied to make a statement about the brand, its context, and its relationship to other brands. In addition to logos, portfolio graphics are also defined by such visual representations as packaging, symbols, product design, the layout of print advertisements, taglines, or even the look and feel of how the brand is presented. Any of these can send signals about relationships within the brand portfolio.

One role of portfolio graphics is to signal the relative driver role of sets of brands. The relative typeface size and positioning of two brands on a logo or signage will reflect their relative importance and driver roles. The Marriott endorsement of Courtyard, shown in Chapter 8, is visually larger and stronger than its endorsement of the more downscale Fairfield Inn. The fact that the ThinkPad brand name has a smaller typeface than IBM on laptops tells the customer that IBM is the primary driver of the product.

Another role of portfolio graphics is to signal the separation of two brands or contexts. In the case of John Deere lawn tractors, color and product design played a key role in separating a value product branded as "Scott from John Deere" from the classic, premium John Deere line. By departing from the familiar John Deere green, the Scott line provided a strong visual signal that the customer was not buying a premium John Deere product. For its home products lines, HP developed a different color set (purple and yellow), a unique package (people are portrayed, unlike in the white corporate-logo packaging used for business customers), and a different tagline ("Exploring the possibilities").

Still another role of portfolio graphics is to visually denote the brand portfolio structure. The use of color and a common logo or logo part can signal a grouping. The use of the Maggi color and package layout, for example, provides a very strong master brand impact over its many subbrands, indicating that they form a grouping with common brand associations.

The brand portfolio audit discussed in Chapter 3 includes illuminating exercises to help review the brand graphics for all contexts. One simple test starts by putting all the visual portrayals of the brand from all geographics and contexts on a large wall. Do they have the same look and feel? Is there visual synergy, whereby the brand graphics in one context support the graphics in another? Or is the brand presented in an inconsistent, confusing, cluttered manner? This visual test is a good complement to the logical test of the brand structure presentations. It is also useful to compare the brand graphics to those of competitors.

BRAND PORTFOLIO OBJECTIVES

The goals of the portfolio are qualitatively different from the goals of individual brand identities and positions. Creating an effective and powerful brand is still a prime goal, but others are also key to achieving brand leadership. The objectives of the brand portfolio are to foster synergy, leverage brand assets, create and maintain market relevance, build and support differentiated and energized brands, and achieve clarity.

Foster Portfolio Synergy

A well-conceived brand portfolio should result in several sources of synergies. In particular, the use of brands in different contexts should enhance the visibility of the brands, create and reinforce associations, and lead to cost efficiencies (in part by creating scale economies in communication programs). Conversely, the brand portfolio should avoid negative synergies. Differences between brand identities in different contexts and roles have the potential to create confusion and diffuse the brand image.

Portfolio synergy involves allocating resources over the portfolio to support the overall business strategy. Funding each brand merely according to its profit contribution starves high-potential brands with modest current sales, as well as those with important roles in supporting the portfolio. The identification of brands with portfolio roles to play is a key first step in making optimal allocation decisions. In particular, the brand driving a potentially large emerging business needs to be given extra resources, even though the justification based on short-term results may be difficult.

Leverage Brand Assets

Underleveraged brands are unused assets. Leveraging brands means creating strong brand platforms and then making them work harder, increasing their impact in their core market, and extending them into new product-markets as endorsers or master brands. Another dimension of leverage is a vertical extension—moving a brand upscale, or into a value market. The brand portfolio management system should provide a structure and process to create brand extension opportunities, assess their risks, and adjust the portfolio accordingly. A portfolio perspective will help identify and assess risks of extending the brand, particularly when there is a vertical extension involved.

A brand portfolio strategy should also have its eye on the future and develop brand platforms that will support strategic advances into new product-markets. That might mean creating a master brand with significant future extension potential even if doing so may not be easy to justify with the business of today.

Create and Maintain Relevance

Most markets are affected by trends driven by customers, technology, channels of distribution, and the introduction of a flow of new offerings by competitors. The brand portfolio needs to be capable of adapting existing brands, perhaps by adding subbrands or endorsed brands, and even creating new brands when needed to support offerings that are needed to maintain relevance. A static brand portfolio is likely to invite the risk of losing relevance.

Develop and Enhance Strong Brands

It would be self-defeating not to have strong brands as a brand portfolio architecture goal. Creating strong brand offerings that resonate with customers, have a point of differentiation, and convey energy is the bottom line. A well-conceived brand portfolio strategy can contribute in several ways. It can make sure that each brand is assigned a role in which it can succeed, and it can focus resources to create more muscle behind the most promising brands. Branded differentiators can be developed and actively managed over time. Brand energizers can be employed to add energy and create or change associations.

Achieve Clarity of Product Offerings

A portfolio goal should be to reduce confusion and achieve clarity among product offerings, not only for customers but for employees and partners (such as retailers, advertising agencies, in-store display firms, and PR firms). Employees and partners should know the roles that each brand plays and be motivated to help the brands achieve their objectives. Customers should not be frustrated or annoyed by an overly complicated brand portfolio strategy.

Achieving these portfolio objectives becomes especially critical as markets become more complex. Most firms face multiple segments, new product opportunities, varied competitor types, powerful and disparate channels, reduced differentiation everywhere, and cluttered communication avenues. In addition, nearly all firms have multiple brands reaching a variety of markets and need to manage them as a team that will work together, helping each other rather than getting in each other's way—a challenge made more difficult by the dynamic setting.

QUESTIONS FOR DISCUSSION

1. Think through the football-team metaphor. How do the concepts apply to your brand portfolio strategy?

2. Pick two product-market contexts and identify the product-defining brand set for some of the major competitors. Why are they different? Is one superior?

3. For each of your major brands, identify the brand's scope as a master brand and as an endorser. Are the brands fully leveraged?

4. Identify examples in your brand portfolio of the five portfolio roles.

5. Put on one wall all of the ways that one of your brands is visually presented. Is there consistency?

6. Detail your current portfolio structure using one of the approaches discussed. Is it logical and clear, or a mess? If it is a mess, what alternatives would improve it?

CHAPTER 2

THE BRAND RELATIONSHIP SPECTRUM

Beware of all enterprises that require new clothes.

—HENRY DAVID THOREAU, *WALDEN*

Architecture starts when you carefully put two bricks together. There it begins.

—LUDWIG MIES VAN DER ROHE

THE DISNEY BRAND FAMILY

Disney is simply an awesome brand supported by a brand family that has been nurtured for around three-quarters of a century.* How awesome? Young & Rubicam has measured the brand equity of more than 13,000 brands in some three dozen countries four times over the past decade. Their key brand dimensions are differentiation, relevance, esteem, and knowledge. A super brand, according to Y&R, is a brand that scores over 80 on each dimension; Disney has scored over 90 on each dimension in all four surveys. In the second year of a study of the strength of some 1,300 brands in Japan conducted by Nikkei BP, Disney vaulted into a share of the top spot with Sony, long the strongest brand in Japan. This accomplishment was based in part on the visibility of a new theme park, Tokyo DisneySea, but also reflects the heritage of Disney among Japanese.

The *Business Week* 2002 Interbrand study of brand values concluded

---

* Sources for this piece included the Disney website; Disney annual reports for 1999, 2000, 2001, and 2002; Michael C. Rukstad and David Collis, "The Walt Disney Company: The Entertainment King," Harvard Business School case 9-701-035; Bill Capodagli and Lynn Jackson, *The Disney Way,* New York: McGraw-Hill Book Company, 1999; and Tom Connellan, *Inside the Magic Kingdom,* Austin, TX: Bard Press, 1997.

that over 50 percent of the value of The Walt Disney Company was attributable to the Disney brand, which thus was valued at 29 billion dollars.[1] And this valuation undoubtedly understates the worth of the hundreds of strong brands in the Disney family.

Certainly the Disney story is not without flaws. A Mickey's Kitchen fast food concept proved to be too much of a stretch in the 1980s. An effort to create a local entertainment venue for young kids failed to attract weekday business needed to make it successful. Disneyland Paris struggled during the early EuroDisney days, and the Go.com web concept failed.

In general, however, for an extended time period Disney has set the standard for leveraging a brand to make it richer and stronger, continually injecting energy into it, and virtually never disappointing customers. The story of the Disney brand and the management of the Disney brand portfolio is impressive, providing instructive insights. The Disney brand portfolio strategy tying together the extensive Disney brand family started with Disney's original big brand extension: Disneyland.

The Really Big Idea—Disneyland

At the risk of hyperbole, one could argue that Disneyland Park had more brand impact than nearly any brand-building initiative in business history. Disneyland took magical family entertainment to a whole new level in terms of both breadth and depth. Prior to Disneyland, the audiences for Mickey Mouse, Snow White, and *Fantasia* were absorbed into a magical world, but it was a world based on movies and books that created a passive experience.

In contrast, Disneyland was a hands-on experience. You didn't just see Fantasyland, you were *inside* it, experiencing being a cowboy and eating in the Western bar. You interacted with Mickey and Donald up close. You had sensations on rides that were placed in a context not found in other amusement parks. Moreover, the experience was probably with a family unit. The memory of that experience lingers, creating nostalgia surrounding Disneyland—the place where those warm feelings surrounded you as a kid, or as a parent. Magical family entertainment now had a depth of expression rarely attached to any brand.

The Disneyland experience is firmly attached to Disney as a brand. The Disney name is on the door, of course, but also Disneyland provides a showcase for a host of symbols and characters that are closely associated with the brand. Not only are the Disney characters walking around and participating in parades, they are represented everywhere from Tarzan's Treehouse to the Many Adventures of Winnie the Pooh to Meet Your Favorite Disney Princesses. There is no way that the Disneyland experience could be separated from the total Disney brand.

Disneyland also has a host of branded differentiators—branded features that set it apart from other theme parks. There is only one place where a child can experience the Matterhorn Bobsleds, the "It's a Small World" ride, Tom Sawyer Island, and on and on. These features provide a sense of familiarity, another link to Disney, and unique experiences.

Brand Extensions: Leveraging, Enriching, and Supporting

Many of the Disney brand extensions could also be categorized as "big ideas." Disney is a role model for aggressively extending the brand to strengthen assets and build new business areas, using descriptors like "land" and "Cruise Ship," subbrands like Disney's Boardwalk and Disney World, endorsed brands like "The Lion King" or Disney's Animal Kingdom, or co-brands like Disney-MGM Studios while maintaining a true-to-brand discipline. Consider the path of the Disney brand and how every initiative fits and enriches.

In 1954, a few months before the Disneyland theme park opened, the Disneyland (later "Wonderful World of Disney") television show appeared, a solid hit that is still on the air today. Hosted for many years by Walt Disney himself, it had a rotating subject that often was related to the Disneyland park themes of Fantasyland, Adventureland, Tomorrowland, and Frontierland. The Davy Crockett series was particularly popular and garnered for Disney yet another family of characters and symbols. The Disney brand continued to expand into the television space with the "Mickey Mouse Club" in 1955 and eventually the Disney Channel in 1983. After a slow start (in part from choosing not to be a "free" channel), the latter was poised to overtake Nickelodeon in 2003.

Disney has extended the Disneyland park concept to other geographies, opening the Walt Disney World Resort in 1971, Tokyo Disneyland Resort in 1983, and EuroDisney in 1992. These were supplemented by other theme parks endorsed by Disney, such as Epcot in 1982, Disney-MGM Studios in 1989, Disney's Animal Kingdom in 1998, and Disney's California Adventure in 2001. Making these parks endorsed brands rather than subbrands served to accentuate the perception that they were substantial and would warrant extending a planned stay at the destination. Surrounding the theme parks are a set of resort hotels, each with a distinctive personality that is very Disney, such as the Disney-endorsed Paradise Pier and Disney's Grand Californian at Disneyland, and Disney's Animal Kingdom Lodge (with rooms facing the "African Safari") and Disney's Yacht and Beach Club Resort at Walt Disney World. In part to make the destination vacation experience complete, there is Downtown Disney at Disneyland Resort and the Walt Disney World Resort as well.

And that is only part of the story. The Disney Stores were launched in 1987 as another vehicle to interact with the brand, offering dolls, games, videos, and CDs based on Disney characters. Walt Disney Pictures continued to put out a stream of both animated pictures (such as *101 Dalmatians*) and feature films (such as *The Parent Trap* and *Mary Poppins*) that enriched the Disney family of brand assets. And there is also Disney on Ice, Disney Cruise Line, *The Lion King* on Broadway, Disney Auctions (in conjunction with eBay), Disney's Visa card and Radio Disney.

One characteristic of good extensions is that the brand brings something to the party. The potential customer should be able to specify how the new entry will be different from the competition based on his or her knowledge of the brand behind it. In each extension, the Disney brand brings expectations of magical family entertainment, as well as a host of associations. For example, even those who have never experienced a cruise can probably describe what the Disney Cruise Line will look like, and how its cruising experience will differ from other cruise lines. Further, the Disney brand provides a level of trust that others must spend considerable resources to earn.

An extension should also support and enhance the parent brand. Think how much Disneyland, Disney Channel, and Disney Stores have helped make the Disney brand richer. These extensions enhance associations, provide visibility and energy, and strengthen the brand relationship by providing more opportunities for customers to interact with Disney.

Branded Energizers

Disney has hundreds of branded energizers, brands, or subbrands that energize or enhance the Disney brand. Most brands are lucky to have any. Mickey Mouse appeared in 1928 and was followed by Donald Duck in 1937, Snow White and the Seven Dwarfs in 1939, and Pinocchio in 1940. Think about it: Disney owns the characters of Snow White as well as Sneezy, Dopey, and the others. How valuable is that? Yet before the animated movies made them part of the Disney family, the characters existed solely in the public domain, gathering dust.

And it goes on and on. Disney not only co-opted such existing characters as Snow White, Pinocchio, Davy Crockett, Aladdin, and the Little Mermaid, but has created its own. *The Lion King* and *Lilo & Stitch* both contain properties and characters that enrich the Disney experience. Perhaps more important, they create vitality; there is always something fresh in the Disney portfolio.

The Disney family of brands is actively managed. Aggressive licensing programs contribute on-going visibility for many characters that could have faded quickly after they appeared in a movie or TV show. Mickey Mouse watches and model trains were available in the early 1930s, and the Davy Crockett character got legs when his coonskin hat was licensed and became popular. Licensing has grown to be a major source of both brand visibility and income for Disney. During the 1990s, the program has been tightened to make sure that exposure of the characters and symbols are "on-brand."

In managing its brand portfolio, Disney understands better than most firms the value of achieving synergy across products. "The Lion King" is not only a film but supports a video, merchandise, publishing, games, and promotional tie-ins, and even a Broadway show. "Pirates of the Caribbean" is not only a theme park ride but an eponymous hit movie, loosely based on the attraction. Each of these efforts not only contributes revenue but also builds equity in the symbols.

Branded energizers, of course, are of value only if they are linked to the parent brand. Disney carefully creates those links. Most of the symbols and characters first appear in a movie or TV show that is distinctively Disney. This initial association is then reinforced with a presence in the theme parks, videos, items sold in the Disney Store, and promotions—most of which link the characters and symbols with not only the parent brand but other Disney characters and symbols. Thus the Disney link is continuously reinforced. Best of all, this reinforcement is basically free, as there is no advertising primarily geared toward supporting the link.

FIGURE 2-1
THE DISNEY FAMILY—A PARTIAL VIEW

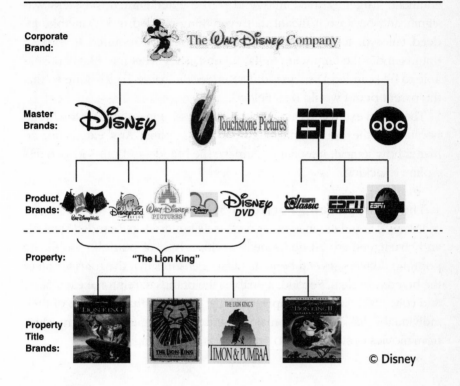

© Disney

The Disney Organization

Imitating Disney is not easy, because much of its success is based on the heritage and culture established in the early days of the firm. In particular, a relentless, uncompromising drive for operational excellence started with Walt Disney's fanatical concern for detail in the cartoons and theme parks. This drive is manifested in the insistence that all Disney ventures—from the Cruise Line to the movies to the theme parks—exude the trademark magic and live up to Disney standards down to the last detail. There are numerous stories about how the organization went the extra mile to make sure that the parks were clean or the cruise ships were just right. In fact, Disney's excellence in culture-driven operations is so well known that Disney provides consulting service to other companies who want to emulate its approach.

Another asset is the tradition of knowing what the brand stands for.

Disney's wide span of extensions could not have happened without a clear brand identity: making people happy with magical family entertainment. Targeting the family end of the entertainment business was significant, because it meant that everything needed to be suitable, indeed tailored, to kids and families. Discipline is required to protect brands under the family umbrella. When Disney went into films not suitable to be branded Disney, it did so under the name Touchstone so that the parent brand would be shielded.

The brand extensions at Disney are successful in enhancing the brand because of the operational culture and discipline. Any extension, no matter how logical, may fail or damage the brand—or both—if such discipline is lacking.

The Disney Brand Portfolio Strategy

Disney's brand extensions, as well as its hundreds of branded symbols and characters, are all tied together with a host of portfolio tools. The portfolio delivers several benefits. First, it ensures that the roles for all of the brands are clear. Second, it enables the brands to reinforce each other and collectively leave an impression that is greater than the sum of their individual roles. Third, the major brands are leveraged in many ways, from movies to store items to promotions to licensing.

MASTER BRANDS, ENDORSERS, SUBBRANDS, AND DRIVER ROLES

To create effective brand portfolios that will achieve their objectives, it is imperative to understand the basic product-defining building blocks—namely, master brands, endorsers, subbrands, and the concept of a driver role. Much of the task of creating and adapting portfolios to support an evolving business strategy centers on these building blocks. Knowing when to leverage a master brand by using it as an endorser, or how to empower a master brand in a new context through the use of a subbrand, are examples of how these tools can help the portfolio adapt and enable business strategies.

Relationships between brands matter as well. What is the relationship of Disney Cruise Lines or Disney Channel to the parent brand? How much do the Epcot or "The Lion King" brands impact the Disney brand, and vice versa? What is the relationship between Touchstone Pictures and Disney? Why are some relationships between Disney brands closer than others?

We start below by reviewing some definitions. The brand relationship spectrum (a tool to understand brand relationships) is then introduced, followed by a discussion of its four pillars—the house of brands, endorsed brands, subbrands, and a branded house. Finally, the selection of the optimal spectrum position is addressed.

Master Brand

A master (or parent) brand is the primary indicator of the offering, the point of reference. Visually, it will usually take top billing. GE is a master brand under which the company sells refrigerators, aircraft engines, and a variety of other goods. Crest is a master brand that defines a line of dental products from P&G. Toyota is a master brand that defines a line of cars. A master brand can have a subbrand, such as the Toyota Corolla, or can be endorsed, as the Band-Aid brand is by Johnson & Johnson.

Endorser Brands

An endorser brand serves to give credibility and substance to the offering. When, for example, IBM endorses Lotus, the IBM organization implicitly affirms that Lotus will deliver on its brand promise (which, of course, is very different from that of products for which IBM is a master brand). Endorsers are usually organizational brands—that is, they represent organizations rather than products—because organizational associations such as innovation, leadership, and trust are particularly relevant in endorser contexts. Endorsements are powerful because endorsers are somewhat insulated from the brands they endorse. Thus, they can contribute with reduced risk that their associations will be affected by the performance of the endorsed brand.

Endorsements can take several forms. For example, Fiber One bran cereal is endorsed by General Mills, but a note on the package adds that Fiber One is a proud sponsor of the American Diabetes Association (ADA), whose logo is shown. Because customers correctly surmise that the logo would not be there unless the ADA was comfortable with the product, the association has an endorser relationship with Fiber One.

Subbrands

Subbrands are brands that modify the associations of a master or parent brand, which remains the primary frame of reference. The subbrands can add associations (Sony Walkman), a brand personality (Calloway Big Bertha), a product category (Ocean Spray Craisins), and even energy (Nike Force). In doing so, they stretch the master brand. In fact, one role of a subbrand is usually to extend a master brand into a meaningful new segment.

Subbrands are brands in that they are uniquely associated with an organization and can capture equity. Descriptors, in contrast, merely describe what is offered. For the brand GE Appliances, "Appliances" is a descriptor. There is no brand called "Appliance," because that characteristic cannot be owned by GE or any other firm. The same can be said of the descriptors in Ziploc Sandwich Bags or Tylenol Extended Relief.

Unlike descriptors alone, a product brand—a master brand plus a subbrand or master brand plus a descriptor—can capture equity. For example, GE Appliances is a product brand and can potentially differ in its equity from GE Aircraft Engines. Similarly, descriptors define the product brands for Cadbury Chocolate Biscuits and Marriott Resort Hotels, and each potentially merit active management and can capture equity. Some suggestive descriptors (as in Holiday Inn Express, Wells Fargo Advantage, Fisher-Price All-In-One Kitchen Center, or Visa Gold) have more potential to help define a distinctive product brand.

Subbrands and endorsed brands are important portfolio tools because they allow brands to be stretched beyond their existing zone of comfort. As such, they provide vehicles to do the following:

- Address conflicting brand strategy needs as when a brand image needs to be adapted to a new product-market context
- Conserve brand-building resources in part by leveraging existing brand equity
- Protect brands from being diluted by overstretching
- Signal that an offering is new and different without starting over with a new brand

Without these product-defining tools, the choice of a new offering would be limited largely to either building a new brand (an expensive and difficult proposition) or extending an existing brand with a descriptor (and thereby risking image dilution).

Driver Roles

The driver role reflects the degree to which a brand drives the purchase decision and defines the use experience. When a person is asked, "What brand did you buy?" or "What brand did you use?" the answer given will be the brand that had the primary driver role responsibility for the decision. A driver brand has earned some level of loyalty; customers would be less comfortable with the product with the brand missing.

Thus, Toyota is the primary driver for Toyota Corolla, as users will say they own a Toyota rather than a Corolla. Similarly, users of Hershey's Sweet Escapes will tend to say they had a Sweet Escapes rather than the endorser, Hershey's. Hershey's is relegated to a minor driver role. Courtyard is the driver of the Courtyard by Marriott offering. Courtyard associations were the primary influence in determining the selection of the hotel and augment the use experience by adding richness and emotional or self-expressive content. Walkman has the primary driver role for the Sony offering.

Of course, the driver role can vary by segment. For some corporate buyers of the IBM ThinkPad, IBM may indeed play more of a driver role than it would among those buying for home use. Similarly, some Hershey's loyalists might buy Sweet Escapes because of the parent brand and may be satisfied with any Hershey's product.

A driver brand is usually a master brand or subbrand. Endorsers, descriptors, and second-level subbrands (which are subbrands to subbrands), however, can have some driver role. In fact, when multiple brands are involved, the driver role of each can vary from zero to 100 percent. The ability of the brand portfolio strategy to refine the driver role in this manner is flexible and powerful. It is sometimes productive to divide 100 points among the involved brands to represent the relative driver roles.

While a business may have hundreds of brands, there are usually a smaller number that have major driver responsibility. These brands are candidates for active management and brand building, both individually and as a group, as a misstep with a driver brand is a serious problem. Some very basic brand architecture issues involve the composition of this group. What are the major driver brands, those brands that collectively control the relationships with customers? Should some be retired or de-emphasized? Should others be added or elevated? Should some be extended, or have they been stretched too far and should contract?

The balance of this chapter will focus on a tool to help understand and select product-defining roles, termed the *brand relationship spectrum*.

LINKING BRANDS—THE BRAND RELATIONSHIP SPECTRUM

A key brand portfolio strategy issue is how to brand an acquired or newly developed offering. There are four options, each with several variants:

- A house of brands (a new brand)
- Endorsed brands
- Subbrands under a master brand
- A branded house (an existing brand with a descriptor)

The most independent option is to have a new brand unconstrained by any past associations. That is termed a "house of brands" strategy because it reflects the fact that the new brand needs its own house; it cannot share an existing brand in the portfolio. The second is the endorsed brand strategy, in which an existing brand provides a limited association (think of them as neighboring houses). The third is the subbrand strategy, where the new offering is marketed under an existing master brand (sort of like a visiting or live-in relative). The final option, to market the new offering under an existing master brand with a descriptor, is termed a branded house option because the offering shares the brand with other household members (like a family member living at home).

The brand relationship spectrum, portrayed in Figure 2-2, helps to position the various product-defining role options. It recognizes that these options define a continuum that involves four basic strategies and nine substrategies. Each of the four strategies represents a relationship between brands:

RELATIONSHIP BETWEEN PRODUCT-DEFINING BRANDS

House of brands	Two master brands (e.g., Pantene–Head & Shoulders)
Endorsed brands	Endorsers–endorsed brands (e.g., Disney–"The Lion King" from Disney)
Subbrand	Master brand–subbrand (e.g., Honda–Honda Accord)
Branded house	Master brand–two descriptors (e.g., GE Appliances–GE Capital)

The position on the spectrum reflects the degree to which brands are separated in strategy execution and, ultimately, in the customer's minds. The maximum separation occurs at the right side of the spectrum in the house of brands, where the brands stand by themselves (just as ESPN is separate from the Disney brand family). Moving to the left, there is a relationship between an endorser brand and the one being endorsed, but the brands are still very separate. For example, Pfizer can be very different from its endorsed brands such as Viagra. Moving further to the left, a master brand/subbrands relationship is more confining. A subbrand such as Toyota Camry can refine and augment the master brand, but it cannot stray too far from the latter's identity. In a branded house, which is at the far left, the master brand is the driver and the offerings are defined by descriptors. The perception of the master brand will not be modified by a subbrand.

The relationship spectrum, as suggested by Figure 2-2, is related to the driver role. At the far right, in the house of brands, each brand has its own driver role. With an endorsed brand, the endorser normally plays a smaller (perhaps very much so) driver role. Subbrands tend to share the driver role with the master brand. At the far left, in the branded house, the master brand generally has the driver role, and any descriptor has little or no such role.

Figure 2-2 shows that beneath the four brand relationship strategies, there are nine subcategories. Each of these is positioned on the spectrum based on how much brand separation they imply. To design effec-

FIGURE 2-2
BRAND RELATIONSHIP SPECTRUM

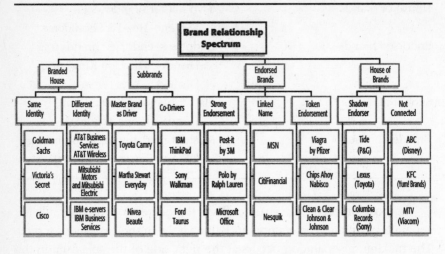

tive brand strategies, one must understand the four strategies and nine subcategories in the brand spectrum. Each will be reviewed and explained in the following sections.

A House of Brands

A branded house and a house of brands (as shown in Figure 2-3) vividly describe the two extremes of alternative brand portfolio strategies. While a house of brands contains independent, unconnected brands, a branded house uses a single master brand to span a set of offerings operating with only descriptive subbrands. For example, Harvard, Virgin, Caterpillar, Toshiba, Canon, GE, and Healthy Choice operate a large number of products (although most have exceptions) under the master brand using the branded house strategy.

In contrast, the house of brands strategy involves an independent set of stand-alone brands each focusing on maximizing the impact on a market. Procter & Gamble operates more than eighty major brands, few of which have any link to P&G or to each other. In doing so, P&G sacrifices the economies of scale that come with leveraging a brand across multiple businesses; each brand needs its own brand-building investment. Those brands that cannot support investment themselves (especially the third or fourth P&G entry in a category) risk stagnation and

FIGURE 2-3
BRANDED HOUSE VS. HOUSE OF BRANDS

HOUSE OF BRANDS

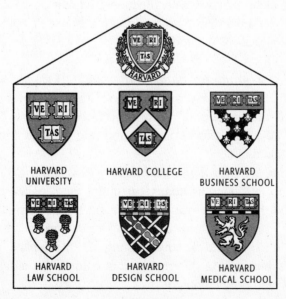

BRANDED HOUSE

decline. P&G also sacrifices brand leverage in that its brands tend to have a narrow range and potentially could be used more broadly.

The house of brands strategy, however, allows firms to position brands clearly on functional benefits and to dominate niche segments. No compromises have to be made in positioning to accommodate the brand's use in other product-market contexts. The brand connects directly to the niche customer with a targeted value proposition.

P&G's brand strategy in the hair care category illustrates the house of brands strategy. Head and Shoulders dominates the dandruff-control shampoo category. Pert Plus targets the market for a combined conditioner and shampoo product (where it is the category pioneer) and has its own personality. Pantene, "for hair so healthy it shines," a brand with a technological heritage, focuses on the segment concerned with enhancing hair vitality. The total impact of these three distinct brands would be lessened if they were restricted to the brand "P&G shampoo" or were sold as P&G Dandruff Control, P&G Combo, and P&G Healthy Hair. P&G detergents are similarly well positioned to serve niche markets: Tide (tough cleaning jobs), Cheer (all-temperature), Bold (with fabric softener), and Dash (concentrated powder) each provide sets of focused value propositions that would be difficult to achieve with a single P&G Detergent brand employing descriptors.

Targeting niche markets with functional benefit positions is not the only reason for separating brands through a house of brands strategy. Five additional reasons include:

- *Avoiding a brand association that would be incompatible with an offering.* The Budweiser association with the taste of beer would prevent the success of Budweiser Cola. Likewise, Volkswagen would adversely affect Porsche's and Audi's image if those brands were linked to it.
- *Signaling breakthrough advantages of new offerings.* Toyota's decision to introduce its luxury car under the separate Lexus name signaled that the car was truly different from any predecessors at Toyota. Similarly, General Motors decided to create the Saturn brand unconnected to any existing GM nameplate so that the brand's message ("A different kind of company, a different kind of car") would not be diluted.

- *Owning a new product-class association with a name reflecting a key benefit.* Gleem toothpaste and Reach toothbrushes are examples of this approach.
- *Avoiding or minimizing channel conflict.* L'Oréal has cosmetic brands that are channel specific. The L'Oréal and Maybelline brands are sold through drugstores and mass merchants, while Lancôme and Helena Rubinstein appear in high-end department stores and Redken is sold to professional hair stylists. When unconnected brands are sold through competing channels, conflict is usually not an issue.
- *Targeting multiple and conflicting product lines or segments.* For example, Nestlé and Purina (food and petfood) need brands with no connection between them.

The unconnected subcategory represents the most extreme house of brands strategy, maximizing the separation between the brands. Few people know that Head & Shoulders and Pantene are made by the same company.

SHADOW ENDORSER

A shadow endorser is not connected visibly to the endorsed brand, but many consumers know about the link. It represents a subcategory in the house of brands strategy that provides some of the advantages of having a known organization backing the brand, while minimizing any association contamination. The fact that the brands are not visibly linked makes a statement about each brand, even when the link is discovered. It communicates the organization's realization that the shadow-endorsed brand represents a totally different product and market segment.

Lettuce Entertain You, a Chicago-based group with roughly forty restaurants (such as Shaw's Crab House and Brasserie Joe's), was a shadow endorser for some twenty-five years after opening its first concept restaurant in 1971. Each restaurant had its own image, personality, style, and brand name; the absence of a visible endorsement from Lettuce Entertain You meant that there was no chain connotation. Patrons need to discover the shadow endorsement themselves through word-of-mouth and public relations. Discovering the endorsement and having some intriguing "insider knowledge" only increased its impact. In the late 1990s, Lettuce Entertain You found through a survey that it had substantial brand equity, and so it decided to become more visible. They risked losing their mystique but were able to advertise, develop a frequent diner program, and cross-promote their restaurants.

Disney, of course, is the shadow endorser of a host of brands, including Mickey Mouse, Davy Crockett, and Snow White. The absence of a visual Disney endorsement allows each to develop a personality and set of characteristics largely unencumbered by the parent brand's associations and other Disney characters, even though it is well known that they are part of the Disney family.

A shadow endorser strategy can protect the endorsed brand from unwanted associations while still providing the benefits of endorsement. For example, many people are reassured by knowing that Toyota's financial strength and reputation support Lexus. However, Lexus still delivers self-expressive benefits that would be diminished by a visible connection with Toyota. A shadow endorsement can minimize the impact on the endorsed brand because the connection is recessed in memory.

A shadow endorser, while having a minimal impact on the brand's image or ability to deliver emotional and self-expressive benefits, can be important to non-customer segments. Dockers and Mountain Dew both get more respect from retailers because of their association with Levi-Strauss and Pepsi, respectively. The concierges at major Chicago hotels were more likely to recommend a Lettuce Entertain You restaurant when it was a shadow endorser. The shadow endorsement of Touchstone by Disney helps it attract high-potential scripts. The shadow endorsement by Viacom of its properties such as CBS television, Blockbuster, Simon & Schuster, Paramount Pictures, and Nickelodeon affects investors and advertisers.

Endorsed Brands

Brand portfolio strategy is not limited to the house of brands (a new brand) or branded house (existing brand with a descriptor) options. The brand portfolio solution is much more complex because of the existence of two powerful tools—namely, endorsed brands and subbrands/co-brands. Endorsed brands are explained in this section.

With an endorsed brand (such as Miracle fragrance from Lancôme) the endorser brand represents an organization providing assurance that the endorsed brand will live up to its claims. An endorsed brand (Miracle) is not independent of the endorser (Lancôme), but it has enough freedom to develop product associations and a brand personality that are different from that of the endorser.

The endorser brand usually has only a minor driver role. For example, Hanes endorses the Revitalize collection, a line of sheer hosiery designed to promote daily leg health and wellness. The driver brand is Revitalize because customers are primarily focused on the functional benefits, not the Hanes name. As the endorser brand, though, Hanes provides assurance that Revitalize will live up to its quality and performance claims.

Although the primary role of the endorser usually is to provide credibility, a strong brand can impact the endorsed brand image and even play a modest driver role. The endorsement of Ralph Lauren, for example, can modify the image of the endorsed brand (Polo) by signaling a fashion-forward line of clothing. Although people buy and use Obsession, the endorsement by Calvin Klein gives consumers permission to buy something that would otherwise, on its own merits, be too tacky. In this case, the endorsement by Calvin Klein is like a wink at the consumer, saying that the name is just a game, a bit of self-expression.

Do endorsers make any difference? A study of confectionery brands in the United Kingdom provides some empirical evidence that organizational brand endorsers pay off.[2] The study involved customers evaluating nine confectionery offerings, each of which was backed by one of six corporate endorsers (Cadbury, Mars, Nestlé, Terry's, Walls, and a control). The results showed that all of the corporate endorsements added significantly more value than the control (no endorsement) even for Walls, an ice-cream brand whose associations are with a different category. Cadbury, which received the highest ratings, consistently endorsed a range of leading confectionery products. Second was Mars, which endorses only a few of its confectionery brands. Third was Nestlé, which endorses a wide range of products. The conclusion from the study was that endorsement is helpful, and that the best endorsement comes from an organization with credibility in the product class.

Making the endorser strategy work involves understanding the role of the organizational brand. Consider the Hobart brand, the top-of-the-line industrial mixers used by larger restaurants and bakeries. Purchasing a Hobart provides significant self-expressive benefits to chefs who want only the best brands for their kitchens. Responding to an emerging value segment served by offshore suppliers, the company introduced the Medalist by Hobart brand, with the Hobart endorsement in small type. Now there were two Hobart brands involved in the marketplace—the Hobart product brand, and the Hobart organizational brand used to endorse the Medalist mixers.

Two implications of this dual Hobart brand reality are worth noting. First, the integrity and self-expressive benefits of the Hobart product brand are maintained, because it is distinct from the organizational brand. Second, the Hobart organizational brand is now an important part of the brand portfolio and needs to be actively managed. In particular, the organizational brand will have its own distinct identity and, as a result, its own set of associations to develop and maintain. It is possible to make clear that the endorser is an organizational brand by representing the product as "from Hobart" or "a Hobart company." This is not always necessary, however, because the endorser role by itself has an organizational brand connotation.

Another motivation for endorsing a brand is to provide some useful associations or energy for the endorser. For example, when Nestlé bought Kit-Kat, a leading chocolate brand in the United Kingdom, the addition of a Nestlé endorsement enhanced Nestlé's image in that country by associating the firm with quality and leadership in chocolate. In another industry, the endorsement by 3M of Post-it Notes probably does as much for 3M as it does for Post-it Notes.

The form of the endorsement can affect the relationship, sometimes in a subtle way. Dreyer's ice cream licensed Mars candy products such as Snickers and Three Musketeers. Mars, who wanted more distance from Dreyer's than a normal endorsement would suggest, agreed to have a "Dreyer's presents" endorsement, suggesting more of a Mars product and reducing the suggestion that Dreyer's was a master brand.

TOKEN ENDORSER

A variant of the endorser strategy is a token endorser (usually a master brand involved in several product-market contexts) in which the endorsement is substantially less prominent. The token endorser can be indicated by a logo like the GE bulb or the Betty Crocker spoon, a statement such as "a Sony company," or by another device. In any case, the token endorser will not have center stage; the endorsed brand will be featured. Nestlé puts a seal of guarantee on the back of packages—for example, "All Maggi products benefit from Nestlé experience in producing quality foods all over the world." The role of the token endorser is to make the connection with the endorsed brand visible and provide, especially for new brands, some reassurance and credibility while still allowing the endorsed brands maximum freedom to create their own associations.

A token endorser can be especially helpful to brands that are new or not yet established. The token endorsement will have more impact if the endorser:

- Is well known already (for example, Nestlé or Post)
- Is consistently presented (the visual representation—the Betty Crocker spoon or the GE bulb—is in the same location in the visual setting of the ad, package, or other vehicle)
- Has a visual metaphor symbol (such as the Traveler's umbrella)
- Appears on a family of products that are well regarded, such as the Nabisco product lines, so that the endorser provides credibility from its ability to span well-regarded products

A token endorsement is more useful than a strong endorsement when the endorsed brand needs more distance from the endorser. This situation may arise because the endorser has undesirable associations, or the endorsed brand may be an innovation that needs more perceived independence to make its position credible.

A common mistake is to exaggerate the impact of a token endorsement when the endorser is not well known and well regarded, or when the endorsed brand is well regarded and established and thus does not need the reassurance of an endorser. Two studies make the points well.

Providian, a major financial services firm, was once a combination of businesses connected by a forgettable phrase (something like "a Capital Holding Company"). In a survey of 1,000 customers all of whom had been exposed numerous times to the phrase, only 3 (or 0.3 percent) knew the endorser. This sobering statistic led to the renaming of the firm as Providian, and to a new brand portfolio structure.

Nestlé once conducted a U.S. study to determine the impact of the token endorsement by Nescafé (a strong coffee brand elsewhere, but a weak one in the United States) on Taster's Choice, a strong American brand. Because of Taster's Choice's brand strength, the token endorsement had little impact either positively or negatively in terms of image or intention measures. When the endorser was elevated to a co-brand status, however, it had a negative impact.

LINKED NAME

Another endorsement variant is a linked brand name, where an endorser is linked to brands through a name with common elements. This creates a family of brands with an implicit or implied endorser. This option allows a way to have multiple distinct brands, each with its own personality and associations but also a subtle link to a master or umbrella brand.

McDonald's has registered around 100 names with *Mac* or *Mc,* including Big Mac, Chicken McNuggets, Chicken McSwiss, Egg McMuffin, McDonuts, McFortune Cookie, and McRib. It has even developed a McLanguage that includes McCleanest, McFavorite, and McGreatest. In the Far East, it is rolling out McCoffee to compete with Starbucks. The company protects the *Mc* word part aggressively and has objected to a bakery named McBagels and a McSushi restaurant. The result is an endorser brand with a powerful range.

The prefix *Mc* creates an implied McDonald's endorsement, even though a traditional endorsement is not present. Linked names allow more ownership and differentiation than a descriptor strategy; just consider the value of the Big Mac brand name as opposed to "McDonald's large hamburger" or Chicken McNuggets vs. "McDonald's fried chicken morsels" or McKids vs. "McDonald's children's clothing."

HP has the Jet series—LaserJet, DeskJet, OfficeJet, InkJet and others—that covers a variety of price points and applications. LaserJet is the strongest brand in this group (the others have little equity), but its associations with quality, reliability, and innovation transfer to the other Jet brands. In effect, LaserJet is endorsing the rest of the family. Nestle's Nescafe, Nestea, and NesQuik (in the United Kingdom) provide a compact but strong link to the parent brand. The Netscape e-commerce brand, Netscape CommerceXpert, has the linked subbrands ECXpert, SellerXpert, BuyerXpert, MerchantXpert, and PublishingXpert.

A linked name provides the benefits of a separate name without having to establish a second name from scratch and link it to another brand. Consider Ofoto by Kodak. The brand name Ofoto needed to be established, an expensive and difficult process. In addition, it had to be linked to the Kodak brand, another nontrivial task. In contrast, the name DeskJet itself accomplishes 80 percent of the task of linking this HP product to the established brand, LaserJet. Furthermore, the communication of what DeskJet stands for is also partially accomplished by what is known about LaserJet. The linked brand name also achieves these goals in a more compact way than, for example, "DeskJet from LaserJet."

STRONG ENDORSERS

A strong endorser is visually indicated by a prominent presentation. Examples of strong endorsers include Simply Home from Campbell's, Highland by 3M, Polo Jeans by Ralph Lauren, Optiquest by Viewsonic, Lycra by DuPont, and Paramount's Kings Dominion. A strong endorser usually has more of a meaningful driver role than does a token endorser or linked name relationship. Therefore, it has credibility in the product-market context and associations that fit.

A continuum of endorsement options are available. In the relationship spectrum, three are explicitly identified: token, linked names, and strong endorser. The availability of multiple endorsement levels adds valuable flexibility to the brand portfolio.

ENDORSEMENT AS AN INTERIM STRATEGY

An endorsed brand can play a key role as an interim step in a broader strategy. For example, token endorsement is often a first step in a gradual name change. A token endorsement becomes a strong endorsement, and then a co-brand, and finally a master driver brand. The process involves transferring the brand equity from the endorsed brand to the endorser.

An endorsed brand can also go the other way. Thus, Levi's endorsed Docker's at first in order to give the then-new brand credibility (with channel members as much as with customers). When Docker's became established, however, the endorsement was no longer needed—and, in fact, became something of a liability. So it faded away.

Subbrands

The subbrand, another powerful brand portfolio strategy tool, modifies a master brand by adding to or changing its associations (such as an attribute, a benefit, or personality). For example:

- Black & Decker Sweet Hearts Wafflebaker (which makes heart-shaped waffles) and the Black & Decker Handy Steamer (which makes steaming fresh vegetables easy) have subbrands that add points of attribute differentiation while offering emotional benefits to the Black & Decker brand.
- The Smucker's Simply Fruit subbrand strengthens the fresh/healthy/quality associations of the Smucker's brand.
- Audi TT has the TT subbrand that adds energy and personality to an established master brand that is considered high in quality but lacking the interest and personality of its competitors.
- Revlon Revolutionary (lip color) and Revlon Fire and Ice (fragrance) represent two subbrands that add energy and vitality to the parent brand.
- Dodge Viper has a subbrand that can create associations that make the master brand seem more differentiated and appealing to customers.

A subbrand can allow a master brand with too broad an appeal to access niche segments. For example, Pepsi with its huge, broad brand basically hit a wall and needed to create subbrands around the Pepsi and Mountain Dew franchise in order to find pockets of growth.[3] So they introduced lemon-flavored Pepsi Twist and berry-flavored Pepsi Blue and the cherry-flavored, caffeine-loaded Mountain Dew Code Red. Code Red has attracted urbanites, women, and African-Americans who had not previously been attracted to Mountain Dew. Pepsi Blue is aimed at teens.

A subbrand can also stretch the master brand, allowing it to compete in arenas in which it otherwise would not fit. For example, KNBR, a radio station in San Francisco, is known for its all-sports programming; it calls itself "The Sports Leader." But during the morning commute time, the audience is too broad to stick to a purely sports-talk format, so KNBR has what it calls the John London "Not Just Sports Show." The subbrand makes the point that this segment is different, and listeners normal impression of the radio station will not apply. It not only defines the John London show but actually serves to reinforce the sports format that applies to the rest of the day. So instead of having that show confuse the format, it does the reverse.

Another potential subbrand function is to signal that the new offering is novel and newsworthy. Intel developed the Pentium subbrand in part to signal that this new-generation chip was significantly more advanced. Without the subbrand, it is harder to create excitement around a new innovation.

Subbrands are closer to a master brand than endorsed brands are to endorsers, even strong endorsers. Because of this proximity, a subbrand has considerable potential to affect the associations of the master brand, which in turn can be a risk or an opportunity. In addition, the master brand will usually have a major driver role in a product brand using a subbrand. Thus, if Revolutionary is a subbrand to Revlon rather than an endorsed brand, it will have less freedom to create a distinct brand image.

Unlike a descriptor that will have little or no driver role, a subbrand can have a significant driver role, sometimes more than the master brand that it modifies. In developing a subbrand strategy, it is important to recognize the extent of the driver role to be assigned. It is all too common to manage as if the subbrand had a substantial driver role when in fact it basically acts as a descriptor. The result is wasted brand-building resources and marketplace confusion. If the subbrand has a driver role equal to the master brand, a co-driver situation exists. If the subbrand is the dominant driver, it is no longer a subbrand, but an endorsed brand.

THE SUBBRAND AS A CO-DRIVER

When both the master brand and the subbrand have major driver roles, they can be termed co-drivers. The master brand is performing more than an endorser role. For instance, customers are buying and using both Gillette and Sensor; one does not markedly dominate the other. Usually for this to be the case, the master brand already has some real credibility in the product class. Gillette, with its innovation over the years, has become a brand that enjoys loyalty in the razor category. Sensor is a particularly innovative razor, and it too merits and receives loyalty.

The cosmetics product Virgin Vie uses a subbrand as a co-driver. While the Virgin brand provides presence, visibility, and attitude, it is associated with a generation older than the target market for Virgin Vie. The use of the Vie subbrand rather than a subbrand descriptor (such as "Virgin Cosmetics") helps to make the brand more credible in the cosmetics market and to access a younger target market of twentysomething consumers. A young British celebrity used in the Virgin Vie communications creates further separation from the Virgin brand and founder Richard Branson.

THE MASTER BRAND AS THE PRIMARY DRIVER

Another subbrand variant occurs when the master brand is the primary driver. The subbrand is more than a descriptor, but it has a minority role in defining the purchase decision and use experiences. The buyer clearly believes that it is the master brand that is being purchased.

When the subbrand has a minor driver role, one implication is that there should not be a lot of resources placed into the subbrand. The emphasis should be on the master brand. Too often, a subbrand is wrongly perceived to have equity and a co-driver status in part because employees have seen the subbrands for many years. Subbrands like Del Monte's Fresh Cut or Celestial Seasonings Mint Magic or Dell Dimension, however, usually have less equity than is assumed. Thus, in sorting out the brand portfolio, it is important to ascertain which subbrands have significant equity in order to avoid making decisions to build brands that lack equity or equity potential.

A Branded House

In a branded house strategy, a master brand moves from being a primary driver to a dominant driver role. Any descriptor used has a very modest or nonexistent driver role. Virgin has a branded house because the master brand, Virgin, provides an umbrella (or roof) under which most of its business operations operate: Virgin Airlines, Virgin Express, Virgin Radio, Virgin Rail, Virgin Cola, Virgin Jeans, Virgin Music, and many others. Other branded houses include many of the offerings of Healthy Choice, Kraft, Honda, Adidas, and Nike.

The branded house option leverages an established brand and minimizes the required investment on each new offering. It also, of course, puts a lot of eggs in one basket and limits the firm's ability to target specific groups. Toshiba, Mitsubishi, and Kodak, for example, have struggled with a brand that has been an umbrella for a wide product line. Each has found it difficult to maintain a cutting-edge image or a quality position with a large product scope and the presence of aggressive competitors. Even a branded house such as Nike, which has been generally successful over the years, might have had an easier time had it developed multiple brand platforms.

In addition, with a branded house strategy, sales and profit are affected across the board when the brand falters. The problem is accentuated by momentum; when the brand struggles in some contexts the momentum can be very hard to regain. However, the branded house enhances clarity, synergy, and leverage, three of the goals of brand architecture.

The branded house portfolio strategy has the potential to maximize clarity, because the customer knows exactly what is being offered. Virgin stands for service quality, innovation, value, and being the underdog. It has a heritage of being fun and outrageous. The descriptors indicate the business; Virgin Rail is a railroad run by the Virgin organization. It could not be simpler from a branding perspective. A single brand such as Virgin, communicated over products and time, is simply easier to understand and recall than a dozen brands, each with its own identity and associations. Employees and communication partners benefit from greater clarity and focus with a single dominant brand. There should be little question of brand priorities or the importance of protecting the brand when a branded house is involved. Clarity, however, will depend on a consistent brand meaning and message. If the brand is allowed to vary in an undisciplined way across contexts, confusion and dilution can be the result.

A branded house will also tend to maximize synergy, as participation in one product market creates associations and visibility that can help in another. At Virgin, the product and service innovations in one business enhance the brand in other businesses. Every exposure of the brand in one context enhances awareness of Virgin in all other contexts. Further, the ability to allocate resources over product brands may be organizationally easier with a branded house, because the strong subbrands and endorsed brands will not be competing for those resources.

Two anecdotes about GE show the synergistic value of how brand building in one business can affect another. First, GE was the perceived leader (by a big margin) in the small appliance category years after it had exited the business, in part because of the advertising and market presence of GE large appliances. Second, over 80 percent of the respondents in a survey said that they had been exposed to a GE Plastics ad during a time in which none appeared, but ads for other GE products had. Clearly, the accumulation of brand exposures over time and over business units has impact far beyond their intended function.

Finally, the branded house option provides leverage, in that the master brand works harder in more contexts. Virgin brand equity is harnessed and employed in hundreds of contexts. The role of business strategy is to create and leverage assets, and thus the branded house is a logical choice.

Because of its synergy, clarity, and leverage, the branded house should be the default option in establishing a new brand. Any strategy other than introducing a new sibling under the roof of an existing brand requires compelling reasons.

DIFFERENT PRODUCT BRANDS WITHIN THE BRANDED HOUSE

A branded house will not achieve its potential automatically. Just because the same brand is used with descriptors across products or markets does not mean that the portfolio goals will be met. If the brand is managed by silo business units with no coordination, the branded house will be an illusion, regardless of the common name.

Samsung found itself in the late 1990s with seventeen product brands being marketed in seventy countries.[4] Virtually all units, over 100 in number, were managing the brand autonomously, resulting in monumental inconsistency with many units tactical in orientation. The branded house was in existence in name only.

The creation of a true branded house for Samsung started with the development of a single brand identity and essence that would apply across products and markets. Samsung would be a leading innovator in product and digital convergence, led by some flagship products in wireless and display. The process then turned to the distribution of this brand identity to business units so it could be implemented at the product-market level. This effort was supported by the development of an infrastructure that included a single advertising agency, a marketing information system, a brand health measurement system, and a brand council supported by the CEO. A branded house emerged, but not without considerable effort and will.

It is certainly true that a brand identity can and usually should be adapted to different contexts. After buy-in was obtained throughout the organization, the Samsung brand was adapted at the local level. In fact, a brand identity can be adapted to different contexts by interpreting an association differently, or adding an association component or two. For example, GE Capital requires certain associations that are inappropriate for GE Appliance. The ultimate objective is to have strong product brands in each setting that are true to and leverage the GE brand. The goal is not to have identical product brands.

SELECTING THE RIGHT POSITION IN THE BRAND RELATIONSHIP SPECTRUM

Each context is different, and it is difficult to generalize about when to use which spectrum subcategory for a proposed new offering (or an existing one that is being reviewed). There are four options and many variants corresponding to the brand relationship spectrum. The offering can be represented by a separate brand, an endorsed brand, a master brand with a subbrand, or with a master brand and a descriptor. The choice really rests on the analysis of three questions:

- Will the existing brand enhance the offering?
- Will the offering enhance the brands that define the offering?
- Is there a compelling reason to generate a new brand (whether it be a stand-alone brand, an endorsed brand, or a subbrand)?

If the answers to the first two are positive and the third negative, the optimal choice will tend to be to the left side of the spectrum, toward a branded house. However, if the answers to the first two questions are negative and the third positive, the best choice will tend to be to the right side of the spectrum, toward a house of brands.

These three questions and other related issues will be discussed in more detail in the context of the brand extension decision in Chapter 7, the brand extension chapter.

A Closing Thought

Nearly all organizations will use a mixture of all four branding routes on the brand relationship spectrum. A pure house of brands or branded house is rare. GE, for example, looks like a branded house, but Hotpoint and NBC are outside this house. In addition, GE Capital itself has a host of subbrands and endorsed brands. The challenge is to create not a single house, but a village where all the subbrands and brands fit in and are productive.

QUESTIONS FOR DISCUSSION

1. Pick two diverse firms: one that is close to being a branded house, and another that is close to being a house of brands. Look closely at their branded offerings and identify the subcategories represented. Which offerings are endorsed? Which involve subbrands? Are there different levels of subbrands? What problems do you see? What changes would you consider? What research would you do to investigate those changes?

2. Analyze your endorser brands. Should there be more? Fewer? How much of a driver role do they have by channel? What percentage of the buying/use experience by segment does the endorser drive?

3. Analyze your subbrands. What do they add to the brand architecture? Are they confusing and complex? Could they be simplified? Rate these on a driver role scale as well.

4. For what portion of your offerings is a house of brands appropriate? Why? What portion should instead be modeled as a branded house? Why? Under what circumstances would additional subbrands or endorsers be helpful?

CHAPTER 3

INPUTS TO BRAND
PORTFOLIO DECISIONS

Brand strategy is the face of the business strategy.

—DICTUM OF PROPHET, A BRAND STRATEGY CONSULTANCY

Plans are nothing, planning is everything.

—DWIGHT EISENHOWER

Microsoft should invest in building the fewest number of the strongest brands needed to cover and compete in all desired markets.

—DAVID WEBSTER, MICROSOFT

MICROSOFT

Microsoft's big break came when IBM entered the PC world in 1981 and needed an operating system, the indispensable guts of the computer's software.* When the then-leading operating system company was reluctant to deal with IBM, Microsoft, a tiny company making programming languages like BASIC, was asked to do the job. Bill Gates, then the twenty-five-year-old CEO of a firm with a handful of employees, was able to negotiate a nonexclusive license. This meant that when the new Disk Operating System (DOS) quickly became the dominant operating system for personal computing, Microsoft controlled it.

During the first few years, PC companies used their own operating system brand—IBM called it PC-DOS, for example—but Microsoft's

---

* This section is based on the Microsoft website; Microsoft annual reports for 1999, 2000, 2001, and 2002; Jim Frederick, "Microsoft's $40 Billion Bet," *Money*, May 2002, pp. 66–80; Daniel Ichbiah and Susan L. Knepper, *The Making of Microsoft*, Rocklin, CA: Prima, 1991; Michael A. Cusumano and Richard W. Selby, *Microsoft Secrets*, New York: Simon & Schuster, 1995.

MS-DOS brand (the "MS" linking it to Microsoft) soon became the industry standard. As a result, even as they competed vigorously with each other, computer manufacturers all helped build and enhance the MS-DOS brand. Knowledge that a computer was based on MS-DOS gave customers assurance that the computer was in the mainstream and could run current software. The brand MS-DOS certainly helped Microsoft attain its market position.

A holdout to MS-DOS was Apple. In 1984 it introduced the Macintosh, a 32-bit computer whose operating system supported a user-friendly graphical interface that employed visuals and a mouse. Even though the Mac had modest market share, its design and attitude clearly resonated with people. It made MS-DOS, with its text-only interface, seem clunky and limited in comparison. Protecting the operating system business arena was important to Microsoft, because of its business potential going forward but also because it was a linchpin to applications programs.

Microsoft's response was Windows, introduced in November 1985 after having been announced two years earlier (giving the firm a reputation for "vaporware" that still clings). The development of Windows was guided with a clear vision as to the features that the market wanted in addition to the graphical interface. Applications that would run on it were slow to get written, however, and the performance still lagged behind Apple. Further, there were a host of competitors, including an IBM product called Top View.

It was not until Windows 3.0 came out in 1990 that Windows became the undisputed operating system winner for non-Apple computers. The introduction of Windows 3.0 in May 1990 was creative and expensive, featuring twenty gala events throughout the world, with a 6,000-person event in New York City as the centerpiece. The aggressive launch, coupled with a product that was finally competitive if not superior and the availability of a host of application programs, enabled Microsoft to recover from a half decade of struggle. Microsoft's market victory, however, was due to far more than its flair. A less wealthy, less persistent, less talented firm never would have survived, much less won. Periodic Windows updates (such as Windows 95, Windows 2000, and Windows XP) added features and reliability, and in the mid-1990s a networking-enabled operating system was developed under the Windows NT brand.

Windows continues to be a key strategic brand, second in importance only to the Microsoft parent brand.

Windows, like nearly all of Microsoft's products, have branded features that help differentiate it. Not all work as well as planned, though. Windows 95 came out with a perky "assistant" named Bob that was designed to help the novice navigate through the capabilities of Windows—reducing usage frustrations and, not incidentally, overlaying a sense of humor and a personal touch to a brand that could use it. Bob was viewed as intrusive, slow, and annoying to the core user base, however, and this impression spread so widely that the assistant's mission was corrupted. Perhaps the concept would have worked better with Apple users, who might have felt that Bob was part of the Macintosh look and feel. Microsoft had to back off, though, and make the helper (now called Office Assistant) easy to turn on and off, much less intrusive, and faster.

One of the first "killer applications" on personal computers was the electronic spreadsheet. The first such program (VisiCalc, introduced in 1979) demonstrated that personal computers were not just for games. During these early years, about one-fifth of Apple buyers did so just to access VisiCalc. Microsoft, realizing that a similar application would be a worthwhile business and would stimulate sales of computers, entered the fray with Multiplan in 1982. But some months later Lotus 1-2-3, a competing product that was faster, had more features, and facilitated graphical outputs, was introduced and became the winning entry even in the face of new versions of Multiplan.

Microsoft went back to the drawing board and developed new specifications based on customer research and an analysis of competitor products. The result of its development effort was Excel, a product (first introduced in 1985 for the Macintosh and later for the PC) that had visible advantages in speed and features. The introduction was a major campaign, with a PR event in New York plus extensive radio and print advertising. A new brand was considered essential to break into the market controlled by Lotus. In contrast, Windows 3.0 had not faced a winning competitor, as that space was cluttered with challengers who had failed to get any traction.

Another killer app was word processing. The complex but functional WordStar, introduced in 1979, was the early leading brand. WordStar lost its leadership in the mid-1980s to WordPerfect, which by comparison was incredibly customer-friendly in both features and service attitudes. Microsoft introduced Microsoft Word in 1983 with a big promotion that included distributing 450,000 demo disks with a twelve-page tutorial; however, the product was unreliable and unimpressive next to Word-Perfect. It was not until the middle of 1986 with Word 3.0 that Microsoft finally got it right and began to take over the market, thanks in part to extensive brand-building budgets.

In 1990 Microsoft introduced Office as a bundle of discounted applications containing Word, Excel, and PowerPoint, a presentation program. Bundling PowerPoint with the two other leading programs helped enhance its then-modest market position. In 1993, Office 3.0 was launched and became the primary application vehicle. As the application products grew, it became unwieldy to promote the individual brands, and the umbrella brand, Office, captured much of the reason to buy a Microsoft application program. Over time, Office gained functional benefits as the application programs became more and more seamless with common commands and the ability to transfer information from one to the other. It was clear from the beginning that learning multiple programs, each with different commands and interfaces, was a source of customer irritation.

By 2003, Microsoft felt the time was right to create a new category around the Office brand. Instead of offering individual applications, Office 2003 would now represent a comprehensive and integrated system to enhance productivity. To support this new category perception, the stand-alone application brands were changed to subbrands of Office 2003. Different versions of Office 2003 could include subbrands such as Office Word 2003, Office Excel 2003, Office PowerPoint 2003, Office Outlook 2003, Office FrontPage 2003, Office OneNote 2003, Office InforPath, Office Publisher 2003, and Office Visio. The Office umbrella brand became the master brand.

Although Office and Windows continue to provide the bulk of revenue and profit for Microsoft, the firm has looked to other market arenas in which to develop business and brand platforms. Other emerging business areas have generated strategic brands—that is, brands expected to play important roles in the future. For example, the growth of the Internet prompted Microsoft to develop the MSN brand with its brand family, including subbrands HomeAdvisor and Carpoint and the endorsed brand Hotmail (purchased by Microsoft in the late 1990s). MSN also developed the visual of a butterfly that flits around effortlessly, symbolizing the easy-to-use Internet portal and representing a friendly and warm side to Microsoft.

Some of these new areas are distanced from the Microsoft brand. Microsoft, for example, is not linked to Xbox except as a shadow endorser. The Xbox brand was established as a platform to compete in the $20 billion gaming world with Sony and Nintendo. Inspired by the X Games (which feature competition in extreme sports), the Xbox had a target market of young males, that neither needed or wanted a formal endorsement by a firm that ran their parents' computers.

In 2003, Microsoft created a set of six umbrella brands to group products providing similar value propositions to a common primary target market. Office, MSN, and Xbox were three of these brands. Another was Microsoft Business Solutions, an umbrella brand that represented a family of connected applications and services for small and midsized businesses. Subbrands included CRM for customer relationship management tools, Analytics for reporting and budgeting, and Navision for business management solutions. Microsoft Business Solutions, an important Microsoft business initiative, provided a way to talk to this broad segment that none of the dozens of individual brands could do. The other two umbrella brands were Windows Server System, whose primary audience was IT professionals, and Visual, aimed at software developers.

Windows remains a key platform brand. It is the driver for the Windows products (e.g., Windows XP), server-related software (Windows Server Systems), and the emerging mobile arena. Windows Mobile is the Microsoft entry into the mobile world of PDAs and cell phones. The brand leverages the familiarity and credibility of its big brother and provides a way for Microsoft to have a niche in this important space. Prior to Windows Mobile, Microsoft was competing with device-specific brands such as PocketPC and SmartPhone (a brand that Microsoft did not own) that had some brand challenges in a brand-messy environment. Even resource-rich Microsoft decided that a new brand was not the optimal course with the Windows brand available.

The Microsoft brand portfolio revolves around the Microsoft brand, even though the brand is more often used as an endorser than as a master brand. The Microsoft brand itself has a lot of positives. It is considered a software market leader, aggressive, professional, innovative, and successful with a broad, synergistic line of software products. It is associated with the visionary Bill Gates and has a strong global presence. In Japan, both Microsoft and Windows are among the strongest brands in terms of ratings on the "Could not do without it" scale.[1] The brand has been positioned as an enabler with the 1990s theme of "Where do you want to go today?" followed by another based on the tagline "Realize your potential."

However, Microsoft also has several brand challenges. Its product line and brand architecture are complex, in part because of the use of both the Microsoft brand and the Windows brand. Further, Microsoft is seen by some as an arrogant bully because of its anti-trust battles, as well as the vocal opinions of competitors and the frustration of users of complex products. As a result, attitudes toward Microsoft tend to be polarized.[2] The Microsoft brand portfolio strategy has been instrumental in creating and nurturing the positives and dealing with the challenges, often by creating strong endorsed brands.

The Microsoft brand is a strong endorser to many of the key master brands in the portfolio, such as Windows, Office, and MSN. The image of these endorsed brands has undoubtedly been affected by the Microsoft connection (which is well known because of the heritage of the products, as well as the graphical presentation of the brands). Even so, each brand has its own identity and relationship with customers. Most often, people will say they use Windows or MSN rather than Microsoft. Thus, the brands Windows and MSN have some independence from the Microsoft brand—and therefore the potential to draw on its positive aspects while avoiding the negative aspects.

Microsoft is one of the most successful firms ever, and its brand portfolio supports an aggressive and dynamic business strategy involving a complex array of products. From its humble start in 1975, Microsoft has grown to have the largest market capitalization of any firm in the world. The creation and management of a brand platform driven by customer insight and business strategy has been part of the journey.

CITIGROUP

Citigroup, a dynamic, global organization formed by the 1998 merger between Citicorp and Travelers Group, has an evolving brand portfolio

FIGURE 3-1
CITIGROUP BRANDS—PREMERGER

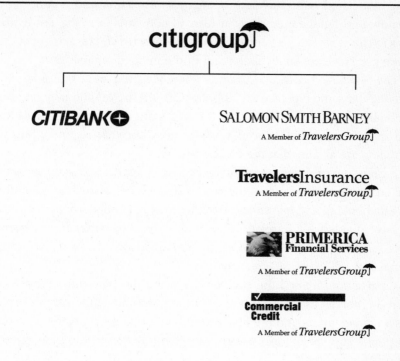

structure to accommodate acquisitions and a complex business strategy targeting diverse segments.[3] At the time of the merger, the brand portfolio (as shown in Figure 3-1) included Citibank, Travelers Insurance, Salomon Smith Barney, Primerica Financial Services, and Commercial Credit.

The merger provided a catalyst for reevaluating the brand portfolio strategy, and a new strategy with new logos resulted. A hybrid portfolio model, summarized in Figure 3-2, was employed to represent the breadth of Citigroup's financial services offerings, covering three primary areas: consumer brands (branded Citi), corporate and institutional brands (branded Citigroup), and specialty brands (neither Citi nor Citigroup branded). The brand logos created visual references to indicate that, while part of the same family, the individual brands represented three broad areas and appealed to different target segments.

The parent brand, Citigroup, reflects the prestige, financial power, diversity, and sophistication of the firm. It was created by combining the "Citi" from Citicorp and "group" from Travelers Group. The brand logo is a simple, lowercase Citigroup followed by a red umbrella, the rights to which were obtained from Travelers Insurance. The familiar umbrella, long associated with Travelers, stands for protection and security in a friendly and lighthearted way (at least in comparison to the Prudential rock). The new logo leverages this well-known symbol and serves to make the Travelers family feel a part of the merged organization.

The revitalized consumer brands reference the parent brand by employing the same typeface and a bold "Citi" prefix. Additionally, the red umbrella is stylized to fit over the Citi wordpart, and is referred to as the red arc. Citibank, CitiFinancial, CitiMortage, CitiInsurance, and a host of CitiCards are all aimed at the end consumer.

A branding problem for all financial services firms is how to separate the consumer offering from the rest of the business—such as high-end private banking and investment banking, whose clients may be reluctant to have a side-by-side relationship with consumer banking customers. This reluctance is due in part to functional reasons, but also has emotional and self-expressive reasons.

Citigroup addressed the problem by using the Citigroup brand with its red umbrella as a master brand for the corporate bank, private bank, asset management, and the investment bank. Citigroup branding on the corporate and institutional brands therefore reflects the corporate parent brand.

Various specialty brands like Smith Barney, Travelers Life and Annuity, Banamex, and Primerica do not fit neatly into either the consumer or corporate areas. The plan was to migrate the Smith Barney brand to the Citigroup brand. However, when Smith Barney got caught up in the conflict-of-interest controversy involving research analysts alleged to have been influenced by the investment banking side of the firm, that distance from Citigroup became very convenient.

The remaining insurance business after the Travelers spinoff could not be broadly labeled as Travelers Insurance, and therefore a transition was made to Travelers Life and Annuity. Banamex, Mexico's largest commercial bank, had strong equity in the market, so it made little sense to convert its brand to a Citi brand. Primerica, a system of more than a hundred thousand representatives in North America, needed to distance itself from the other brands so that it could cross-sell financial services in its niche market, and so it could sell term life insurance without worrying about conflicts with the Travelers products.

The endorsement line, "A member of Citigroup," is used in customer communications as a way to tie together the consumer and specialty brands that do not feature Citigroup as part of their name.

Citigroup's brand portfolio strategy allows a degree of flexibility for acquisitions or the launch of new business divisions. Offerings that fit within either the consumer or corporate side can take on the mantle of Citi or Citigroup, respectively, regardless of whether these are organically grown or acquired businesses. Likewise, acquired companies with significant brand equity can retain that strength and fit into the organization as a specialty brand.

Several aspects of brand portfolio strategy should already be clear. A sound brand portfolio strategy can enable business strategies and enhance the effectiveness of brand-building tactics as well. There is a large upside to getting the portfolio strategy right, and an equally significant downside to a portfolio strategy that fails to generate relevant, differentiated, energized brands and lacks leverage, synergy, and clarity. But brand portfolio strategies are complex both conceptually and organiza-

FIGURE 3-2
CITIGROUP BRANDS—POSTMERGER

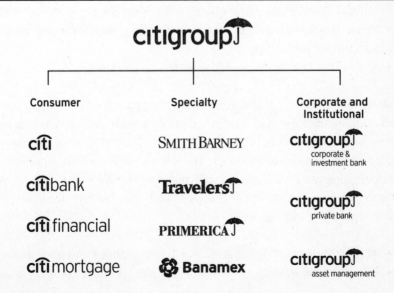

tionally, with a bewildering host of dimensions and contexts. Developing sound, effective brand portfolio strategies is rarely simple or easy; on the contrary, it tends to be situation specific and dynamic, a challenge indeed.

This chapter is designed to assist those who develop, refine, and manage a brand portfolio strategy. The strategy can and should be developed at several levels. At the top level, the strategy could focus on the strategic brands driving major business areas. For Citigroup these might include the brands in Figure 3-2; for Microsoft, they might include Office, Windows, MSN, Xbox, and a half-dozen other strategic brands that represent a distinct business. The strategy could also focus on a particular strategic brand, so there could be a portfolio strategy around the MSN business or the Citigroup Private Banking business. In each case, there will be several strategic brands involved; for MSN, there is Carpoint, Hotmail, and so on. The scope and level of analysis will depend on the needs and responsibilities of the strategist.

The need is to address the many portfolio strategy decisions implied earlier by Figure 1-2. Among the most important will be the following:

- What are the strategic brands, and how should they be managed?
- What brands should have their scope expanded or reduced?
- What brands should be added, deleted, or consolidated?
- Should branded differentiators be added or deleted?
- Should branded energizers be developed or managed differently?
- What changes should be made in defining product categories or subcategories?
- Should the corporate brand be dialed up or down?

Given the complexity and context-specific nature of portfolios, there is no cookie-cutter approach to brand portfolio management. It is possible, however, to provide some guidance by identifying some questions and information areas to consider. These areas will lead the strategist to the development of background information that will lead to the identification of portfolio options and issues. They can be organized around four categories of inputs:

- Market forces and dynamics
- The business strategy
- Brand equities and identities
- A brand portfolio strategy audit

FIGURE 3-3
INPUTS TO BRAND PORTFOLIO STRATEGY DECISIONS

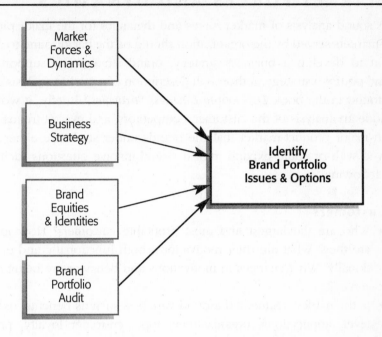

Each dimension involves a checklist of questions and issues from which insights about portfolio problems and options can be derived. These are suggestive and representative, but not exhaustive; they should open doors to information rather than represent a limit or boundary. Avenues that could generate further options or issues should be pursued. Also, a few of the questions will lead to the greatest insight, but it is hard to predict in advance the identity of those few. The subsequent discussion of each of the four components of Figure 3-3 will be followed by a discussion of the management of the portfolio strategy and a preview of the rest of the book.

MARKET FORCES AND DYNAMICS

A sound analysis of market forces and dynamics for the major product-markets served by the organization should be the background to any effort to develop a business strategy, brand strategy, or supporting brand portfolio strategy. A thorough description of a market analysis can be found in the book *Developing Business Strategies*.[4] Briefly, it would include an analysis of the customer, competitors, and market trends for each major product-market that the brands under study are either involved with or could expand into. It would involve questions such as the following:

Customers

- Who are the largest and most profitable customers? How loyal are they? What are their motivations, both functionally and emotionally? What changes in motivations and behavior are being observed?
- Is the market segmented around variables such as benefits, usage level, applications, organizational type, customer loyalty, price sensitivity, life stage, lifestyle, purchase drivers, or motivations? How does this segmentation inform the brand portfolio strategy?
- What are the motivations of the various segments? Do customers value global reach or a local connection? A systems solution or best of breed?
- What are the unmet needs? Are some customers dissatisfied? Why? What are the imperatives for the next offering?

Competitors

- Who are the competitors? Can they be organized into strategic groups?
- What are the strengths, weaknesses, and business strategies of the major competitors? What are the white-space opportunities afforded by their weaknesses and strategies?
- What brand equities do competitors possess? What is the brand portfolio strategy of each? What are their brand vulnerabilities?
- What trends are competitors betting on?

Market Trends

- What are the growth dynamics of the category and subcategories?
- What are the current and emerging cultural, demographic, technological, and economic trends that could affect the business?
- How is the perception of the product categories changing? What are some emerging product categories or subcategories?

The end goal is to precipitate portfolio options and issues. The process of obtaining an informed feel for the customers, competitors, and trends should advance this goal. The options and issues raised will, of course, be the subjects of focused, in-depth analysis and evaluation.

Most of these inputs will have some relevance to brand portfolio decisions. In particular, segmentation will have a close link to brand portfolio strategy, because the role of brands will often be to define a segment-driven offering. Citigroup defined offerings around such distinct segments as consumers, private bank customers, or institutions. At Donna Karan, life-stage segmentation has led to lines of offerings that range from young professionals to more mature customers seeking a classic look. The portfolio needs to be clear and compelling at the segment level, so the strategy needs to be based on an understanding of and sensitivity to segmentation.

The brand portfolio strategy will include scope and extension decisions that start with an analysis of current and potential product-market options. Decisions to extend to a new product-market, for example, will need to consider the prospects, the competitive intensity, the existence of unmet customer needs or areas of dissatisfaction, and the relevant market trends. Certainly Microsoft has its eye on an emerging area for future business when deciding to develop Microsoft Business Solutions, MSN, or Xbox.

The brand relevance problem, the topic of the next chapter, will hinge in part on how the perceptions of the product category and subcategory are changing. If the product category or subcategory attached to the brand is declining, or perhaps being replaced by another, a serious portfolio problem can emerge.

BUSINESS STRATEGY

The brand portfolio needs to support and reflect the business strategy. Thus, it is important to have a sound knowledge of the business strategy, to understand what the business model is in each product market in which it competes. That leads to two basic questions: What is the business strategy, and how are the firm and its strategic brands performing with respect to the strategy? At its essence, a business strategy includes the following:

- *The product-market scope*—where the business is going to compete. What products and markets will be emphasized, and which will be de-emphasized or avoided?
- *The value proposition*—what the customer offer is. Why should the customer buy? What is the basis of loyalty? What is the point of differentiation?
- *Strategic assets*—assets, including brand assets, that create a sustainable competitive advantage. What assets will allow the business to be successful over time in each product-market? (A strategic asset might be a talented R&D group, an installed customer base, a manufacturing competence, skill at product design, or a set of brands.)

The Product-Market Scope

The specification of the product-markets in which the business will compete will directly affect the portfolio strategy. The products a firm offers (or chooses not to offer) and the markets it seeks (or does not seek) serve to define the scope of a business. The analysis should start by looking at the present product-market profile. The heart of the business strategy, however, is found in the dynamics of the product-market scope. What new markets are targeted, and/or what new products will be introduced? What is the growth trajectory?

Knowing the product-market areas the business is targeting is critically important to the portfolio strategy. Usually, such business decisions are based on finding an overlap of market opportunities with organizational competence. The brand portfolio insight is that the organization also needs to assess brand relevance. (Davis and Dunn call the intersec-

FIGURE 3-4
THE CREDIBILITY FOOTPRINT

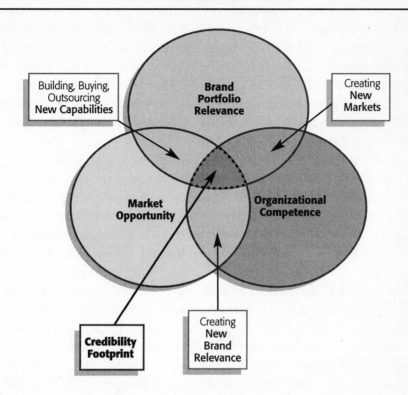

tion of these three factors a "credibility footprint," using Figure 3-4 to show the issues involved.[5]) Even if opportunity and competence exist, a brand needs to be available to carry the flag in the new product-market arena. This need implies a new brand or a brand extension, perhaps with a subbrand or an endorsed brand, determining which of these is most appropriate as a particular product-market area is a central brand portfolio strategy issue.

The business strategy scope dimension involves setting priorities among current and future product-markets—in particular, determining the investment level for each product-market served. This important business strategy decision will depend on market opportunity and organizational competence, as suggested by Figure 3-4. A growth investment level means that a strategic brand will be needed, just as Microsoft made a business decision to invest in Microsoft Business Solutions and other umbrella brands. To be competitive, this brand will likely also need to be surrounded by subbrands to create a full line, and possibly some branded differentiators as well.

A business decision to milk a position to conserve resources will similarly affect the portfolio. If Microsoft were to declare the Office family to be cash cow brands, it would have a reduced number of branded energizers and silver bullets. Further, the office family of brands will likely be reduced to descriptor status and receive few resources. If Citigroup were to decide to dial down retail banking, a similar contraction effect should be an outcome.

When different product-markets share a brand, it is particularly important that the brand portfolio be designed so that the firm will have a strong brand entry in the most important competitive arenas. If brand risks are to be taken, it should be in important arenas rather than unimportant ones. The business strategy can make sure that decentralized decision makers in product-markets that are not strategic do not misuse the brand.

In that spirit, a sequential portfolio development process can be useful. For example, a global financial services firm was trying to reconcile several major acquired brands with the corporate brand. Clarity emerged when the company first picked the most important business area going forward (which was investment banking) and identified a brand to support that business and enhance its success chances. Then the second most important business arena was identified (private banking) and the optimal brand established for it, taking into account the brand that was selected for investment banking. This process continued for the other two major business areas. The result was a brand portfolio strategy that worked for the whole firm and did not in any way compromise the most critical business areas. Any alternative might have given excess weight to less strategically important areas.

The Value Proposition

Ultimately, the offering needs to appeal to both new and existing customers. It must have a value proposition that is relevant and meaningful to the customer and is reflected in the brand identity and positioning of the brand(s). To support a successful strategy, the customer value proposition should be sustainable over time and be differentiated from competitors. It can involve providing the following elements:

- A good value with high-quality store brands and a personal touch (Wal-Mart)
- Excellence on an important product or service attribute, such as safety (Volvo) or cleaning power (Tide)
- Cool products in colorful stores (Gap)
- Luxury cars with a sophisticated taste and feel (Jaguar)
- Product line breadth, items that are easy to find and order, and reliable delivery (Amazon)
- Innovative offerings (3M)
- A shared passion for an activity or a product (Harley-Davidson)
- Global connections and prestige (Citigroup)

Sam Palmisano, who became the new CEO of IBM in 2003, had to follow the remarkable success of his predecessor.[6] IBM had achieved a dramatic turnaround under Lou Gerstner during the 1990s, in part by making the synergy and technology of the organization work for the customer. Palmisano's strategy was based on a new value proposition: "On Demand." The core idea was that IT systems would include customers and suppliers and information and computer resources would be available on-demand, when needed. "On Demand" ultimately implied that computer systems, data software, and networks seamlessly connect with each other. All IBM business units were charged with delivering the value proposition.

Strategic Assets

Strategic assets are needed to underlie the strategy and provide a sustainable competitive advantage. Assets can involve a wide spectrum, from buildings and locations to R&D expertise to a metaphoric symbol (such as the Michelin man) to a strong brand (such as the Johnson & Johnson brand). The ability of the assets to support a strategy will in part depend on their power relative to competitors'. To what extent are the assets strong and in place? To what extent are they ownable because of a symbol trademark or long-standing investment? To what extent are they based on the synergy within a unique organization that others cannot duplicate? It is only logical that multiple business organizations that can achieve synergistic effects will have an advantage over those that ignore or fail to achieve synergy.

Brands and subbrands, including potential branded differentiators and energizers, are key assets. They provide a way to leverage a temporary product or technology advantage into one that is sustainable over time. A feature can be copied, but a branded feature that is actively managed is more formidable.

Brand assets need to be linked to the value proposition. For example, a value proposition of being a global, full-offering player has implications about what brands should be created or dialed up to have credibility in the relevant product-defining settings. If a premium position is to be the strategy, certain brands would not be suitable, and others may have to be enhanced. A value strategy also would have portfolio implications; a value brand or subbrand would have to be created or acquired if one did not exist.

Business strategy dynamics need to be supported by a dynamic brand strategy. When Microsoft established Xbox, it created a personality suitable for the target market through an edgy brand name and a decision to dial down the "corporate" Microsoft brand. The ability of the Office family to deliver synergistic value because of the convenience and appeal of the suite made it logical to dial up the Office brand name.

Business Performance

The performance of a business unit attached to a strategic brand can suggest portfolio issues and options. What are the sales and profit trends? What about market share? Growing sales with declining market share can be a red flag. How is the performance by segment? What are the healthy, growing segments, and which ones are declining? What is the source of the problem? Competitor initiatives? Changes in customer purchase habits, perceptions of product categories, use patterns, attitudes toward the brand, or motivations?

Unsatisfactory performance, if properly diagnosed, can be relevant to brand portfolio strategy. It can suggest, for example, the need for branded differentiators or branded energizers. A relevance problem might be remedied with new offerings and the introduction of strong subbrands. Shifting the brand portfolio role from strategic to a cash cow could also be an option.

BRAND EQUITIES AND IDENTITIES

Among the basic inputs to any brand portfolio decision are the equities and identities of the brands. Brand equities will influence what portfolio strategy is optimal or even feasible. For example, a weak brand may not be suited to a strategic or silver bullet role and/or may need a branded differentiator or energizer. A brand constrained to a product class may not be a good extension candidate, whereas a lifestyle brand may have unrealized extension potential. A brand might have an image profile that would make it a co-brand candidate. The image will affect product-defining rules. The Microsoft image, for instance, influences how associated it will be with the strategic brands in its portfolio.

The equity of the involved brands should be determined using a structure that fits the product category. The equity structure should address the major dimensions of brand strength, as outlined in the boxed list on page 84, in order to identify areas of strength and weakness.

The brand's identity is often as important as its equity. Where is the brand going aspirationally? The brand identity will have a core set of from three to five elements that will be the most important drivers of the future brand vision. It may also involve a brand essence, a single concept that captures much of the identity.[7] The brand's role in the portfolio needs to reflect the brand identity because that is the future of the brand. If reliability is seen as becoming the brand's salient position, then the brand may be more suitable for an endorsement role than if it had an edgy, bold identity.

The brand identity and the portfolio strategy are so intertwined that it is hard to develop one without the other. Without knowing the portfolio roles, it is hard to define a brand identity by deciding which associations should be enhanced or dialed down. Conversely, without knowing the brand identity, it is hard to assign a brand to roles within the portfolio and to know where to take the portfolio strategy. When some

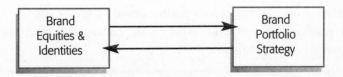

or all of the brands' identities are not in place when developing a portfolio strategy, it is sometimes necessary to create a set of identities based on some assumptions and quick analysis. This way, at least some feel will emerge as to the feasible roles to which a brand might be assigned.

In addition, the brand portfolio can improve or damage brand equities and affect the ability to realize identities. Branded differentiators and energizers, for example, can build or enhance target brands. Subbrands can influence master brands, and vice versa. Citigroup's decision to distance itself from Smith Barney and to use the Citigroup brand on its high-end offerings was influenced by the desire to protect and build the namesake brand. Microsoft is continually evaluating the status and use of silver bullet brands.

The portfolio strategy should place brands in the right contexts—those in which the brand has a chance to win, given its equity. Even with substantial brand-building resources, a brand in the wrong context

---

Elements of Brand Equity

- Awareness. Is the brand well known in the marketplace? What is the unaided awareness among key segments?
- Reputation. Is the brand highly regarded in the marketplace? Does it have a high level of perceived quality?
- Differentiation. Does the brand have a point of differentiation? A personality? Does or could it deliver emotional or self-expressive benefits?
- Energy. Does the brand have energy? Or is it tired and bland?
- Relevance. Is the brand taken seriously by today's customers for today's applications? For what other product categories or subcategories could the brand be relevant?
- Loyalty. Are customers loyal to the brand? How many of them? Who are they, and how do they differ from the general customer base? On what is the loyalty based?
- Extendibility. Does the brand have the potential to extend to other products, either as a master brand or endorser? Can it be a platform for growth? What is the association that travels across product categories?

may have little chance to succeed. Knowing the brand's equity, identity, and position strategy is a factor in making sure that the context is right.

THE BRAND PORTFOLIO AUDIT

The fourth input, a brand portfolio audit, provides a systematic way to critically examine the current brand portfolio and to identify problems and issues that merit further analysis and responsive programs. Figure 3-5 provides a set of just over two dozen questions to provide a structure and agenda for the audit. They also provide an overview of the scope of a brand portfolio strategy. Each question is potentially important and can lead to significant analysis and change, but the set is not meant to be exhaustive. As the agenda is pursued, additional questions will become helpful and relevant.

The audit is shown to start with an appraisal of the portfolio strategy objectives, which often results in useful insights that would not otherwise emerge. For example, the other audit questions will not necessarily identify points of confusion in a portfolio that lacks clarity.

Starting with the objectives means raising general issues that will then be explored with the subsequent, more detailed examination. A judgment that some brands are not leveraged, for example, will inform the more detailed look. However, the analysis can also proceed from the detailed to the general; the objectives would then be appraised when a close examination of the strategy has been accomplished.

The identification of the portfolio brands to be included in the audit is the next dimension shown in Figure 3-5. Rarely will any audit take on all the brands in the portfolio. Rather, it will focus on a manageable set, such as the top-level strategic brands or the brands associated with one business area. However, branded energizers and brand alliances should not be ignored. Brands owned and managed by other firms, at least those that are important influences of brand equity or determinants of business success, should be included.

The purpose of the audit questions is to challenge the existing portfolio strategy and to suggest options and issues that will merit further analysis and consideration. The options can involve changing role priorities for a brand, or creating different role contexts entirely. They can involve the need to develop new brands or subbrands, or an opportunity

FIGURE 3-5
THE BRAND PORTFOLIO AUDIT

Portfolio Objectives

- Is the portfolio delivering synergy, with brands teaming to support and enhance other brands? Are the brands consistent across product-market contexts? Are brand-building resources allocated optimally across brands? Are the future strategic brands and brands with clear roles given adequate resources to fulfill their assigned roles?

- Are all the brands fully leveraged? Could they be extended horizontally or vertically without damage to equities? Are future growth platforms being developed?

- Are the brands, especially brands with a driver role, losing relevance? Are they adapting to market dynamics? Is there an opportunity to create new categories and subcategories?

- Are the brands strong enough to perform their role? Do they have enough energy and vitality? Enough differentiation? Is the differentiation sustainable?

- Is there customer-facing clarity? Or is there confusion and clutter among the offerings?

Brand Portfolio

- Identify the brands in the portfolio or portfolio subset, including subbrands, endorsed brands, branded differentiators, branded energizers, alliance brands, and corporate brands.

Portfolio Roles

- Which brands are the strategic brands—that is, the ones representing substantial current or future profits or points of leverage (linchpin brands)?

- What brands or subbrands are playing (or should play) branded energizer roles? Are additional ones needed? Can existing branded entities be packaged to play that role, or are new programs needed? Are brand alliances needed?

- What branded energizers have the potential for significant impact? How? Are there organizational problems holding them back?

- What branded energizers should be a priority, which should be silver bullet brands?

- Are flanker brands needed? Why? What is the threat? Can existing brands be adapted, or are new ones needed to play the flanker role?

- Are strategic and silver bullet brands, brand energizers, and flankers being supported and actively managed?

- What brands should be playing cash cow roles? Do they require the resources they now receive?

Brand Scope

- Are driver brands and subbrands adequately leveraged? What would be candidates for horizontal brand extensions? Are subbrands or endorsed brands needed to more fully leverage the brands?

- Is there the potential to extend brands vertically, with or without a subbrand or endorsed brand?

- Can a brand be exported into new markets?

- Are some brands overextended? Are their images being jeopardized?

Product-Defining Roles

For major and/or representative product-market contexts:

- Identify the brands and subbrands with substantial driver responsibility. How much equity do they have? How strong is their link to customers? What are the group of brands that need active management and brand-building?

- Identify the subbrands and scale them on the driver-descriptive subbrand spectrum. Given that appraisal, are they all receiving an appropriate amount of resources and management? Should some be relegated to descriptor roles?

- Do the existing endorser brands add value as endorsers? Do they detract? Is their identity appropriate for that role? Should their role as endorsers recede or be deleted in some contexts? Are there other contexts in which an endorser should be added or made more pronounced?

- Does the endorser role enhance the endorser brand in all contexts? If not, is the potential damage to the brand worth it?

- Identify the branded differentiators. Should these be given a greater or lesser role? Are more needed? Where?

- Identify co-brands. Are they well conceived? Should new ones be considered? What types of partners would serve to enhance the brand?

- Are umbrella brands needed to provide clarity, focus, and better communication strategies?

Brand Portfolio Structure

- Create for each brand in the portfolio a disk with the brand's logo and ask people to arrange the disks using a universe model. Identify the "suns" and, around each sun, the planets with their moons. Ask the participants to explain the logic. Compare the results. What is common? What is different?

- Portray the brand portfolio structure by one or more of the following:
  - Showing a grouping of brands using logical descriptors such as segment, product type, application, or channel.
  - Diagramming all of the brand hierarchy trees.
  - Specifying the structure with a network graphic.

- Evaluate the brand portfolio structure (and meaningful subparts) as to whether it generates clarity, strategy, and direction rather than complexity, ad hoc decisions, and strategic drift.

- Should existing brands be deleted or given a greater or lesser influence in existing contexts? Should new driver brands or subbrands be created?

Portfolio Graphics

- Lay out a sample of the way that the brands are presented visually, including logos and communication material. Are the presentations clear, consistent, and logical? Or is there confusion and inconsistency? Is the relative importance of each brand reflected in the visuals? Is there visual energy?

- Does the visual presentation of the brand across the portfolio create clarity or confusion? Does it support the portfolio structure? Does it support the context roles? Does it support the brand identities?

to extend existing brands. Branded differentiators or branded energizers can be created, refined, or dialed up or down. The relationships among brands can change. The key is to look for portfolio implications when the analyses are conducted.

Rather than attempt to sort out all the portfolio strategy options, it can be more productive to identify some key issues that will influence major portfolio decisions. One, for example, might be a business strategy decision to push into a new product-market. Another could be to identify the most important business challenge going forward. Still another might be to decide whether to revitalize a brand. Do not get bogged down in the complexity of the portfolio decisions, though; the goal is to rise above the complexity and focus on the key issues.

MANAGING THE BRAND PORTFOLIO

Managing the brand portfolio starts with structures and systems of brand management. A person or group should be in charge of each brand. There should be a common brand planning system across all brands, and for each brand across all product-markets. The planning templates should be the same, using shared inputs, outputs, and vocabulary. But brand portfolio management also requires a mechanism to achieve portfolio goals, as well as the goals of a brand in a given product-market context.

The person or group managing the portfolio must have access to brand knowledge, market knowledge, and the necessary authority and resources to implement portfolio decisions. Brand knowledge is needed because there are complex difficult brand strategy implications. Market knowledge is required because many of the portfolio objectives are customer facing and, without credibility in the marketplace, a person or team can make arbitrary, suboptimal decisions. Finally, having the needed authority and resources is critical. Without these components, the portfolio manager will fail to get the needed support to design and implement portfolio refinements, because most are extremely organizationally sensitive.

That person can be the CEO or a top operating executive. If it is not, the person or team in charge needs to have the visible support of the CEO. There is little question that the sensitive issues of brand portfolio management cannot be addressed effectively, nor solutions implemented, without the active support of the top management of the organization. In the firms that have made progress at improving portfolio strategy (such as Dell, Nestlé, Sony, Henkle, GE, HP, IBM, 3M, P&G, and UBS), the CEO has had direct involvement with brand portfolio decisions and issues. Brand management in general—and certainly brand portfolio management—is not a brand issue or even a marketing issue; it is an organizational issue. Without interest and involvement starting at the very top, it is very difficult indeed to achieve brand portfolio objectives.

The process should be supported by procedures and organizational structures to create, review, and improve the brand portfolio strategy. There should be a periodic audit to uncover emerging problems with the portfolio. Such audits should be made when a new product or group of products is being considered, or when an acquisition is made. An acquisition that introduces a set of brands into the portfolio almost always raises serious portfolio issues. The key is to make sure these *are* raised, not assumed away and relegated to a tactical implementation phase.

Several portfolio issues are organizationally sensitive, and it takes a determined force to address them. The following paragraphs profile a few of these.

One sensitive issue is the allocation of resources across brands and roles. This involves interfering with the decentralized structure and culture that often provide healthy vitality and control for an organization. Yet without analysis and discipline at the portfolio level, mature brands and markets are inevitably going to get excess resources at the expense of future strategic brands and emerging markets.

A second issue is the decision whether to add brands or subbrands. This decision needs to be made with clear guidelines and discipline, because there is such an organization bias toward adding brands. Managers are inclined to inflate the prospects and the newness of proposed offerings, and their frequently maternal attachment to these offerings may be symbolized by a brand name. The introduction of new brands, though, is costly in terms of managerial, organizational, and financial resources. Further, it is cumulative in that it represents a commitment to the future that needs to be added to obligations for other brands.

To control brand proliferation, clear criteria for adding a brand to the portfolio must be in place and communicated to the organization. In general, a new brand must be needed because an existing brand would be either a liability or at risk, because the new offering reflects a major departure from existing offerings, and because the new business has sufficient future prospects that investments in a new brand can be justified.

In addition to clear criteria, some person or group must have enough authority to make the criteria stick in all markets. There cannot be country managers beyond the system who are free to introduce brands. A host of firms have a formal person or group at a high level who must approve any new brand. When the criteria is clear and communicated, however, requests generally decline; managers themselves can evaluate against the criteria and decide not to go forward with a new brand proposal.

A third portfolio issue, maybe the most sensitive, is the deletion of brands or even dialing them down. Organizations and people within them get extremely attached to brands, which become a symbol of the value of their activities and the status of their position. Deleting a brand is therefore extremely threatening. Further, it is always easy to find reasons why a brand's equity is important and why attempting to transfer it is risky. And, of course, there is always a turnaround program in hand. It is always very difficult to see the view of the whole portfolio and the total business strategy. Sometimes an arbitrary decision, such as the one that Unilever made to reduce the portfolio by eliminating 75 percent of the brands, is needed.

A fourth sensitive portfolio issue is the decision to leverage a brand by extending it horizontally or vertically, or adding it as an endorser to new contexts. In many organizations, such decisions are made in a decentralized manner—if a business unit feels that the brand can help, that brand is used even if its use places its equity at risk. An entity with strategic perspective and the necessary market knowledge and feel for the brand and its identity needs to be able and willing to intervene to protect the brand. Nestlé, for example, has a person from the executive team who acts as the brand champion for one of its major global brands. One responsibility of that person is to make sure the brand is not extended into a context in which its equity will be degraded.

A fifth issue—not usually sensitive, but potentially troublesome—is the policing of the visual presentation of the brands to make sure they are presented in a consistent way that will result in more impact. Toward that end, basic principles need to be communicated to all who will be presenting the brand visually, with easily accessible rules and models that show the right colors, type sizes, and fonts that should be used in each context. And there should be a specific person or group who can interpret and ensure consistency in the visual presentations. The person(s) charged with this assignment should not be viewed negatively, always saying no and labeled as a logo cop. The role and process is healthier when the role can be expanded to include more than logos and be a more positive influence in brand building.

Dell ensures consistency in its visual presentations in part through a quarterly meeting in which the CEO and the president display on a large wall all of the Dell visuals throughout the world. They can then pick out those presentations that are off brand or inconsistent in some way; the problems identified tend to be corrected before the next quarterly review. In contrast, a "logo cop" can make pronouncements that line managers find ways to avoid or delay compliance with.

A PROFILE OF THE NEXT SEVEN CHAPTERS

In the next seven chapters, we will see brand portfolios in action—how they can be used to advance and enable business strategy, as well as support ambitious brand strategies. Figure 3-6 provides an overview, and each element is briefly summarized below. Good fishing!

Part II. Creating Relevance, Differentiation, and Energy

Chapters 4 and 5 explore how a brand portfolio strategy can potentially help build brand equities by creating relevance, differentiation, and/or energy for brands. Chapter 6 discusses brand alliances, an option when the organization lacks adequate time and capability. Brand alliances are to respond to market dynamics or brand problems.

Achieving and maintaining brand relevance. A business needs to stay relevant in a dynamic market by participating in the emerging market niches that represent future growth. The goal of any strategy is to compete in attractive markets where the business has or can create enduring strengths. Maintaining relevance often means shifting a business in a new direction, a potentially dangerous and difficult task. Brand portfolio

FIGURE 3-6
BRAND PORTFOLIOS IN ACTION

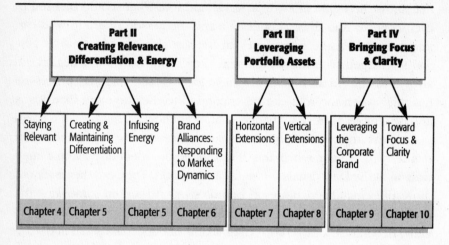

tools such as subbrands and endorsed brands can help reduce the risk. The Citigroup brand, for example, helps distance the company's offerings to institutions and private bank customers from its retail banking business, thereby making those offerings more acceptable.

Creating differentiation and energy. Nearly all brands need more differentiation and energy. It is hard to maintain a point of differentiation through innovative product features, however, because in most product classes features are ultimately easy to copy. In contrast, a branded differentiator that is actively managed over time can be protected more effectively. The need for energy is keen for heritage, market-leading brands like John Deere, AT&T, Campbell's, Bank of America, and IBM. The great assets of reliability, prestige, and history also make these brands feel stodgy. Branded energizers, such as a branded sponsorship linked to the brand and its customers, can provide vitality.

Brand alliances to respond to market dynamics. A firm in these dynamic times will often face relevance challenges created by market shifts or an urgent need to create branded energizers or differentiators. Many companies, though, may lack the resources, capabilities, programs, or brands to respond in a timely manner. The solution may be to create a brand alliance yielding a co-branded offering—an immediate, credible response based on the resources and brand strengths of the two firms.

Part III. Leveraging Brand Assets

Most organizations want and need to grow. One avenue is to leverage brand assets to enter new product-markets. Chapters 7 explores horizontal brand extensions, and Chapter 8 looks at vertical extensions (that is, going into superpremium or value markets).

Leveraging the brand to enter new product-markets. Brand extensions need to consider not only the new product-markets but also the impact of the new brand context on brand health, the brand's roles in the portfolio, and portfolio health. Suppose that Oracle wanted to market a specialized software product in Japan. Should the Oracle brand be used? If so, should the brand mean the same thing in Japan as elsewhere? Should a subbrand or endorsed brand be used? Will the Oracle brand be perceived as more global as a result? Should the product be co-branded with an established Japanese brand? If so, exactly what role should each of the co-brands play in the offering? And what impact in the business strategy of the future will these branding options have?

Participating in the upscale and value markets. Businesses are often struggling with margin pressure and need to participate in the superpremium arena, where there are high margins plus brand energy. But what is the brand strategy to reach that market? It can be a challenge to make existing brands credible, and expensive to create new ones. Another attractive market can be at the value end, because of the volume rather than the margins. The brand challenge in this case is to participate without risking brand equity.

Part IV. Bringing Focus and Clarity to the Brand Portfolio

One key objective of brand portfolio strategy is to achieve clarity and avoid confusion (and frustration). Another is to focus resources behind the strategic brands and avoid wasting them on brands with little future. One approach to these problems, to leverage the corporate brand, is the subject of Chapter 9. Chapter 10 takes a more general look at achieving focus and clarity.

Leveraging the corporate brand. The corporate brand—or, more generally the organization brand—has some special characteristics that make it an important player in most brand portfolios and a vehicle to provide differentiation as well as focus and clarity. Representing the firm, it has the potential to span many of its products and be the home of organizationwide brand-building efforts like the World Cup sponsorships. Representing an organization, it can reflect a culture, set of values, and strategy to customers and employees, unique characteristics that can provide points of differentiation and clarity to the offerings. It is particularly well suited to be an endorser brand that creates powerful portfolio flexibility. GE, for example, is a corporate brand that is used in business arenas from aircraft engines to appliances to finance (GE Capital).

Achieving focus and clarity. A firm, especially one that is decentralized and entrepreneurial, may proliferate brands and subbrands. The result can be debilitating confusion and a dilution of brand-building efforts. What is often needed is a no-compromise, disciplined examination of the role of each brand, with the objective to combine, delete, or de-emphasize brands for greater focus and clarity of offering. Canon, for example, struggles to avoid confusion with its five camera options, each with many variants. While complexity works fine for the camera enthusiast, many consumers would be less frustrated with and more inclined to buy a brand that could simplify the choice option and the use experience.

QUESTIONS FOR DISCUSSION

1. For a brand or brand set, assess or review the market, the company's brand equities and identities, and the business strategy. Do any brand portfolio strategy problems or opportunities emerge? Are any portfolio refinements suggested?

2. Conduct a brand portfolio audit. What implications emerge for the existing portfolio strategy?

3. Develop and evaluate refinements to a brand portfolio strategy.

4. Assess a brand portfolio management structure and system.

PART II

Creating Relevance, Differentiation, and Energy

CHAPTER 4

BRAND RELEVANCE

Even if you're on the right track, you'll get run over if you just sit there.
                                                        —WILL ROGERS

I realized that my competition was paper, not computers.
                            —JEFF HAWKINS, FOUNDER OF PALM SOLUTIONS

The best way to predict the future is to invent it.
                                    —ALAN KAY, COMPUTER SCIENTIST

Minicomputers, pioneered by Digital with its PDP series in the mid-1960s, opened up a new market for which mainframe manufacturers were not relevant. For several years, minicomputers were defined by the PDP, a subbrand that contributed to Digital's market leadership. When the PC arrived in the early 1980s, Digital clung to a belief that it was limited in application and audience, whereas minicomputers were still a growth area. (The CEO of Digital had been quoted in 1977 as saying, "There is no reason anyone would want a computer in his or her home.") As a result, in just two years, the company went from a leadership position with an admired strategy attractive to investors to a struggling also-ran that lost its relevance in an important growing segment. The life cycle of the minicomputer subcategory largely mirrored the fortunes of Digital during that era.

Home Depot, with some 1,500 stores, in effect created a new product category by offering a selection of products and services for do-it-yourselfers that combined the offerings of retailers dealing in hardware, paint, flooring, lumber, lawn and garden, and tool rental, among other specialties. Started in 1978, the company defined concepts such as a warehouse feel, a one-stop shop for home repairs, and offering extensive advice. As a result, Home Depot created a relevance problem for many firms trying to compete with a partial offering. In the mid-1990s

Home Depot had some relevance issues of its own as it attempted to become more acceptable to women (who were attracted by the "softer" feel of Lowe's), to professional customers (some of whom were uncomfortable shopping side-by-side with homeowners), and upscale customers looking for high-end design services.

POWERBAR

Decades ago a candy bar, Snickers, successfully positioned itself as a source of energy.* If you were dragging a bit, a Snickers bar would pick you up. Breakfast bars created a category around a use occasion; people who lacked the time to sit down for a good breakfast could eat a bar on the road. Diet bars helped define another category with a similar product. A person on a diet could eat a bar to replace a snack or even a meal, reassured that the bar was designed to enhance the effectiveness of his or her diet by supplying requisite vitamins and minerals. Granola bars were the "healthy" candy bars. Very different application areas defined each of these four very similar products.

Then the PowerBar firm in 1986 developed the original PowerBar, singlehandedly creating the energy bar category. Positioned as athletic energy food, the original PowerBar was distributed at bike shops and events usually involving running or biking. The target segment was the athlete who needed a convenient, effective energy source. Six years later, stimulated by the need to provide an alternative to the sticky nature of the PowerBar, a competitor developed a product with superior taste and texture and branded it the Clif Bar. Another competitor, Balance, introduced an energy bar offering a blend of protein, fat, and carbohydrates based on the 40/30/30 nutrition formula associated with the so-called Zone diet.

Thus, in the early days of energy bars, at least two product subcategories were defined—bars that tasted good, and bars that were nutritionally balanced. PowerBar was not relevant to either, nor were its erstwhile competitors (candy bars, breakfast bars, diet bars, and granola bars) despite their functional similarity. Significantly, the energy bar cat-

---

* Information for this section was drawn from the websites of the relevant brands. Thanks to Cindy Vallar of PowerBar for helpful comments.

egory moved from bike shops to supermarkets and became a mainstream snack item for anyone in need of an energy boost, no longer just long-distance runners or cyclists.

Faced with these relevance challenges, PowerBar developed two new products, for which it adapted an endorser strategy. The Harvest Bar had a much more accessible taste and texture, while ProteinPlus became the PowerBar entry into the high-protein subcategory closely related to that defined by the Balance bar. The endorsement strategy was employed because PowerBar was so associated with a distinctive texture that the use of a subbrand was not feasible, especially for Harvest Bar, which was positioned on taste and texture. A PowerBar endorsement was extremely helpful in a messy market arena populated by a host of small start-ups, providing welcome heritage and leadership associations to the new brands.

The makers of the Clif Bar observed that half the population were women, of whom many were athletes and many more were involved in fitness. They further observed that women have unique needs in terms of vitamins and supplements, and that the energy bar industry had yet to recognize or fill those needs. As a result they introduced Luna as the first nutritional (not energy) bar for women, using media and promotions targeting active females.[1] The bar had a light crunchy texture, came in flavors like LemonZest and Chai Tea, and had nearly two dozen vitamins, minerals, and nutrients. The target market was time-strapped women who want taste and nutrition in one bar and would appreciate a firm that tailored a product to what they needed. A small, token Clif endorsement on the package provided some credibility while creating space for the new bar to prosper in its target segment.

Partly in reaction to Luna's success and partly to expand the populations for which the category was relevant, PowerBar did some research as to why women did not use its own product, which was nutritious, convenient, tasty, and addressed a real need for a pickup in mid-morning or mid-afternoon. One answer was the calorie hit was simply too great to justify using. In response, PowerBar created a tasty, even indulgent, PowerBar-endorsed Pria bar that had only 110 calories and was designed to answer Luna, as well as to attract new users into the category.

The Balance strategy was to introduce a series of products, all of which stuck to the established 40/30/30 blend but had different tastes

Figure 4-1
The Energy Bar World

and textures. There was the Balance Plus, Balance Outdoor (no chocolate coating to melt), Balance Gold, Balance Satisfaction, and the Balance-endorsed Oasis, a bar designed for women. The big success was Balance Gold, which was positioned close to the candy bar category by containing traditional candy ingredients like nuts and caramel. (It even had a tagline of "like a candy bar.") The bar was able to expand its relevance to those looking for candy bar qualities. Obviously such a direction risked the perceived authenticity of Balance as being an energy bar, but as it entered the category from the diet (Zone association) perspective anyway and probably was never considered to be in the center of the energy bar world, the risk may have been acceptable.

The energy bar category exploded from just over $100 million in 1996 to well over $700 million in 2001, with attractive growth prospects extending well into the future. Challengers advanced many subcategories by positioning around seniors, kids, soy, and diabetic- and heart-friendly diets, to say nothing of the variety of textures, sizes, and coatings. Looking at the category from the perspective of the major players and others (such as snack and cereal companies), several questions arise. Which of these subcategories or niches represent a sustainable business in terms of not only market size, but also competitive intensity? What innovation would support a new entry? How should entries be branded? Can brands such as Harvest, Luna, Balance Gold, Satisfaction, and others be leveraged?

There was also the more basic question as to how to expand the category's relevance. Energy bars were one of the few categories that successfully moved from niche to mainstream status. The heritage of being a product to enhance the performance of top athletes like Lance Armstrong (a PowerBar endorser) created credibility and self-expressive benefits, but the household penetration was still under 20 percent. The major firms worked to generalize the concept of athletic performance to be relevant to anyone who needs to perform well during the day. In fact, the industry dream is to get people to label the category "performance nutrition" and think of enhancing their ability in everyday tasks. Clearly, relevance opportunities and challenges remain.

Here is the all-too-frequent problem: A brand seems very strong because tracking studies show that it retains a high level of trust, esteem, perceived quality, and perhaps even perceived innovation. Customers may still be satisfied and loyal. However, its market share is slipping, perhaps dramatically—and fewer customers, particularly new ones, are considering the brand. Why? In many cases, because the product category or subcategory with which the brand is associated is fading, perhaps being replaced or augmented by another. The brand has become irrelevant to one or maybe more important segments.

If potential customers want SUVs, it simply does not matter how good a minivan they think you have. They might believe your minivan is the best quality and value on the market, recommend it to any friend interested in a minivan, and knew that if they ever buy a minivan again, they will buy yours. But, if they are interested in an SUV because of their particular needs, then your brand is irrelevant to them if it is too connected to minivans—sometimes even if your brand has an SUV subbrand. Brands associated with minivans that have not developed interest and credibility in the SUV category, no matter how good their entry is, will be irrelevant to people buying SUVs.

A host of brands or subbrands have seen reduced relevance in key segments in these dynamic times. It is hard to find a CEO who does not worry about staying relevant. AOL faces an ongoing relevance problem with seasoned Internet users as the growth of unsophisticated first-time users slows. Xerox gradually faced a relevance challenge when the market turned to lower-cost Japanese options in many copier subcategories. As such firms as HP, Microsoft, and Canon were carving up the digital systems world, Xerox struggled to find its niche. Similarly, Polaroid clung to a technology that eventually became irrelevant, and it has been unsuccessful in finding a role in the new digital world.

Relevance is an issue as well for brands attempting to open up a new business arena, such as hybrid cars (from Toyota and others) or personal video recorders (from Tivo and others). The challenge is to define the product category or subcategory. What exactly are customers buying? It is very hard to make the brand relevant if the product category or subcategory is not well understood.

The reality is that nearly every marketplace is undergoing changes that are often dramatic and rapid. Examples can be found in industries from computers, airlines, consulting entertainment, golf clubs, and financial services to snack food, beverages, fast food, and toys. Managing these changes is a challenge. Firms that do it successfully are able to develop organizational skills to detect change and respond to it, achieve strategic flexibility, and/or pursue and implement alliances. It involves basic strategic management—selecting product-markets in which to invest, developing differentiated entries with value propositions and creating assets leading to sustainable competitive advantages.

Brand portfolio strategy plays critical roles in enhancing or even enabling responsive strategic options. When the need arises to create a new product category or subcategory or enter one that is already there, a brand, endorsed brand, or subbrand needs to carry the flag. Thus, leveraging existing brands or developing new ones is a crucial component in developing the strategy. In addition, other portfolio tools such as branded differentiators or co-brands can help in what is usually a difficult positioning task.

We turn in the next section to a more extensive description of the relevance concept, its measurement, and the product class dynamics that drive it. Alternative ways to address the relevance challenge are then discussed.

WHAT IS RELEVANCE?

Relevance for a brand for a customer occurs when two conditions are met:

- There is a perceived need or desire by a customer for a product category or subcategory defined by some combination of attributes, an application, a user group, or other distinguishing characteristic.
- The brand is among the set considered by that customer to be relevant for the product category or subcategory.

It is assumed too often that the only brand challenge is to win among the brands within a product category or subcategory. There are two additional relevance challenges. One is to make sure that the product category or subcategory associated with the brand becomes or remains relevant. The problem may not be that the customer picks the wrong brand, but rather that the wrong product category or subcategory (and brand set) is picked. This implies a need, especially among current or potential market leaders, to manage perceptions of and demand for the product category or subcategory as well as that of a brand.

The second challenge is to make sure that the brand is considered by the customers to be an option with respect to a product category and subcategory. This implies that a brand needs to be positioned against a product category or subcategory in addition to whatever other positioning strategies may be pursued. If the brand is not dialed up for those evaluating a product category or subcategory, it will not have a chance to be selected.

To become considered, the brand must have both sufficient visibility and performance credibility. The brand must register when the product category or subcategory is cued. Further, it must be seen as passing the performance threshold in order to be considered. A case in point is the subcompact arena, where the Toyota Corolla and Chevrolet Prism were for many years made to the same design by the same factory. The Prism, until it was discontinued, was discounted more and still had sales less than one-fourth of the Corolla's, because a perceived quality gap had precipitated a relevance problem.

To better understand relevance and the concept of product categories or subcategories, consider a simple model of brand-customer interaction where customer choice involves five steps. First, the customer needs to be motivated by a problem, need, or opportunity, such as the need to buy a car. Second, the customer selects a product category or subcategory that is perceived to be relevant to the problem or opportunity; for example, he or she may decide to buy a luxury sports sedan rather than a sports car or SUV. Third, the customer next needs to determine what brands to consider (let's say Audi, BMW, Lexus, and Cadillac). A brand is not relevant unless it survives both the second and third stage to join the final consideration set.

The remaining two sets define brand preference. The fourth step, perhaps after some evaluation, is to select one brand from the consideration set. Finally, the product or service is used, and the resulting use experience may influence the next cycle.

FIGURE 4-2
THE BRAND–CUSTOMER INTERACTION

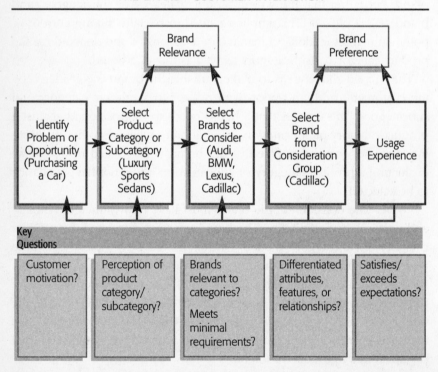

Relevance, then, involves stages two and three. A brand will be relevant if it is included in the consideration set for a particular product category or subcategory, and if that category or subcategory is the focus of the customer's decision. Both are needed. If either is missing, the brand lacks relevance, and no amount of differentiation, attitudes, or relationship will help.

Most of brand management is focused on achieving differentiation among a set of brands being considered for a given application. The goal is usually to gain preference and liking, which are then expected to drive choice and provide a basis for relationships. Of course, achieving differentiation is increasingly hard in the face of reduced product distinctiveness, extensive media clutter, and squeezed margins. The task increasingly requires brilliance and resources to get it done, and many firms realistically lack one or both of these.

Without relevance, however, differentiation and preference may not be worthwhile. The ultimate tragedy is to achieve brilliance in creating differentiation after expending precious resources behind the brand, only to have that effort wasted because of a relevance problem. Consider a brand aiming for a large prestige market but ending up with a Rolls Royce—a highly differentiated brand with too few buyers.

As Figure 4-2 suggests, differentiation and the use experience can also help to enhance relevance. To be considered by a customer, a brand not only has to be recognized as serving the product category or subcategory but must also have a minimal level of visibility, credibility, and perceived quality. If a brand is differentiated with a compelling brand proposition, a strong personality, and a positive customer relationship, then it will be more likely to pass the threshold standard—and its association with the product category or subcategory will be more likely.

Measuring Relevance

A distinction should be made between product classes associated with the brand and brands associated with a product class. Knowing what product classes are associated with the brand is actually not very important strategically, although it does provide clues as to the brand's current image and barriers to changing it. The image of Sony and its management can be understood better, for example, by knowing that it is associated with television sets, consumer electronics, games, and less so with movies and music.

The more strategically important association—and the one that drives relevance—is knowing what brands are associated with the product category or subcategory. Those are the brands that pass the relevance test. If Sony is mentioned as an option by a customer considering video cameras, then it is relevant to video cameras whatever other products the customer assumes Sony makes. In fact, a brand that aspires to be relevant to multiple product categories or subcategories may find that some people may not be able to recall all of them when the brand name is the stimulus. That doesn't really matter because it is product category- or subcategory-driven brand recall that determines market power.

The measurement of relevance needs to start with a well-defined product category or subcategory. A specific label (such as energy bars or minicomputers) is helpful. If no label is accepted, then a tight description is needed (shaving products for women, for example). The basic relevance measure would be unaided recall: what brands do you associate with the product category or subcategory? A stronger indicator would be the consideration set: what brands would you consider buying for the product category or subcategory?

Simple recognition—namely, what brands from a list are associated with a product category or subcategory—is generally too weak a measure. There are brands people have heard of but are so low on the relevance scale that they do not come to mind when considering a product category or subcategory. Such brands with high recognition and low recall are termed "graveyard" brands. Suppose members of an audience segment were asked to name compact cars; later, they were shown a list of twenty brands and asked to check those that they recognized as makers of compact cars. If Dodge had high recognition but few had named Dodge in the prior recall task, then Dodge would be classified as being in the graveyard. When a brand is in the graveyard, extraordinary change is needed in order to resurrect it because it is hard to create news around long-familiar brands. Accordingly, it is usually easier to create a new brand than to get one out of the graveyard. And it is extremely important to avoid the graveyard.

The Techtel high-tech tracking database illustrates how relevance-based measurement can yield strategic insights. During the 1990s, Intel wanted to be associated with attributes such as "fast," "powerful," and "industry standard processors." Tracking data in the later part of the decade showed that the Intel Inside program had worked well for this criteria but was not helping Intel become relevant to Internet applications. While more than 55 percent of respondents found IBM strongly associated with terms such as eCommerce and eBusiness, both Intel (at 12 percent) and Dell were low by this measure. Thus, Intel and Dell had a problem in that few customers thought them relevant to an emerging product category. Over time both firms responded—Intel by expanding the Intel Inside brand "outside of the box" and Dell by dialing up its server line, particularly at the high end.

Product Class Dynamics That Drive Relevance

In bygone times, when markets were clearly defined and competitors were few and well-behaved, visibility and differentiation could carry the day. However, markets today contain emerging and receding product categories or subcategories, making relevance a strategic issue. Coping with a fast-changing market with dynamic product categories and subcategories (and it is hard to find a competitive context, from snack food to financial services to information systems, that does not qualify) starts with understanding some of the drivers. What forces or events create the rise or fall of product categories or subcategories? The following, reflected in Figure 4-3, are examples.

First, the product or service can be augmented to include a new product or service dimension that helps define a new subcategory. Saturn and Lexus, for example, changed the way customers interacted with car dealers and for some created a product subcategory, making most other brands less relevant. In this case, both GM (Saturn) and Toyota (Lexus) used new brand names to support the new dealer experience that in part defined a new product subcategory. A controlled-release dimension to the Paxil anti-depression drug using the PaxilCR brand created a product subcategory. Banquet Homestyle Bakes successfully entered the shelf-stable meal kit market (where Betty Crocker's Hamburger Helper resides); by including meat they created a new subcategory.

A new package can define a subcategory, as L'eggs did in hosiery decades ago. The eat-on-the-go trend led Yoplait to the endorsed brand Go-Gurt, yogurt delivered in a colorful nine-inch tube that was designed to deliver portability (like their advertising said, "Lose the spoon!"), appealing flavors (Berry Blue Blast and Watermelon Meltdown), and fun to kids (what could be better than squeezing out food?). Go-Gurt was a home run that helped Yoplait forge ahead of Dannon, a brand it had

FIGURE 4-3
PRODUCT CLASS DYNAMICS DRIVING RELEVANCE

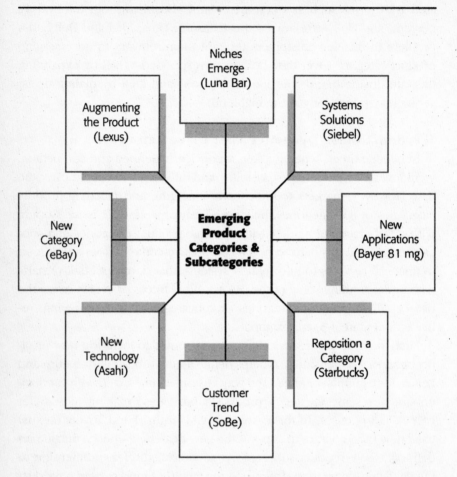

trailed for decades.[2] A new growing subcategory had emerged for which Dannon was simply not relevant.

Second, the product category or subcategory can be broken into niches. The problem then becomes to actively manage and possibly drive the emerging niches. In the energy bar market, Protein Plus, Balance, and Luna were all developed to define niche markets. In the fast food market, there are fast casual brands such as Panera Bread Pan. The task is to predict when a niche will emerge, assess its staying power, and evaluate the firm's ability to compete in that market subset.

Third, the application scope can be expanded from components to systems or turnkey solutions—in essence, an aggregation into supercategories, the inverse of breaking the category up into subcategories. Consumers can now buy the Pioneer Home Theater, which means that component manufacturers are less relevant than before. In the late 1990s, Siebel took the lead in creating Internet-based CRM (Customer Relationship Management) by pulling together a host of application areas including customer loyalty programs, customer acquisition, call centers, customer service, customer contact, sales force automation, and e-business.[3] Part of the remarkable success story surrounding Siebel was their ability to become the most relevant company in the CRM space. Their ongoing challenge is to manage the CRM brand as it adapts to an increasing emphasis on data mining, analytics, and higher levels of integration.

Creating a systems solutions approach is attractive because of the potential to achieve higher margins, create longer, deeper customer relationships, and avoid the perils of commoditizing. But one study suggested that 75 percent of such efforts fail.[4] One reason is that the firms bundle products or offer add-ons rather than providing a true system solution for customers. True customization and integration of products is lacking, as is the necessary in-depth understanding of customers and their challenges. Another reason for failure is that the difficulty of selling solutions is underestimated—it differs markedly from component selling in terms of cost, time, knowledge, and the use of sales teams.

Fourth, the emergence of a new and distinct application can define relevant brand options. Cereal firms saw significant incremental sales when cereal bars became a defined submarket.[5] Rice Krispie Treats was one of the first, but then came others (such as Honey Nut Cheerios Bars and Cocoa Puffs Bars) that drew upon the taste associations and customer loyalty in the dry cereal arena. Bayer aspirin developed a whole new context—taking baby aspirin regularly to ward off heart attacks—with its Bayer 81 mg with Enteric Safety Coating, with the latter feature reassuring those who might be concerned about the effects of regular aspirin use on the stomach.

Fifth, a product class can be repositioned. Starbucks repositioned the retail coffee experience by defining its local outlet as the third place (after home and office) that defines a person's day.[6] The experience involved aroma, a break from routine, an affordable luxury, a social feeling, and some self-expressive benefit of appreciating great coffee. Ford Galaxy in the United Kingdom positioned its minivan experience as being roomy and comfortable, like first-class air travel, and therefore suitable for busy executives rather than soccer-moms.

Sixth, a customer trend can drive a new product category or subcategory. The dual trends to wellness and the use of herbs and natural supplements has supported a new category of healthy-refreshment beverages (HRB), which now contains a host of subcategories such as enhanced teas, fruit drinks, soy-based drinks, and waters. The pioneer and category leader is SoBe, which started in 1996 with SoBe Black Tea 3G with Ginseng, Ginkgo, and Guarana and now has an extensive line of teas, juices, and energy drinks. A trend toward buying video and DVD movies was threatening the relevance of Blockbuster who, perhaps reluctantly, plunged into the sales arena.

Seventh, a new technology like disposable razors, notebook computers, or hybrid cars can drive the perception of a product category or subcategory. Asahi Super Dry Beer destabilized the competitive landscape in the Japanese beer market by creating a subcategory for dry beer, which has a very different taste than lager. As a result, Kirin, for decades the leading lager beer with a dominant 60 percent market share, suddenly was not relevant for many customers. Asahi's market position (an 8 percent share in 1986, when Asahi Super Dry was launched) rose dramatically until it actually took market share leadership in 1998.[7] Soon after Asahi Super Dry appeared, Kirin attempted to respond with Kirin Dry, but its heart and brand were really not into the effort given its lager heritage. Kirin was perceived as a big bully trying to get in on another's innovation, and the firm lacked credibility in the dry beer space.

Adidas developed a technology, termed Clima, that keeps a body dry by drawing sweat away from the skin. Defining a new subcategory, Adidas has applied the technology in a wide spectrum of shoes and apparel, using linked subbrands such as ClimaLite, ClimaWarm, Clima-Shell, and ClimaCool. One challenge for Adidas is to build the Clima brand to compete with Nike Dri-FIT, which has similar properties. The goal is to win, if not own, the new subcategory—and to avoid at all costs having a competitor be the winner.

Finally, a whole new category can simply be invented. eBay created an online auction category that has spawned imitators, who have had difficulty matching both the operational performance and the critical mass of users that eBay established. The Internet space has also seen the development of a search engine category. Google, initially a minor player, emerged as a leader by focusing on being the best search engine while others followed a desire to become portals. Tivo pioneered the personal video player that changed the way that some watched television.

STRATEGIES TO CREATE OR MAINTAIN RELEVANCE

Firms vary along a spectrum (shown in Figure 4-4) in their ability to maintain relevance. At the left extreme is the all-too-common *trend neglector* firm, which is unaware of or ignores market trends and wakes up surprised to find its brand is no longer relevant to a significant submarket. In the middle are those firms, termed *trend responders,* who track closely the trends and the evolution of categories and take responsive action so that their offerings stay current and relevant. At the right end of the spectrum are firms that are actually driving trends that underlie category definition, the *trend drivers*. They are ahead of the trend because they are part of the driving force and are actively participating in the category definition or redefinition.

FIGURE 4-4
THE RELEVANCE RESPONSE SPECTRUM

Firm's Response to Trends	Unaware of Market Trends	Detect and Respond to Trends and Emerging Categories/Subcategories	Drive Market Trends and Create/Influence Categories/Subcategories
Firm's Relationship to the Market	**Trend Neglectors**	**Trend Responders**	**Trend Drivers**

Trend Neglectors

One trend neglector variant has the "stick-to-your-knitting" mindset that is not motivated to stay informed about market trends. The organization is committed and focused on its own model and feels, with some justification, that chasing apparent trends will be a futile waste of precious resources. The "any color as long as it is black" Ford experience of the 1920s is a classic case. Firms of this type need to make sure that disappointing growth and financial strains do not lead to cost cutting that affects the customer experience.

Another trend neglector type sees trends but believes they are fads. Recall how Digital, ignoring the advent of PCs, held on to the minicomputer world too long. This trend neglector often needs to get better at projecting competitor capabilities—as well as do a periodic arrogance check.

The final trend neglector type is the firm that would like to identify, evaluate, and respond to market dynamics but is simply not very good at it. Such a firm is usually characterized by an inadequate external sensing system, executives who are not customer-driven, and organizational inflexibility. Many of the corporate disaster stories can be traced to these organizational limitations. This trend neglector type will benefit from investing in programs that create the capability to become an effective trend responder.

Trend responders and trend drivers represent two strategic reactions to a dynamic market very different from that of trend neglector firms. Both market timing and firm resources have to be in place before the trend driver option is viable. In contrast, being a trend responder is an option for most firms, although it is not always an easy one.

Trend Responders

Trend responders have two jobs. The first is to recognize and evaluate trends. Detecting trends and making them visible to the organization is not easy, and firms that are skilled at it tend to have certain characteristics. Generally, they have an externally oriented, market-focused culture, an information system that captures and distills intelligence, top management who are concerned with market dynamics, and solid business strategists in a position to act. Evaluating trends can be more difficult than identifying them. Which trends are real and substantial? Which are fads? Which represent real threats or opportunities for the organization, given its strengths and weaknesses?

The second job is to modify, reposition, and/or rebrand the offering so that it becomes more relevant given the market dynamics. This task is not easy. Any repositioning or rebranding needs to be respectful of the brand's heritage and compatible with the ability of the brand and the organization to deliver on the promise. The modified brand needs to develop a point of difference from competitors, generating its own unique take on the product category or subcategory. To explore further the issues and options that can arise, the healthy fast food subcategory will be used as a context.

The fast food industry, as abstracted by Figure 4-5, is seeing the development of a healthy subcategory. The market served by McDonald's, Wendy's, Burger King, Pizza Hut, Round Table Pizza, Taco Bell, KFC, and others (represented by the large oval) could be called the historical fast food category. Its customers value upbeat, familiar, convenient, economical offerings. The smaller oval intersecting the larger one can be termed the healthy fast food subcategory. It is populated with brands such as Subway, Souper Salad, and Sweet Tomato, with customers who value the attributes of fast food but also are sensitive to healthy eating. The subcategory is driven by a trend to healthier living and eating, as evidenced by such developments in society as the visibility of child obe-

FIGURE 4-5
AN EMERGING SUBCATEGORY

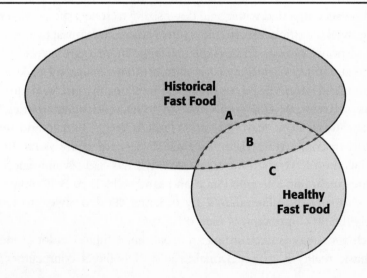

sity, changes in school lunch menus, interest in eating programs, the growth of organic foods, the success of health-oriented food retailers, and the interest in such diets as Weight Watchers, Atkins, and the Zone.

Note that the total fast food market is now larger because it is augmented by the healthy fast food segment, drawing in customers who have previously considered fast food as not relevant. There is thus an opportunity for the existing players. Note also that the new healthy segment is taking customer dollars from the original fast food marketplace. Thus, the threat is not benign in that a do-nothing response could result in a declining marketplace, especially if the new category grows at the expense of the earlier one.

The relevance challenge for McDonald's and others is to execute a response based on an assessment of the new subcategory's level of threat to the existing marketplace (area B in the figure), the opportunity that it represents (area C), and its components and dynamics. This assessment starts with simple numbers: the size and growth of the market, its components, and the major players. However, a deeper analysis will get into the nature of the forces behind the emerging subcategory, the segments it is attracting, and ownable niches that might be scalable.

A variety of strategic responses are available to existing players. They could simply stick to their knitting and pursue sales and loyalty from the core of the A customer group, enhancing quality and the customer experience and attempting to interject energy into the brand. In this strategy, growth might not necessarily be a priority. In fact, the strategy could be accompanied with some downsizing to reflect the revised market, as well as efficiency-enhancing and cost-reduction activities. Four other response options address the challenge more aggressively.

One such option is to alter the current brand image by making the current menu acceptable to those in search of healthy fast food fare. McDonald's, for example, developed a way to make its signature fries with dramatically reduced "bad" fat, offers Fruit 'n Yogurt Parfait, and served the now-discontinued McLean's Deluxe burger for many years. Burger King has the BK Veggie Burger and Wendy's has had several pita brand offerings including a Veggie Pita brand sandwich. Taco Bell allows customers to substitute ingredients, by ordering "Fresco Style," to reduce sharply the fat component of their offerings.

Such a strategy is like turning an ocean liner; there is a lot of inertia. The basic reality is that McDonald's and their direct competitors lack brand credibility in the "healthy" arena. They are too strongly associated with major items such as the Big Mac, Egg McMuffin, and Happy Meals—all very functional brands not associated with healthy eating. Such brand strength can become a liability when attempting to adapt or change an image. It is especially hard to appeal to the B segment that has already been attracted to competitive offerings and is not inclined to look to McDonald's for healthy fare. Further, the loyalty of the A segment could be put at risk when the basic menu is altered. Recall the specter of New Coke, which resulted in such a backlash from the loyal customer base that Coca-Cola sheepishly brought back Coke Classic.

A second response option is to create subbranded healthy alternatives that are so prominent and desirable they create a destination option even for the segment C group. This would require an exceptional product offering with its own strong brand. For example, the Wendy's Garden Sensation Salads line (which includes the Mandarin Chicken and Taco Supremo salads) has the potential to draw customers, even from Segment C. Such a brand not only provides relevance for Segments B and C but also protects the original brand promise from being contaminated by the new initiatives. The need, however, is to hit a home run, a branded product or product line that has buzz and a following—in a ball park with distant fences and incoming winds.

Implementing this option can be a struggle because it is not easy to create new home-run products. A host of McDonald's new products, from McLean Deluxe to Grilled Chicken Flatbread to Salad Shakers (where the containers were packed too tight to distribute the dressing) have failed to gain acceptance.[8] In fact, the last blockbuster product for McDonald's was Chicken McNuggets in 1983, despite trying hundreds of concepts.[9] And the task is even harder for healthier entries which have no constituency among the McDonald's patrons. Further, the prime prospects for a healthier McDonald's is probably already in segment C and will not be exposed to any new menu items.

A third response option is to create healthier options for patrons by co-branding with brands that have credibility in that space. Adding a co-brand relieves the task of creating a brand that can sometimes not be feasible, is always costly, and takes excessive time. McDonald's has gotten traction for a line of premium salads, for example, by offering "all natural" Newman's Own Dressings. The co-brand provides a boost by generating interest, acceptance, and credibility. Applebee's, a brand in the casual dining area which is adjacent to fast foods, has co-branded a line of low-calorie appetizers, entrees, and desserts under the Weight Watchers name. The Weight Watchers brand, with its associated point system, should not only appeal to current members and alumni of the program but provide credibility to the menu items as well.

Co-branding is a powerful tool to provide a fast, effective response to a relevance problem. However, it is not always easy to find the right co-brand, to generate an exclusive arrangement, to develop the right co-branded product that will deliver against the emerging subcategory, and to manage the relationship between two organizations whose needs and priorities may change over time. Further, the end result is that customers may develop a relationship with the co-brand that is in part controlled by another organization and whose long-term availability may not be certain.

The fourth response option is to create or buy a new format, creating a new brand platform. Wendy's has Baja Fresh, a Mexican chain, while McDonald's has invested in Boston Market, the Pret A Manger sandwich chain, and the Chipotle chain of gourmet burrito restaurants. This option recognizes that success in the new subcategory requires a brand that is on-market, signals a relevant, involving value proposition, and requires no brand compromises. It is difficult, though, to find a concept and brand that will resonate with customers, be differentiated from competitors in a cluttered marketplace, and be scalable so that the business is significant. McDonald's wants concepts that can grow to a thousand locations, because anything smaller doesn't affect its numbers, nor does it represent a business that fits the company's operating skills or can use its economies of scale.

The reality, of course, is more complex than Figure 4-5 suggests, because there is a significant trend detection and evaluation challenge surrounding the many components of the healthy fast food subcategory. A healthy burger and fries market, for instance, competes directly with McDonald's and Burger King by offering veggie or soy-based burgers and baked fries. Healthy sandwich markets such as Subway offer parallel products to the hamburger chains, and upscale "fast casual" sandwich shops like Cosí and Panera Bread have developed their own buzz. There are ethnic foods, such as Japanese and Thai, and a variety of new forms, such as the buffet-style Fresh Choice and Sweet Tomatoes and the grilled chicken offerings of Boston Market. An established fast food firm such as McDonald's needs to break down the entire subcategory to identify threats to be countered, the opportunities to carve out a niche, and the location of merging critical masses.

The trend responder task is indeed challenging, but it is also doable. The baby Bells in general have stayed relevant, in part by participating in wireless and then broadband communication. Some fashion brands such as Tommy Hilfiger have managed to be nimble in staying abreast of fashion trends. Barbie has changed with the times, being an astronaut in 1965, a surgeon in 1973, and a presidential candidate in 1992, and appearing in the video "Barbie in the Nutcracker" in 2001. Fuji Film was quick to adapt to the digital age and became a leader with its Super CCD high-quality image sensor for digital cameras (the fourth generation of which was introduced in 2003) and several digital products, such as digital photo printers.

L.L. Bean, a brand built on the authenticity of Maine outdoorsmen, has repositioned itself in response to market dynamics. The brand's heritage (hunting, fishing, and camping) was not relevant to the largest and most important segments. Its challenge was to refocus this outdoors heritage to become relevant to hikers, mountain bikers, cross-country skiers, and water-sports enthusiasts—the heart of L.L. Bean's modern marketplace. The heritage was allowed to evolve in a natural way so that L.L. Bean kept its own distinct outdoor perspective.

Trend Drivers

Trend drivers are those organizations that actually participate in the creation of new category or subcategory definitions. Few firms have the opportunity or capacity to be a trend driver, and even those firms have only a few windows of opportunity. The timing needs to be right. A premature effort to create a category can fail, perhaps because the underlying technology is not ready, or the market size has not reached the tipping point. Witness the failure of the Apple Newton to create the PDA category, only to see Palm be successful only a few years later.

The firm needs to either be an extremely strong player or have the potential to become one. In either case, it needs real ammunition to work with, such as a breakthrough product like the dry beer innovation that allowed Asahi to define a new subcategory. Further, the firm needs to be capable of turning a first-mover advantage into a sustainable position by actively managing the new product category or subcategory perception and asserting a dominant position with its brand in the new arena. All this requires not only resources and recognition of the expanded brand-building task, but competence in brand building.

IBM was a trend driver with its e-business position during the middle to late 1990s, when many firms were attempting to be relevant to the Internet and the emerging network world of business. The terms *network computers* or *information superhighway* or *e-commerce* never got traction, but IBM's creation of an eBusiness category did. IBM ultimately spent over $5 billion building the eBusiness "label" after introducing it in late 1996, and related all its business units to that context. Nearly all the major firms in the computer industry were extremely frustrated that IBM was able to define the new category and essentially own it. In 2003, as mentioned in the last chapter, IBM embarked on an effort to create another subcategory, eBusiness on Demand, which means that firms would develop an IT system that would encompass suppliers, customers, and partners and deliver information and computer resources on demand, when needed. IBM again created responsive products and services throughout the firm to meet this set of customer needs. Rivals with similar strategies struggled to be relevant.

There are not many opportunities to be a trend driver and not many firms that have pulled it off. Asahi Super Dry Beer was a trend driver, as were eBay, Nike, Toyota (with hybrid cars), Starbucks, Home Depot, PowerBar, Gap, Healthy Choice, SoBe, Siebel, and Saturn. Charles Schwab is another example.

SCHWAB: A TREND DRIVER

Schwab has been a firm that has defined product categories or subcategories and been a trend driver several times throughout its history.[10] In the 1970s, Schwab was an early participant in the discount broker industry, which served to make full-service brokers less relevant to an important market segment. During the 1980s, Schwab repositioned itself with state-of-the-art computer systems, reliable execution and service, and exceptional reporting tools. In doing so, Schwab made many of its discount broker competitors, who were competing solely on price, less relevant for many customers.

In 1992, Schwab again changed the boundaries of the product class by adding a vehicle to buy and manage mutual funds. The vehicle was the subbrand OneSource®, which provided Schwab customers with ac-

FIGURE 4-6

cess to a wide variety of mutual funds with no transaction fee. Removing the motivation for customers to search multiple firms for mutual fund options and do cross-firm analysis, Schwab conveniently packaged data on its comprehensive mutual fund list. As the new strategic position evolved over time, Schwab provided increased support for mutual fund buyers. The result was a new product subcategory, one in which a host of major financial services firms faced a low relevance level.

In 1997, after several efforts at providing computer-based transaction options for customers had created confusion, frustration, and resentment, Schwab made a commitment to the Internet and computer trading—even risking much of the commission income that it received through telephone services. As a result of the commitment, Schwab became one of the first recognized e-companies for securities trading, and in the process again helped define a new category in which it was a dominant brand name.

After 2000, Schwab again moved to create a new category by becoming a full-service firm—but one offering advice that is objective, uncomplicated and, importantly, not driven by commission. The effort follows from the Schwab vision "to provide our clients with the most useful and ethical financial services in the world." The new position was supported with a host of innovative branded products and services for individual investors, high net-worth investors, institutional investors, and independent financial advisors. These included Schwab Private Client™ (an advisory service for affluent investors), Schwab Advisor Network (a service that refers clients to fee-based independent advisers), StreetSmart Pro (direct market access for active traders), and Schwab Equity Ratings™ (an objective rating system for more than three thousand publicly traded stocks).

The Schwab experience suggests several observations, the first of which is that business strategy often evolves rather than is the result of a distinct decision. Certainly Schwab's expanding strategic position came about over time and was not a deliberately executed, preplanned strategy. Each step was itself a product of an evolutionary process, sometimes culminating in a watershed decision. There were mutual fund activities at Schwab before OneSource under the Mutual Fund Marketplace brand, for example, and computer trading before the decision to commit to the Internet.

Second, changing the product category context by adding a dimension does not necessarily make the existing dimension irrelevant. The initial Schwab strategic position dimensions were not eliminated or even dialed down but rather augmented, so the brand became richer and deeper rather than different. The firm remained true to its heritage; it did not change so much as it expanded the scope of its brand.

Third, any firm that attempts to create a new product category or subcategory without the support of a subbrand (such as OneSource or

Schwab Equity Ratings) has a difficult branding task. When a master brand is modified in order to represent a strategic response to a trend, it loses some of its flexibility to make future adjustments. There are only so many times you can turn a huge boat in the water in close quarters. The reliance on a subbrand allows the master brand to retain more flexibility and avoid getting boxed in.

Fourth, any first-mover advantage will be short-lived if it is not supported with resources and innovation and actively managed over time. Schwab OneSource was a moving target for competitors: funds were added over time, a method for customers to screen funds was created, and the Schwab Select List®, a concise list of pre-screened mutual fund picks by category, was introduced. A competitor faced more than a static OneSource concept.

Finally, the irony is that strength also creates vulnerability as the market changes; a brand's position can be so strong that it is hard to adapt. So each evolution of the Schwab brand had to recognize where it was coming from. The evolution to a full-service firm was one of the hardest changes, because the Schwab legacy was as a limited service firm. The same issue was raised for PowerBar, as its texture was so distinct that the brand could not be used elsewhere except as an endorser. It also happened to Schweppes Tonic, which was always positioned in Europe as an adult soft drink, but gained a strong position in the American market as a mixed drink. As a result, it did not participate in the fast-growing U.S. adult beverage market, even though in Europe Schweppes was extremely relevant.

Labeling the Product Category or Subcategory

The product category or subcategory label, such as e-business, energy bar, or dry beer, when it emerges, can be similar to a brand in that its associations can be actively managed. Therefore, a firm, particularly a trend driver, can and should seek to create, nurture, and protect the category or subcategory label accordingly. Even trend responders can be in a position to influence perceptions of the category to their advantage. Of course, the emergence of a category or subcategory label will be influenced by a host of factors, and the power of a participating firm will be limited.

Another implication is that the name or label of the category itself can be an important definer of any brand and thereby affect its image. Consider the power of labels such as Enterprise Resource Planning (ERP), desktop publishing, fast food, hybrid car, server, wireless, ATM, or high-protein energy bar. Think, for example, of the shift in a category brand name from private banking (which may imply secrecy and even tax evasion) to wealth management (which has more of an association of effective, active management of assets). Creating a label with positive associations can help firms that are attempting to build a category. Understanding the importance of a label is important as well to trend responders, who need to find ways to link to the emerging product category or subcategory.

A critical task, especially for trend responders, is to identify concepts and their labels, track both over time, and attempt to predict which label will break out and become an industry standard. Category labels like interactive or distributed computing never took off, but minicomputers, a less descriptive term, somehow got traction. IBM struggled with the concept of network computer applications until it struck gold with e-business. If the firm is in a position to drive a trend, the category label used can be especially crucial. The right concept with the wrong label may be dormant until the right label appears.

The use of a descriptive subbrand is one direct way to attempt to achieve relevance, although it can occur at a sacrifice of differentiation. In the Gillette for Women set of products—including Gillette for Women Venus (a shaving system), Gillette for Women Sensor, Gillette for Women SensorExcel, and Gillette for Women Agility—the "for Women" part of the name rather directly attempts to achieve relevance in a relatively new product subcategory. The fact that it spans a large set of products enhances both the credibility and the relevance of Gillette to this subcategory. IBM e-servers similarly use a subbrand to create a new subcategory of servers.

The importance of a label in relevance was shown experimentally by Mita Sujan, a consumer behavior researcher. She described both a 35mm reflex camera and a 110mm camera along five dimensions, including shutter speeds, aperture settings allowed, and film loading. The camera labeled 35mm signaled a higher-quality camera to consumers even when the descriptors for the two cameras were reversed. The label thus has the power to override the detailed factual information.[11]

Some brands such as Kleenex (tissues), Hoover (vacuum cleaners in Germany), A1 (steak sauce), Tesa (sticky tape in Austria), and Xerox (copiers) represent the category as well as the brand. Such brands have more control over the category label and can thus actively manage it, perhaps by making it a moving target for competitors. They also do not have to worry about the task of being relevant by creating a link to the category. Their strong tie to the category also limits their ability to adapt to a new emerging category, however, even if it is adjacent.

Often a consensus name does not emerge, even though an emerging category or subcategory is still driving relevance, or a label (such as systems or solutions) is too ambiguous to provide customers with an anchor term. When a label does not emerge, the resulting position might actually be stronger because competitors may have a harder time aiming at such a fuzzy target. If competitors can be inhibited from making a connection to the category, the relevance position of the competitors will be affected. When Schwab creates the upscale discount brokerage or the full-service firm without commissions, for example, competitors lack an anchor to which to attach their response.

Business-Defining Brands

The challenge is to create or connect to an emerging subcategory with a spin on it that both creates a link and provides a point of differentiation. A business-defining brand, a brand that serves to define a business, can be helpful.

A business-defining brand can be a product brand, a branded program, or a branded initiative. In any case it serves to position the business and affect relevance. The Nike All Conditions Gear is an umbrella brand that provides the Nike spin on outdoor clothing drawing on the Nike brand associations. Another is the Microsoft Business Solutions, which provides a Microsoft take on the needs of small- and medium-sized businesses. An example of a branded program is the American Express Open Small Business Network that allows small business owners to share experiences and problems with others, find articles and resources, save on selected vendors, and participate in an American Express Credit Card Rewards program. It defines for American Express a business relevant to a key segment. A branded initiative like IBM's eBusiness on Demand will define a business from a customer-need perspective.

For a business-defining brand to work, it needs to be supported by substance. Proof points need to be generated that show that the firm is indeed delivering in this business. Proof points should be part of a program to make sure that the firm is connected to the business-defining brand. The worst scenario is to create a sandbox and then have others occupy it.

Strategic Questions

A few strategic questions can help you evaluate potential or emerging product categories or subcategories. Some of these questions are as follows:

IS THE OPPORTUNITY GOING TO BE WORTHWHILE IN TERMS OF SIZE AND COMPETITIVE INTENSITY?

Consider the fragmentation of the energy bar market, with products oriented toward two dozen niches—women, kids, Zone dieters, and so on. PowerBar and others need to make an economic decision as to which of these niches are worthwhile in terms of size, growth, and profitability. The size and growth dimensions depend largely on whether the subcategory involves a value proposition that will appeal to a wide enough customer base and that in turn may depend on the offerings that emerge.

Profitability will depend in large part on the number, strategy, and commitment of competitors. The greatest strategy blunders are frequently caused by underestimating the number and quality of competitors, which results in debilitating overcapacity unless a sustainable advantage can be found. Branding is usually crucial to such an effort. Of course, even a small niche might be worthwhile just to avoid giving competitors a platform from which to expand into the balance of the space. As a result, it may be desirable for the leader brand to participate in small segments defensively.

IS THE TREND REAL, OR IS IT A FAD?

The mistaken belief that certain e-commerce markets represented real trends resulted in some disastrous strategic decisions. One perspective comes from Peter Drucker, who opined that a change is something people do, whereas a fad is something people talk about.[12] The implication is that a trend demands marketplace substance and action supported by data, rather than simply an idea that captures the imagination.

For example, the concept of one-stop financial services got lots of talk in the early 1980s, with a host of highly visible mergers of insurance companies, banks, brokerage firms, credit card firms, and others. It failed because customers did not want one-stop financial services, and because the organizational resistance to cross-selling was substantial—bank or credit card business managers, for instance, did not want an insurance representative calling on their customers. In his book recounting his career at IBM and American Express, Lou Gerstner has noted that "after twenty years of talking there are no true financial supermarkets . . . and there are plenty of financial services companies spinning off their insurance and/or money management businesses."[13] Two decades later, the concept of one-stop financial services is again driving some strategies. The verdict is out as to whether new products, technologies, organizational structures, and brand strategies will make the concept viable or whether it is just a flawed idea that will not die.

DOES THE FIRM HAVE THE ABILITY TO DEVELOP THE ASSETS AND SKILLS NEEDED TO COMPETE?

If these are lacking, the responsive strategy might be doomed. A large set of firms, including IBM and HP, attempted to become direct-model players in personal computers in response to the success of Dell and Gateway, only to struggle or fail because they lacked not only the manufacturing and logistics capability but also the organizational culture and brand strength to succeed in that context. Full-service retailers have struggled in discount retailing because they lacked the cost structure and culture.

DOES THE FIRM HAVE THE BRAND ASSETS NEEDED?

Can an existing brand be leveraged, perhaps with a subbrand, to have credibility? Can a spin on the current image and heritage of an existing brand be created to link to the new product category or subcategory? If not, can a new brand (perhaps endorsed by an existing brand) be purchased or developed? Entering a new product category or subcategory generally requires a brand, or even a set of brands, to be successful.

Consider Snapple's attempt at adapting to the new healthy-refreshment beverage category when its brand was too tied to an existing category. Snapple responded with a new line of enhanced juices under the Elements brand (Atomic, Diet Air, and Diet Ice), all endorsed by Snapple. In addition, Snapple developed a line of energy drinks under the Lizard brand and an energy fruit drink line under the Power-line brands, which are separated from the Snapple brand. The Snapple experience illustrates the use of endorsed brands and new brands in the quest for relevance when subbrands seem inadequate.

RELEVANCE VS. STICK TO YOUR KNITTING

There is a natural tension in both business and brand strategy between "stick to your knitting" focus and consistency of message over time on one hand, and adapting to create or maintain relevance on the other.[14]

The former approach basically says to focus on what you do well and strive to improve it over time. Do not be diverted by market fads or competitor initiatives that might gain short-term success; be patient and invest to improve your process and product. Be as consistent in your message as possible, and don't stretch the brand boundaries. It is true that many of the strongest brands, like Harley, Apple, and Southwest, have been remarkable consistent over a long time period.

The latter says to be sensitive to changes in the environment and to have the flexibility to adapt to changing conditions. Be entrepreneurial and willing not only to adapt, but to lead; allow the brand to stretch and adapt to the industry dynamics. Don't be trapped in a losing position. Strong brands like Nike, Mercedes, and Kraft have exhibited this ability to adapt over time.

The tension between these two strategic orientations need not be unhealthy. The challenge is to reduce the tension by being in both camps, and the brand portfolio can be a significant help in doing so. A firm can stick to its knitting, yet use subbrands and endorsed brands to stretch enough to maintain or create relevance in a dynamic market. Branded differentiators and branded energizers can help develop credibility in new product categories and subcategories. With relevance as the objective and a strong brand portfolio, it may not be necessary to make large departures from the core business strengths of the organization. As a result, the strategic focus can live and the business can still adapt.

When the existing brand portfolio is inadequate even with endorsed brands and subbrands, brand portfolio strategy can guide as well. When new organizational assets and skills are needed, alliances and co-brands are an option. The ultimate branding initiative would be to create new brands or even new brand platforms. Consider where Levi's would be without Dockers and Slates, or Toyota without Lexus, or GM without Saturn. Would Nike be stronger and more flexible today with a second or third major brand platform?

QUESTIONS FOR DISCUSSION

1. What trends do you see in the marketplace? Consider changes in customer motivations, competitor strategies and plans, technology developments, and forces outside your product and industry. Consider the customer's lifestyle and use contexts, as well as motivations to buy your product or service.

2. What are the product subcategories in your industry? What defines them? Which are emerging, growing, maturing, or fading? Who is the dominant competitor in each? What is that competitor's sustainable advantage?

3. Identify some trend drivers in your industry and in related industries. How did they do it? Was their advantage sustained? Identify unsuccessful efforts to be trend drivers. Why were they not successful?

4. Look at a dynamic industry, such as the enhanced drink industry. What are the emerging product subcategories? Who is driving them? Who will win? Why?

CHAPTER 5

ENERGIZING AND DIFFERENTIATING THE BRAND

You do not merely want to be considered just the best of the best. You want to be considered the only one who does what you do.

—JERRY GARCIA, THE GRATEFUL DEAD

Imagining the future may be more important than analyzing the past. I daresay companies today are not resource-bound, they are imagination-bound.

—C. K. PRAHALAD, UNIVERSITY OF MICHIGAN

When you do the common things in life in an uncommon way, you will command the attention of the world.

—GEORGE WASHINGTON CARVER

SONY

Sony is one of the strongest brands in the world. Each year since 1995, the Harris Poll has asked people in the United States to name what they believe are the top three product or service brands. In 2002, Sony was the top-named brand for the third year in a row; during the seven years of measurement, Sony has never been lower than third.[1]

In Japan, it is the strongest brand in the country. Nikkei Business Publications sponsors an annual survey of consumers that evaluates some 1,200 brands along fifteen measures summarized into five dimensions. Sony was the top brand among consumer audiences by a large margin in 2001 and 2003, and in 2002, as noted in Chapter 2, it was essentially tied with Disney, which benefited from the massive publicity surrounding its opening of a new theme park. Its rating on the dimension of being innovative was substantially higher than any other brand. In 2003, Sony had

three subbrands (VAIO, PlayStation 2, and Sony Plaza, a retail chain selling Western-lifestyle merchandise) in the top 100. In 2002, when the
study was expanded to business audiences, Sony was second to Honda,
and in 2003 it moved to a decisive number-one position, with the highest
rating on the vitality dimension.

One reason behind Sony's brand strength is its' disciplined brand
identity (the aspirational associations). Sony has been guided by the
"Digital Dream Kids" vision that CEO Mr. Nobuyuki Idei developed in
the mid-1990s. In this phrase, "Digital" represents a drive to lead the
convergence of audio, video, and information technologies. "Dream"
refers to the astonishing technology that once was only a dream, both to
development engineers and to customers; Sony France once had a
tagline, "If you can dream it, we can make it," that captured this innovative spirit. "Kids" is intended to associate the Sony brand with the fun
and exuberance of being youthful. There is a lot of kid in all of us, and
Sony wants to have that spirit. Sony people are said to remember the
dreams they had as children.

Guided by this brand identity, the Sony brand portfolio serves to support and build the brand and its participation in a variety of product-
markets. The brand portfolio, particularly the product scope and its use
of subbrands and endorsed brands, has helped Sony in several ways to
attain both energy and differentiation.

The Scope of the Sony Brand

The Sony brand spans a spectrum of categories, many of which were
literally invented by Sony. The categories include consumer electronics,
music, electronic games, movies, theaters, and even (in Japan) insurance
and banking. Most of these provide exceptional visibility and reinforce
and broaden the Sony vision. Idei has hypothesized that the pervasive-
ness of Sony in so many product areas is one key to its brand success.[2]

The wide brand scope helps to generate both energy and differentiation. Energy comes via the frequency with which Sony is associated with
major technological innovations or new entertainment vehicles or
events. Because there are so many sources of energy, it is easier to have
a more continuous flow.

The broad scope of the brand creates differentiation as well; no other
brand can claim such breadth. And the digital convergence thrust, with

its implication on managing the digital home (with its entertainment center) and living a digital lifestyle, means that the Sony breadth has relevance.

The Family of Sony Subbrands and Endorsed Brands

The Sony brand portfolio also contributes energy and differentiation because of its family of strong subbrands and endorsed brands. Many Japanese companies, including Toshiba, Mitsubishi, and Canon, rely on a single brand. In these firms, the corporate brand receives virtually all of the brand-building effort, while the other brands in the portfolio have little equity. Sony is an exception because it has developed dozens of strong brands, each of which is focused on a product area and offers valued functional benefits. Some are stronger than others in terms of awareness and impact, but all are more than descriptors.

The brands, some of which are shown in Figure 5-1, include the Walkman (personal audio player), AIBO (personal entertainment robot), Trinitron and Wega (television), Car Audio (mobile entertainment), PlayStation (games), CLIÉ (handheld PDA), VAIO (notebook computer), Cybershot (digital camera), and Handycam (camcorder). All serve as branded energizers for the Sony brand. Some of these brands, such as Handycam and Walkman, have helped define a category that is associ-

FIGURE 5-1

ated with Sony—making the firm a trend driver in the terminology of Chapter 4. Others, like PlayStation and VAIO, have come from nothing to become very strong brands.

Introduced in Japan in 1994, and in the United States in 1996, the PlayStation series grew to where it had nearly 60 percent of the enormous worldwide videogame console market in 2001 and provided Sony with half of its profits.[3] Interestingly, it started out as the Sony PlayStation, leveraging the Sony brand name to get into the business. Over time however, the Sony endorsement was reduced until it virtually disappeared and became a shadow endorser. The PlayStation brand could get edgier, closer to its target audience, without being connected to such an established brand.

VAIO was also a big winner. In 2001, according to surveys conducted by Techtel (a firm that tracks high-tech brands), there were two portable or notebook computers with significant differentiation and equity—PowerBook and VAIO. Both were considerably stronger than the IBM ThinkPad (which had faded because of reduced product and brand-building support from IBM) and Toshiba notebooks, the early leader in this category.

Sony gets its energy and reputation as an innovator from the brands in its portfolio. Sony marketing executive T. Scott Edwards noted that the Sony "value proposition is innovation. Part of innovation is constantly providing consumers with news. Primarily we do that with new products."[4] The brands in the portfolio do more than just create new product news, although that is important. As Denise Yohn, another Sony executive, explained, "There never has been a real marketing program for the Sony corporate brand. We speak about Sony through its subbrands. We are trying to make these subbrands more emotive, lifestyle, toward certain types of customers rather than product oriented. For example, the Walkman brand is going from meaning portable audio to a lifestyle brand for Generation Y."[5]

Some documentation of the role of the subbrands comes from a unique study conducted in Japan in 2000 by the Dentsu advertising agency. The agency asked a sample of people in Japan the extent that they agreed with two statements. "The brand contributes toward Sony's image" and "I would choose it because it's a Sony product or service." The results are shown in Figure 5-2.

The data suggest a substantial influence flow between the Sony brand

FIGURE 5-2
THE SONY BRAND/SUBBRAND INFLUENCE

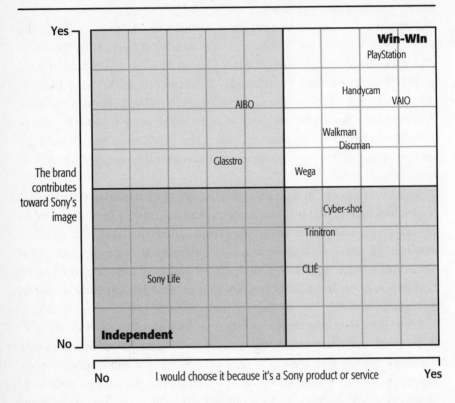

and its subbrands. The subbrands PlayStation (actually an endorsed brand), Handycam, VAIO, Walkman, and Discman demonstrated a strong two-way flow of influence. They supported the Sony image, but the Sony brand also helped make these brands more attractive. However, the influence was neither always symmetric nor strong. AIBO (also an endorsed brand) was a brand whose contribution to Sony was high, but one that relied less on the Sony connection. Trinitron and CLIÉ, in contrast, drew on the Sony brand strength and were relatively low on the scale of helping to support the Sony brand. Sony Life (a life insurance company), which is a brand used in the Japanese market that does not fit the Sony image or identity, was perceived as disconnected from the Sony brand in that it neither helped nor benefited from the brand.

A critical point behind the data of Figure 5-2 is that each of these brands is intimately linked to Sony. The linkage is in part tied to innovation. During key innovating phases in each subbrand context, Sony helped make the innovation credible, and strengthened the link between Sony and the subbrand. Even when Sony plays a shadow endorser role, as it does for PlayStation, the link is well known. Other technology brands have subbrands that may have moments of strength, but their link to the parent brand is weak.

These subbrands or endorsed brands energize Sony by keeping the innovation associated with a product area from being dissipated in the marketplace. An innovation will simply have more impact, both in the marketplace and on the Sony brand, if it is linked to one of Sony's subbrands or endorsed brands. Indeed, because most of these subbrands/endorsed brands represent the essence of innovation—the creation of a new category—advances are naturally associated with them. Ironically, most of these brands are so strong that *any* innovation in the category would likely be attributed to a Sony brand, even if it came from a competitor. Sony innovation would become a vague, generic concept were it not associated with Handycam or one of the other brands.

Many of the Sony subbrands and endorsed brands have potential branded differentiators, such as technology brands, that could help them gain market position. The MICROMV technology, for example, improves video quality on the Handycam, while Super Steady Shot Picture Stabilization makes picture-taking easier and the Memory Stick Media allows you to e-mail pictures right from the camera. The i.LINK digital interface makes the VAIO computer easier to use. The Dualshock analog controller helps differentiate PlayStation 2, as do some of Sony's proprietary games (such as the "Grand Theft Auto: Vice City" blockbuster). These brands, especially for the loyalist or the product enthusiast, provide a vehicle to capture the Sony dream.

There are also branded programs attached to the Sony brand that serve as differentiators. In the DreamLink program, members receive weekly notification of news about the world of Sony, special offers on new products, and a chance at sweepstakes contests such as tickets to the Grammys. They also earn DreamLink points, which can be redeemed for Sony CDs and other products. This loyalty program exploits the breadth of the Sony world and is an important point of differentiation for devoted customers.

Stretching the Brand

When a brand like Sony is strong and when the organization is highly decentralized, with business managers having a high degree of autonomy, there is a tendency to stretch the brand aggressively. Such stretching can create risks as well as rewards, as can be seen by examining three examples in the life of the Sony brand.

When Sony acquired a chain of theaters from Loews, the Sony brand was immediately employed on the rationale that theaters were entertainment, and Sony was in the entertainment business. Most of the theaters were from ordinary to shabby, however, without high-end audio and picture capabilities. Sony corrected this mistake by removing its name from all theaters except those that were physically and technically up to Sony standards—theaters that would be a showpiece for Sony innovation and technology and serve as brand energizers. But without question a branding mistake had been made.

Sony also used the prestige and power of its brand to launch a series of financial services companies in Japan, including Sony Life, Sony Assurance, Sony Finance, and Sony Bank. Although the banking and finance operations do have a technology spin that is not the case with the insurance entries, overall these ventures have little connection with "digital dream kids" and risk turning Sony into just another big Japanese conglomerate. It seems like a no-brainer to use another brand or at least an endorsed-brand strategy to separate the Sony brand from this new context.

A seemingly easy brand strategy judgment becomes more complex, however, if it is assumed that financial services is a strategic business at Sony (as GE Capital was for many years at GE). Further, the financial services business is growing rapidly and is very profitable. In fact, in fiscal 2003, although financial services were less than 7 percent of Sony's revenues, it represented 12.5 percent of profits.[6] Thus, a business strategy rationale for the use of the Sony brand made the risks tolerable. Further, some separation was obtained because the Sony logo was not used. Rather, Sony was written out in Katakana, the Japanese alphabet used for Western words (and, in the case of Sony Bank, was written in English).

A third example involves a vertical stretch. Over the years, Sony has used its brand to span a wide quality spectrum without proactively shielding it from low-end associations with subbrands, endorsed brands, or value brands (although the Sony-owned Aiwa value brand is beginning to be employed more extensively). The Walkman, for example, is sold at a wide variety of price points, from under $20 to over $350. Two rationales for this vertical stretch explain but fall short of reassuring the observer that the problem is mitigated. First, the Sony brand at a value price point is still the quality choice; the point of comparison for a $25 Walkman is a $15 Casio product rather than a high-end Sony. Second, value subbrands have been tried, but the Sony name is so strong that it overwhelms them, limiting their potential to protect the Sony brand. The complex issues surrounding vertical brand extensions will be pursued in Chapter 8.

Allocating Brand Building: Sony vs. Product Brands

The power of the Sony family of brands represents a competitive asset but also a dilemma: How much brand building and management should be placed behind the individual brands, and how much behind the Sony parent brand? IBM, facing a similar question, chose to dial up the master brand, emphasizing what the synergistic IBM organization could do for customers. One of Lou Gerstner's first decisions when he took over IBM in 1992 was to shift brand-building resources from 10 percent behind the IBM brand to 50 percent, requiring a painful adjustment for the product-marketing teams. While the Sony brand is supported by a brand-building program, its subbrands and endorsed brands are allowed to dominate budgets, accumulate equity, and play a key role in making the Sony brand strong.

DIFFERENTIATING AND ENERGIZING A BRAND

The competitive landscape for most brands is difficult to brutal. Most are facing overcapacity, vigorous price pressures, and eroding margins. One product class after another is maturing, becoming boring and life-less. Leading brands seem tired. Product proliferation, often involving little real product improvement, creates confused and ultimately disinterested customers. In their eyes, most brands are essentially the same, with nothing newsworthy, little differentiation, and an absence of energy.

In this context, a reasonable brand goal would be to add differentiation and energy. All brands and contexts are different, but it seems clear that few brands are saturated on either of these dimensions. This chapter will discuss the role of branded differentiators and branded energizers as a way to help create and maintain strong brands. The focus will be on brands that are owned and managed by the firm; contexts in which branded differentiators and energizers are controlled by another firm will be the subject of the brand alliance discussion that follows in Chapter 6.

BRANDED DIFFERENTIATORS

The role of differentiation in building brand strength has been documented by the Young & Rubicam Brand Asset Valuator (BAV) study, a global survey of brand equity conducted every two or three years. BAV covers over three dozen countries, 13,000 brands, 450 global brands and more than fifty measures. BAV is regularly repeated, allowing brands to be compared over time as well as with other brands.

The measures are organized into four key dimensions—*differentiation* (perceived distinctiveness), *relevance* (personally appropriate), *esteem* (perceived quality and increase in popularity), and *knowledge* (awareness and understanding). Using the database to study brand dynamics, differentiation has been found to play a key role. New brands that succeed are consistently found to have high differentiation. In fact, a healthy pattern early in a brand's life is to have differentiation higher than relevance, relevance higher than esteem, and esteem higher than knowledge. Mature brands that start to fade usually lose differentiation and can falter even when remaining strong on the other three dimensions. In the words of Stuart Agris, a brand guru who was instrumental in the development of the BAV, "Differentiation is the engine of the brand train. . . . If the engine stops, so will the train."[7]

There is considerable logic behind the importance of differentiation. If a brand fails to develop or maintain differentiation, all brands will start to look the same to consumers, and price will become the dominant decision determinant. Further, without differentiation there will be little basis for commitment, and it will be difficult to develop and retain a loyal customer base—the core of any brand and its associated business.

Obtaining points of differentiation is a challenge. It is difficult to come up with new products, features, services, or programs that in the eyes of customers are truly distinctive and deliver worthwhile benefits. Worse, when a point of difference is achieved, aggressive competitors too often quickly copy it. As a result, the incentive to advance offerings is reduced. The answer is to brand it. While a specific point of differentiation can be copied, a brand can be owned. The "branded differentiator," like other brands, can be actively managed to create a lasting point of difference in the customer's mind.

A branded differentiator is a branded feature, ingredient, service, or program that creates a point of differentiation for a branded offering that is meaningful for customers and merits active management over an extended time period.

For example, the Westin hotel chain in 1999 created the Heavenly Bed, a custom-designed (by Simmons) mattress set with 900 coils, three versions of a cozy down blanket for three climates, a comforter with a crisp duvet, three sheets of exceptional quality, and five goose-down pillows. The Heavenly Bed became a branded differentiator in a crowded category where differentiation is a challenge.

A branded differentiator does not occur simply by slapping a name on a feature. The definition suggests that rather demanding criteria need to be satisfied. In particular, a branded differentiator needs to be meaningful to customers. It needs to be both relevant and substantial enough to matter when customers are purchasing or using the product or service. The Heavenly Bed was meaningful in that it offered a substantial improvement in the bed, which represents the core purpose of a hotel room—to provide a good night's sleep. Its acceptance in the market demonstrated that it was meaningful to customers. During the first year of its life, hotel sites that featured the Heavenly Bed had a 5 percent increase in customer satisfaction, a noticeable jump in perception of cleanliness, room décor, maintenance, and increased occupancy.

A branded differentiator also needs to warrant active management over time and justify brand-building efforts. The Heavenly Bed has received that treatment with an active and growing set of brand-building programs. Now featured in Westin hotels, it has been made available for purchase; a significant number of buyers undoubtedly generated some buzz for both the bed and Westin. The Heavenly Online Catalog is a place to order not only the bed but accessories as well. The concept has also been extended to the Heavenly Bath, which has custom-designed showers with dual shower heads. Shower components and accessories

FIGURE 5-3
BRANDED DIFFERENTIATORS

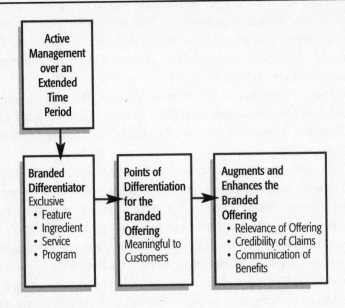

were added to the Heavenly Online Catalog, where there is even a bridal registry.

A branded differentiator needs to be linked to the target offering, giving it a product-defining role. A challenge for Westin is to generate a link to the Heavenly Bed so that customers recall which hotel has this feature rather than being confused or, worse, attributing it to another chain.

A branded differentiator in some settings provides not only differentiation but also relevance. A substantial segment of computer buyers, for example, would only consider those computers with Intel Inside. Similarly, the Heavenly Bed has elevated the importance of bed quality to the point that for some it affects relevance.

A branded differentiator, as suggested by Figure 5-3 and the definition, will be either a feature, ingredient, service, or program affecting the offering. Each of these possibilities is examined below.

A Branded Feature

A branded feature often provides a graphic way to signal superior performance and a vehicle to own that point of superiority over time. To accomplish this mission, it must be something of value to customers, truly differentiating, and linked to the branded offering.

In the automobile industry, as models proliferate, a branded feature becomes a key point in differentiation. BMW iDrive is a dashboard computer that can control all devices in the car, including cell phones and navigation systems. It is designed to reduce distraction and thus make the driving experience safer and less stressful. General Motors pioneered the OnStar system, which provides automatic notification of air bag deployment to roadside assistance agencies, stolen vehicle location, emergency services, remote door unlocking, remote diagnostics, and concierge services.

A branded feature can differentiate by reflecting an organization's heritage and promise. Krispy Kreme doughnuts have enjoyed incredible buzz and sales growth after starting retail sales in the early 1990s. Early on, one enterprising Krispy Kreme retailer put a "hot light" sign in the window; when it came on, passersby would know that hot doughnuts were ready. For loyalists who would line up at 5:30 in the morning for hot, fresh doughnuts, the sign was a beacon. It was also a symbol of the product, a key element of which is its freshness. The symbol has been redesigned and nurtured as part of the brand promise and company culture.

A branded feature can support an innovation association particularly for a high-tech firm. As noted above, Sony has a host of brand features—such as MICROMV technology (digital cameras), the Dualshock analog controller (PlayStation 2), i.LINK digital interface (Vaio), and Super Night Shot (Handycam)—that make a difference, especially to the involved customer. All of these have the potential to be branded differentiators. GE's Mammography System has the SharpIQ grid system to improve performance. Like Sony's features, it signals a point of differentiation that is on target for a key point of interest for customers.

Oral-B has created a position for itself over the years as the toothbrush "more dentists use." The company makes its innovations visible with branded features. For example, its Indicator bristles, which change color as the brush becomes worn, have been well received. And the market leader, the Oral-B Advantage Plaque Remover toothbrush, has two branded features that help communicate its points of differentiation: the Power Tip bristles at the end of the brush that help clean hard-to-reach areas and the Action Cup shape that conforms to teeth and gum contours.

A Branded Ingredient

Another perspective is to brand an ingredient (or component or technology). Even if customers do not understand how the ingredient works, the fact that it was branded lends credibility to the explicit or implied claims. Of course, the brand will only work in the long run if there is substance behind it; building a brand that cannot deliver is a recipe for failure. To fully appreciate the potential of ingredient brands, imagine if Chevron attempted to explain why its gasoline was different without mentioning the Techron brand. The effort would not be persuasive or even feasible. Thus, the brand provides a communication aid. Customers may not know how Techron works, but they do know that it is meaningful and that Chevron thought enough about an ingredient to brand it.

Canon uses its Digic (digital imaging integrated circuits), a process that provides improved signal processing and longer battery life, as a branded differentiator for its digital cameras.[8] Because digital camera buyers generally know little about the purchase beyond the number of pixels, the Digic brand name serves as a crystallized reminder of Canon's advertising tagline: "Digital revolutionized photographs; we revolutionized digital."

Many car models brand ingredients to help communicate points of differentiation. The Cadillac DeVille, for example, includes the Northstar engine, which not only delivers exceptional mileage and smooth riding but interacts with the steering, braking, and traction systems to enhance system performance. Notably, the Northstar engine is a moving target, because it is always being improved. One reason the Northstar brand works for Cadillac is that it provides an explanation as to why Cadillac does well in owner satisfaction ratings. Owners (and others as well) need a reason for the high satisfaction, and Northstar becomes a part of the reason. Reinforced by that reason, owners (and others) are that much more inclined to rate Cadillac highly.

A Branded Service

The classic way to differentiate a brand in a mature category is to add a service. Branding that service and actively managing it over time can create a significant branded differentiator.

Consider Tide, a detergent that is inherently a low-involvement product for most users. A branded service, the Tide Stain Detective, allows a customer to go to the Tide website and get advice for removing most stains that will be encountered. The service provides both credibility and differentiation for Tide. By presenting itself as an authority on stains, Tide's credibility as a detergent can only be enhanced. Further, by actively managing and improving the service over time, Procter & Gamble can not only extend but expand its impact as more customers are exposed to it.

A branded service can help enhance a differentiated position by helping to communicate a set of features. In the credit card arena, American Express staked out the high end with its American Express Platinum Concierge services, whereby cardholders have around-the-clock access to a concierge to make reservations, locate hard-to-find items, or deal with any request.

An image problem for a service organization can be addressed by packaging and branding service components relevant to the problem. For example, a large HMO was perceived by current and prospective members as an impersonal bureaucracy that emphasized efficiency and lacked human compassion. The image was caused in part by a semi-automated system (instead of a doctor's secretary) for making appointments, and a policy of same-day visits being serviced by one member of a pool of physicians (rather than by a patient's regular doctor).

One way to attack the problem was to brand the HMO's same-day appointment systems as "Urgent Care," with an identity emphasizing responsiveness ("We are there for you"). The brand helped to reposition a negative signal as a positive attribute.

Similarly, a program by which elderly people with heart risk factors meet regularly might be given a brand name such as HeartClub and a personality that reflects the care and support this group is receiving. A symbol such as a pair of cheerful heart-shaped characters could represent the support and feelings engendered by the program. These brands and perhaps others could be the differentiators needed to modify the identity of the HMO.

A branded service can help redefine the business, making competitors who lack the perceived willingness or ability to provide that service less relevant. For example, when everyone else is selling a product, the firm that offers a systems solution (perhaps by adding ordering and shipping services to the product) could change what customers want to buy. Thus, as discussed in Chapter 9, UPS changed from a package delivery company to a firm that performs a set of services under the umbrella brand UPS Supply Chain Solutions. Such branded differentiators have the potential to create a product category for which some competitors may not be relevant.

Branded Programs

Some branded programs can provide a differentiated basis for a more satisfying and even intense relationship with their loyal customer base. Harley-Davidson, for example, is more than a brand—it is an experience, and a community supported by several branded programs. The Harley-Davidson Ride Planner allows a person to create a ride plan, given starting and ending points plus desired stops. The output is a detailed map that the person can save and share with friends. The Harley-Davidson Photo Center provides a place to post snapshots of memorable trips. Friends can access the site, relive experiences, and be a part of the community.

Or consider Pampers, a packaged consumer good that struggles to create and maintain points of differentiation. The Pampers website has several branded programs (in addition to the Pampers Perks loyalty program) that serve to differentiate its offering. The Pampers Vantastic Sweepstakes gives customers a chance to win a Chrysler minivan filled with diapers. The Pampers Parenting Institute provides authoritative advice from world experts in child care, health, and development; it also provides a customized e-mail parenting newsletter and is the visible driver of such programs as a campaign to reduce sudden infant death syndrome. In part because of the institute, Pampers in 2001 was measured as the second most popular baby care site with around one million unique visitors per month, many times that of Huggies. The bottom line is that those visiting the Pampers site and accessing these branded programs are 30 percent more likely to purchase Pampers.[9]

Kraft Kitchen is another brand that has used its website, one of the most popular among food brands, as a vehicle to distribute differentiating branded programs. Such programs as "What's for Dinner," "Dinner on Hand," "Wisdom of Moms," and "Sweet Thoughts" enhance a brand that has a difficult time breaking out of the clutter of low-involvement activities.

Loyalty programs have added a new basis for differentiation to many categories. The airline programs, pioneered by American Airlines more than twenty years ago, have a lot of vitality and sources of ongoing differentiation today. United Mileage Plus has the Star Alliance (whereby customers can access 13 airlines through Mileage Plus), upgrade programs, a host of promotions, and a whole family of partners including hotels, rental car companies, and restaurants. Branded loyalty programs have become a key avenue for differentiation in the hospitality industry as well, with Hilton Honors becoming one of the key assets of Hilton. The challenge is to keep innovating and building the loyalty program brand as it matures and competitors develop similar programs.

The Value of Branding It

A valued feature, ingredient, service, or program will serve to differentiate a product whether or not it is branded. So why brand it? There are several reasons, most of which go back to the basic value of a brand in any context. A brand adds credibility, aids memory, helps communication, and can provide the basis for a sustainable competitive advantage.

First, as noted, a brand can add credibility to a claim. The brand specifically says that the benefit was worth branding, that it is meaningful. The observer will instinctively believe that if an organization was willing to commit to developing a brand, there must be a reason why it was branded. Suburu has long emphasized four-wheel drive, and many car brands now offer this feature. Audi, however, has a branded version, Quattro, which gives it a credibility and relevance that the others lack. In essence, there are four-wheel drives, and then there is Quattro.

The ability of a brand to add credibility was rather dramatically shown in a remarkable study of branded attributes. Three prominent academic researchers found that the inclusion of a branded attribute (such as "Alpine Class" fill for a down jacket, "Authentic Milanese" for pasta, and "Studio Designed" for compact disc players) dramatically affected customer preference toward premium-priced brands. Respondents were able to justify the higher price because of the branded attributes. Remarkably, the effect occurred even when the respondents were given information implying that the attribute was not relevant to their choice.[10]

Second, a brand name can make it easier to remember the feature, ingredient, service, or program. It is just much easier to recall a brand name than the details of why a branded differentiator works. Thus brands like HeartClub or Pamper's Parenting Institute can represent complex information that would be difficult to keep in mind. The job of linking the point of differentiation to the parent brand is also made much easier.

Third, a brand makes communication more efficient and feasible. A new product feature, for example, may be important to its designers, but there is likely a monumental lack of interest among the target audience. Even when the communication registers, it can sound like typical puffery and thus lack credibility. A name such as Action Cup, though, provides a way to crystallize one of several detail features, making it easier to both understand and remember.

Fourth, having a brand provides the option of actively managing it, creating a basis for a sustainable competitive advantage. A competitor may be able to replicate the feature, ingredient, service, or program, but if it is branded, it will also need to overcome the power of the brand. As mentioned earlier, sometimes a strong branded feature gets credit for innovations by others because the association between the feature and the brand is so strong. An advance in audio technology, for instance, may be attributed to Dolby no matter where it originates.

Amazon developed a powerful feature—the ability to recommend books or other items based on a customer's interests, as reflected by his or her purchase history and the purchase history of those that bought similar offerings—but they never branded it. How tragic is that? As a result, the feature became basically a commodity that is an expected element of many e-commerce sites. If Amazon had branded it and then actively managed that brand, improving the feature over time, it would have become a lasting point of differentiation that today would be invaluable. Instead, the firm missed a golden opportunity. It did not make that same mistake with One-Click, a branded service that plays a key role in defining Amazon in what has become a messy marketplace.

BRANDED ENERGIZERS

There is also solid logic behind the need for most brands to generate more vitality. Successful brands seem to have energy. Visit a retail shopping area and observe the successful shops; there will be shoppers, music, displays, and storefronts that are interesting, involving, and energetic. Other stores, in contrast, seem boring and dead.

The tradition brands of the world (such as AT&T, John Deere, Sears Roebuck, Brooks Brothers, Toshiba, and Pillsbury) all have incredible profiles. They are usually portrayed as being reliable, honest, dependable, accessible, and often innovative as well. But they often struggle with impressions that they are old-fashioned, out of touch, and boring—an impression that can affect their relevance for some segments. It is amazing how frequently such an image profile is seen, and the conclusion drawn that injections of energy and vitality are desperately needed. This is often especially true with respect to a key younger segment, the lifeblood of future business.

When a brand lacks energy, it often resides in what is termed the graveyard, a concept introduced in Chapter 4. A graveyard brand, one that has low levels of unaided recall but high levels of aided recall, will not get into the consideration set. One way to avoid this graveyard is to maintain an adequate energy level.

Effective Branded Energizers

How do you energize a brand especially when there is little interest not only in the brand but in the product category as well? It can be a tough assignment. The solution might be to use another brand, which is not part of the offering per se, but has energy, and then use that "branded energizer" to energize the master brand or subbrand.

A branded energizer is a branded product, promotion, sponsorship, symbol, program, or other entity that by association significantly enhances and energizes a target brand, with both the branded energizer and its association with the target brand being actively managed over an extended time period.

In this chapter, the focus is on branded energizers owned by the firm. In Chapter 6 on brand alliances, examples are introduced in which the branded energizer is owned by another organization (including celebrity endorsers, countries or regions, and sponsorships owned by others).

A example of an effective branded energizer is Heinz EZ Squirt ketchup, launched in late 2000, which has invigorated a tired brand and category. Kids, who consume 55 percent of all ketchup, told Heinz that the existing bottle was hard to use, and different colors would be fun. In response, EZ Squirt came in colors like Funky Purple and Blastin Green, with a kid-friendly container that allows the product to come out in a

FIGURE 5-4
BRANDED ENERGIZERS

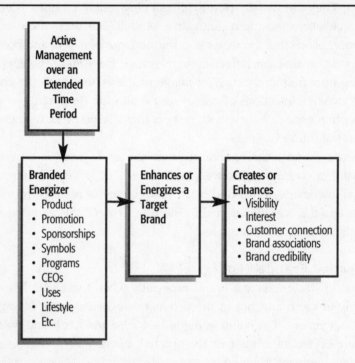

small, smooth stream. As a result, kids can be creative, drawing pictures with the ketchup.

As Figure 5-4 and the definition suggest, a branded energizer can be any of a wide variety of branded entities. It should also have several characteristics, which will be discussed in the following paragraphs.

First, a branded energizer should itself have vitality. An effective branded energizer should do well when asked whether it would be described as being:

- New vs. old, stale
- Youthful vs. mature, older
- Interesting vs. boring
- Dynamic with movement vs. static, unchanging
- Contemporary vs. traditional
- Assertive vs. passive
- Involving vs. separated

Certainly, the Heinz EZ Squirt was new, interesting, involving, and aimed at the key youth segment.

Second, the branded energizer needs to be connected to the master brand, even though (unlike a branded differentiator) it is not part of the master brand offering. This connection task can be difficult and expensive. Even the Energizer bunny, one of the top icons among U.S. brands, is associated by some with Duracell rather than Eveready despite its exposure over a long time period.

There are several routes to creating a link to a brand. One is to use a subbrand such as Ronald McDonald's House, where the master brand has a connection in the name. A second is to select a program or activity so clearly related to the brand that the link is easier to establish. A baby-oriented program, for instance, would require little effort to connect to Gerber. A third is to simply forge the link by consistently building it over time with significant resources. If a branded energizer is regarded as a one-time event rather than an entity to be leveraged in several ways over time, links will be harder to create.

Third, a branded energizer should significantly enhance the target brand. Having energy and being connected is not enough if the energy is misdirected or diffused. Evidence of a change in image or a surge of sales is often the best measure of success. EZ Squirt by several measures had home-run impact for Heinz ketchup, creating a 13 percent sales increase for Heinz and more than 4 percent growth in the category during its first year. In addition, it created significant buzz not only with the media but also with parents, who were alternatively disgusted and amazed by the colored-ketchup concept.

Be careful not to compromise the brand identity, however, in an effort to find or create energy. A branded energizer should not make customers uncomfortable with the brand's association or participation. An off-beat, underdog brand such as Southwest Airlines, Virgin, Apple, Mountain Dew, or Abercrombie & Fitch can do outrageous things to create interest and energy. For the "senior" brands, however, it is quite a different story. In their case, a lot of options may be foreclosed, although a branded energizer can still be edgier than the parent brand (which is often the advantage of using an energizer).

Fourth, if the energizer is ownable, it will have a stronger and more sustained impact. There is such an upside to owning a branded energizer. Ownability means that competitors would have difficulty imitating it, and even better, that it has a chance to have an on-going life. In general, it is difficult and costly to create effective branded energizers and if one can be reused again and again, the economics become more attractive. In the brand alliance chapter that follows, branded energizers owned by other firms will be discussed.

It may be helpful to review the difference between a branded differentiator and a branded energizer. A branded differentiator must involve the product or service directly or indirectly; it has a product-defining role. For example, a branded feature or ingredient (such as the Heavenly Bed) is a part of the functional benefits provided by the product offering. In contrast, a branded energizer involves a wider assortment of branded initiatives, none of which are functionally part of the offering, even though they are linked to it. Thus, instead of having a product-defining role, an energizer has a portfolio role.

There are many types of branded energizers. Some of the most useful include products, promotions, sponsorships, symbols, programs, a use, a CEO, or even a lifestyle.

New Branded Products

The gold standard for creating "on-brand" energy is a flow of new products, products that are worth branding because they are sufficiently different and promise to support sales over time that would justify the branding cost. For example, the EZ Squirt brand clearly achieved this standard for Heinz. A new product brand, subbrand, or endorsed brand linked to the target brand is the ultimate statement of the brand and the firm, and the heart of the customer relationship. Further, it provides the basis for future sales and revenue. An exciting new product is a branded energizer that is likely also qualified to play a silver bullet role.

Nowhere is the power of a new product brand clearer than in the automobile space. Consider how the new Beetle, introduced in 1998, created enormous interest in Volkswagen with a contemporary design yet clearly was linked to the cult-like Beetle heritage. It led a sales revival of the Volkswagen brand, which was on its back. One of the first affordable sports cars several decades ago, the 240Z provided enormous energy to the Nissan (then Datsun) brand. Nissan currently plans to bring back the Z with an eye toward revitalizing its current brand. Consider also how:

- The Miata created a buzz around Mazda.
- The retro PT Cruiser model added interest to Chrysler because it was so novel, while linking the company and the customer to the Chrysler heritage.
- The TT sports car contributed design and a sports-car energy and feel to Audi.

Some new products with strong subbrands that have energized their master brand include the following:

- Bose Wave Radio, which sells for over $300 but delivers performance far superior to other radios, provides energy and brand reinforcement for the Bose brand.
- Apple iPod, a portable digital music player capable of storing a thousand songs, was a dramatic sales success and also expanded and energized the Apple brand.
- Nike's Presto shoe had a versatile, unique design that permits S-M-L sizing with a comfortable fit. As a result, the shoe was available in thirteen colors, which led to a variety of brand-building programs and a stretch into the fashion arena for Nike. The product was a huge hit among the target teen audience and created energy for the Nike brand among that group.
- Crest got an energy boost by buying the Dr. Johns SpinBrush (a disposable, battery-powered toothbrush) and promptly changing its name to Crest SpinBrush.[11] During its first year as a Crest brand, it outsold its Colgate rival (ActiBrush) by two to one, giving Crest something newsworthy in its line and adding to its visibility and credibility as a leading oral health brand.
- Mountain Dew got energy and an expanded customer base with its caffeine-loaded, dewy flavored Mountain Dew Code Red, which attracted urbanites, women, and African-Americans to the brand.[12]

Often energy is needed among a segment, typically younger consumers. Such a problem faced Cover Girl, which was a bit tired and struggled particularly among the key teen market.[13] However, it emerged as the number three "coolest brand for teens" (after Nike and Abercrombie & Fitch) in early 2002. One reason was some product vitality led by

Outlast, an all-day lip color, and Aquasmooth makeup, which changes to a liquid during application. These innovations supported the new, cool look and feel of Cover Girl.

Toyota suffers from an aging customer base, a problem common to several automobile brands. The average Toyota driver is forty-four years old, and this number, already above Honda and Nissan (both at forty-one), is moving up. To address the problem, Toyota in 2003 introduced the Scion, a car to be targeted to younger drivers.[14] The first versions will be a minivan and a five-door hatchback, each with a simple, funky design geared to the target market.

Branded Promotional Activities

Kraft's Oscar Mayer Wienermobiles have provided energy for decades to a very boring category. There are eight vehicles touring the United States shaped like a huge Oscar Mayer weiner, with license plates with appropriate wording (like "HOT DOG"). They turn up at events and parties and support the annual contest to find a child to sing the signature Oscar Mayer jingle. The Wienermobile, which has been shown to bump the product sales, also lives on the web where it can be taken on a tour of Oscartown, visiting such places as the Oscar Museum, the OscarMart, and Town Hall. The Weinermobile's linkage to the product category also links it to Oscar Mayer.

Branded Sponsorships

The Adidas Streetball Challenge is a branded weekend event centered on local three-person basketball tournaments and featuring free-throw competitions, a street dance, graffiti events, and extreme sports demonstrations, all accompanied by live music from bands from the hip-hop and rap scenes. The Challenge was right in the sweet spot of target customers, a party. And it was connected to Adidas by its brand and supporting signage and Adidas-supplied caps and jackets. It revitalized Adidas at a critical time in its history. Five years after the first test in 1992, over a half million people participated, and the finals in Berlin attracted 3,200 players and 40,000 spectators. More than thirty countries were represented in the world finals in Milan. The challenge was extended to a soccer-based Adidas Predator Challenge (subsequently renamed the DFB-Adidas Cup) and the outdoor-oriented (mountain biking, rafting, etc.) Adidas Adventure Challenge.

Memorable Branded Symbols

Brands that are blessed with strong relevant symbols such as the Pillsbury Doughboy, the Maytag repairman, or the Michelin man can actively manage and use the symbols to become energizer brands. Such symbols can give a personality to even the blandest of brands. They can also suggest attributes. The Pillsbury Doughboy is upbeat with a sense of humor, for example, and signals freshness and superb quality. The Maytag repairman is relaxed and confident, and symbolizes the reliability of Maytag. The Michelin man is strong and positive and means safety.

Symbols can have a life of their own. It is often much easier to connect with a symbol than a product. Budweiser's Frank and Louie lizard characters had such a following that customers would go to the Budweiser website and re-watch ads. They would even buy shirts and dolls and send e-cards from the site. And the characters were firmly linked to Budweiser because they were the stars of Bud ads.

Branded Programs

A branded program, such as one in the corporate citizenship arena, can be an effective energizer. Consider the Avon Breast Cancer Crusade, which covers a wide-ranging set of branded programs involving research, early detection, clinical care, support services, and education. With an emphasis on underserved women, the program has substance and significance, one measure of which is the fact that it raised $250 million over a ten-year period. It gives "The Company for Women" a higher purpose and a heart. Or consider Ronald McDonald House, the program by McDonald's to provide housing for families with children with serious illness. It not only does good works of real substance, it contributes to McDonald's relationship with kids and families.

Branding Uses

An entire category can be revitalized if a new application can be found. If that application is branded and linked to the parent brand, the impact can be significant. Angostura Bitters, a 160-year-old brand used primarily in Manhattan cocktails, decided to promote nonalcoholic drinks, starting with the Charger (which consisted of sparkling water, bitters, and lime).[15] Canada Dry was enticed to promote it by putting a packet of bitters, with a recipe, on the necks of bottles of its seltzer. Tastings were organized at museums and street fairs. Radio ads with a

"Charger" theme were run. Other drinks such as the Caribbean (made with cranberry juice, pineapple juice, and bitters) followed.

Branded CEOs

Some firms have branded CEOs who capture and magnify the energy in the brand, or create energy that can be transferred to the brand. Lee Ioccoca helped save Chrysler by exuding confidence and competence when customers and investors had assumed the firm would collapse. William Clay Ford attempted to reassure drivers that Ford was on top of safety problems in part by dialing up the heritage and commitment of the Ford family. Richard Branson's outlandish stunts (some involving hot-air balloons) are a large part of the energy and personality of the Virgin brand. Herb Kellner has personified the Southwest Airline brand with his visible and colorful expression of its culture. Steve Jobs and Bill Gates have driven much of the energy of Apple and Microsoft, respectively, with their visible thought leadership.

The CEO "brand" has many good attributes. These individuals are linked to the brand and can have access to media that other spokespeople and brand-building programs lack. Their ability to energize, however, is in part based on their public presence, reputation, and personality. Thus there are only a few CEOs who are able to play this role. Further, being human, they are subject to adverse publicity, in which case their visibility can backfire. Also, they will eventually leave the scene, which can create an uncomfortable brand void.

Branding a Lifestyle

Many brands attempt to position against a lifestyle, but AT&T Wireless is one of the few to brand a lifestyle itself. mLife is the ultimate in a mobile lifestyle, with the phone in the center. mLife is never being bored, because you can make a call or surf the web, play games, get sports scores, and even shop with your phone. mLife is expressing yourself with your own ring and by communicating silently. mLife is never being lost again, because an AT&T wireless operator will know where you are. And more. When the mLife brand was introduced during the 2002 Super Bowl, the hits on the mLife website that day were over 680,000 (compared to 30,000 on the previous day), and 5 percent of those who visited signed up.

The Value of Branding It

Most of these energizing programs could have been accomplished without brands, but a brand makes it so much easier to achieve the energizing objectives and to own the program. As noted in the discussion of branded differentiators, a brand makes it easier for the firm to communicate what might otherwise be a complex concept, and to link that concept to the parent brand. It also makes it easier for the customer to remember a key point of differentiation. But do not slap a brand on just anything. Having a brand alone will not make an effective brand enhancer. Rather, a worthwhile energizer that involves the investment of resources will be more effective and capable of being leveraged *if* it is branded.

MANAGING BRANDED DIFFERENTIATORS AND ENERGIZERS

It is critical to know that the concepts of branded differentiators and energizers do *not* provide a rationale to add brands indiscriminately. Both can be powerful brand builders, but recall the definitions of both. A branded differentiator needs to create a meaningful, impactful point of differentiation, and it should justify being actively managed. If it does not pass this test, the branded differentiator role is inappropriate, and another justification for the brand will be needed. A branded energizer should significantly enhance the brand, and it too should justify active management. If these criteria are not met, a brand energizer role is probably not warranted.

Identifying branded differentiators and energizers is not easy, or there would be a lot more than there are. However, the following questions can be helpful:

- What is the brand identity and position? What about the brand will potentially resonate with customers and differentiate it from competitors? Why? What are the proof points?
- Are there existing features or services that could be branded? Would their potential be enhanced if they were bundled or extended?

- How does the market segment? For each segment, what are the current and emerging benefits that the customer is seeking? What possible branded differentiators would affect purchases and loyalty?
- What activities and interests that are important to customers have some relationship to the brand? How could the brand be linked to those branded activities and interests? What branded energizers could be developed and owned by the brand?
- Are there sources of brand differentiators and energizers outside the firm? How might they be connected to the brand?

Branded differentiators and energizers need to be linked to the target brand. If they are linked by subbrands, as with the Adidas Streetball Challenge or Heinz EZ Squirt ketchup, the task might be easy. Otherwise, the linkage can require resources and management to make it happen. There is nothing more tragic than to develop a powerful branded differentiator only to learn that most of the market attributes it to your competitor's brand.

Take a strategic, long-term view. Branded differentiators and energizers should have a relatively long life, otherwise the cost of brand building will have to be amortized over too short a period to make it worthwhile. They also need to be actively managed so that they can be successful in their roles over time. Some might need their own development programs in order to maintain the strength needed to perform the assigned role. If, for example, a branded service stays static, then competitors will copy it, and the power of the brand will eventually erode. If the branded service becomes a moving target because it is always advancing, however, then it will be more difficult to neutralize.

If a brand lacks a branded differentiator and developing one is either too expensive or will take too much time, there is the option of "renting" or "leasing" one from another firm. This task involves brand alliances. The potential, risk, and management of such alliances are discussed in the next chapter.

Setting Priorities: Silver Bullets

In some contexts, there will be many branded energizers and several branded differentiators. If so, priorities need to be set. The priorities should be based on two criteria, as suggested by Figure 5-5. The first is the impact on the target brand—in terms of the definitions, you should be looking for meaningful, impactful branded differentiators and branded energizers that significantly enhance the brand. The second is the amount of resources required to build and support the brands or brand linkages. Brands that have a modest impact but can be implemented and managed for little cost can be attractive.

Priority setting often needs to be done by segment. In the Sony case, for example, cutting-edge graphics for PlayStation would have the highest potential to energize the Sony brand for the teen market, while Handycam would have higher potential for families concerned with memories, and VAIO might be superior for businessmen concerned with quality.

The highest-priority brand differentiators or energizers are given silver bullet status. Within the set of branded differentiators or energizers, a silver bullet brand will have high strategic impact and will warrant a

FIGURE 5-5
SILVER BULLETS

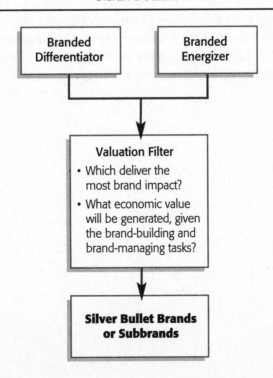

high level of brand management resources. There will normally be at most one or two silver bullets for any target brand, and many will not have any.

Brands that merit silver bullet status usually have an advantage in terms of establishing relevance, differentiation, and energy. However, that does not mean that creating or nominating a brand for this role will be helpful; in fact, it can easily be wasteful, illusory, and distracting. There needs to be substance and a strategic perspective behind a silver bullet, plus a willingness to invest in it over time.

QUESTIONS FOR CONSIDERATION

1. Consider your major brands. How differentiated are they? Do they have any branded differentiators? Are there features, ingredients, services, or programs that could be packaged and branded? If so, what brand-building budget, if any, would you recommend to support those brands?

2. Consider your major brands. Rate each of them on an energy scale. Which rate high? Why? For the ones that need more energy, propose a set of branded energizers. Evaluate your current branded energizers with respect to their energy, whether they are compatible to the brand, their ownability, and their linkage to the target brand.

CHAPTER 6

ACCESSING STRATEGIC ASSETS: BRAND ALLIANCES

If you can't reach where it itches, strike a deal with someone else to help to scratch.

—MATTHEW GRIMM, BRANDWEEK WRITER

Where there is no wind, row.

—PORTUGUESE PROVERB

The man that goes alone can start today; but he who travels with another must wait till that other is ready.

—HENRY DAVID THOREAU, WALDEN

FORD EXPLORER
EDDIE BAUER EDITION

Eddie Bauer opened its first store in Seattle in 1920 with an emphasis on quality and a pioneering money-back guarantee, both of which are still in place today.* During its first fifty years, the brand was focused on the outdoors, making clothing products for serious expeditions as well as for the recreational outdoorsperson. The company was also an innovator; one of its creations was the first-ever garment insulated with goose down, introduced in 1936 and termed the Skyliner. A few years later, during World War II, more than fifty thousand Bauer flight jackets contributed to the war effort and became one of the icons of the period.

After 1970, the firm began an aggressive expansion of its Seattle retail presence, growing to more than five hundred stores by 2000. The focus of the brand expanded as well, to casual-lifestyle apparel for both

---

* Information in this section is based on Eddie Bauer and Ford websites, 2003; Steve Gelsi, "A Marryin' Mood," *Brandweek,* September 2, 1994, pp. 24–28.

women and men. However, it did not walk away from its outdoor heritage. Bauer advertisements feature photographs of outdoor scenes with text describing the ability of the clothing to withstand the elements. A partnership with American Forest and an "Add a Dollar, Plant a Tree" retail program resulted in millions of new trees. A "Building Cities of Green" tree-planting tour brought trees to urban areas. In 2000, Eddie Bauer joined with National Geographic to sponsor a film on Lewis and Clark and a National Public Radio series on expeditions.

In 1983, Eddie Bauer licensed its brand to Ford to create the Ford Explorer Eddie Bauer Edition. This remarkable partnership has not only endured for two decades but has sold over 1 million vehicles. The co-branded car offers an Eddie Bauer fashion and comfort statement in the context of a Ford Explorer. The car thus is distinguished from other SUVs, a product type in which there has been increased brand proliferation and product confusion, by providing an Eddie Bauer influenced interior. The partnership provides enormous benefits to both Ford and Eddie Bauer.

Ford receives from the Eddie Bauer co-brand a link to the outdoor segment and associations of outdoors, active people, comfort, quality, and discriminating taste and style. Ford also gets exclusive exposure in the Eddie Bauer catalogues, which have a circulation of more than 100 million. These associations allow Ford to provide not only functional benefits but self-expressive benefits because of the comfort and style provided by the car.

Eddie Bauer gets incredible exposure from the advertising, the publicity, the showroom experience, and, most importantly, the interactions of the Ford Explorer owners with their friends. Further, the SUV association enhances the outdoors heritage and casual lifestyle that is central to the Eddie Bauer brand. The fact that the partnership creates a sustainable win-win program is why it has survived the test of time, the ups and downs of the car market, and the changing tastes of customers.

The risk to the Eddie Bauer brand was limited. First, the Ford Explorer brand took the lead brand role—customers were buying a Ford Explorer, with the Eddie Bauer quality, taste, and style reflected in the interior. Second, the portion of the vehicle with which the Eddie Bauer brand was associated was relatively easy to deliver to Eddie Bauer standards.

In the 1990s, Eddie Bauer leveraged and broadened its associations in

FIGURE 6-1
FORD EXPLORER EDDIE BAUER EDITION

EDDIE BAUER

The Explorer Eddie Bauer Edition has defined SUV style for more than a decade. For 2003, exterior trademarks include an Arizona Beige lower-body treatment and a satin nickel finish on the grille and cast aluminum wheels. Luxury two-tone leather seating surfaces create a warm interior feel, and you can really heat things up with the standard 290-watt Audiophile 6-disc CD sound system. The 6-way power adjustable heated front seats with driver's-side memory, as well as power adjustable accelerator and brake pedals with memory, make the front row a very comfortable place. In fact, with its generous room, optional 7-passenger seating and fashionable good looks, the Eddie Bauer is really a comfortable choice for everybody.

part by a host of co-branded entries. In 1997, Lane Home Furnishings created a line of reclining furniture and sleep sofas under the brand Eddie Bauer Lifestyles by Lane. Well received by the market, the line has been expanded and even includes a "for kids" version. In 1998, the Eddie Bauer Bicycle by Giant was introduced. In 2000, Signature Eyewear launched Eddie Bauer performance sunwear. In 2001, Eddie Bauer teamed with American Recreation Products to launch a collection of camping equipment. In 2003, Skyway Luggage created a new luggage collection. In the process the Eddie Bauer brand gained visibility and association reinforcement. Further, the brand became broader, more of a lifestyle brand, which helped enable it to stretch its boundaries.

Extending the brand has had risks as well, in part because the brand was out in front and because some of the extensions did stretch the brand beyond its comfort zone. In light of the risks, it became critical that the design and production of the various products deliver quality, taste, and style in casual living that the brand aspires to stand for. Any departures would put the brand equity at risk.

Most firms compete in an environment in which the dynamics make it difficult to stay relevant, differentiated, and energized. Nearly every market is changing because of new technologies, evolving customer applications and tastes, and competitor initiatives.

This demanding context creates significant internal challenges. New offerings are needed at an accelerated pace, and these offerings need to include some home runs among the also-rans. New business capabilities and brand assets need to be developed in order to create and support new offerings, as well as changes in existing ones. Paths to differentiate and energize existing offerings need to be found in mature product arenas. And brand building needs to become more efficient and effective, as margins simply no longer tolerate the mediocre and the inefficient.

Accompanying these challenges are severe constraints in resources, time, and organizational capabilities. New resources are required in R&D, production, brands, and brand building at the same time that existing businesses require resources to maintain vitality and increase efficiency. In terms of the credibility footprint introduced in Chapter 3, there may be either a brand-relevance or firm-competence gap, or both. Where will these resources come from, especially when market environments force shrinking margins? And how can all this be done quickly, before the threat overcomes or the opportunity recedes? The era in which time was a friend is gone. There is usually a short window of opportunity.

Further, even if there were unlimited time and financial resources, it is not clear that some of these challenges would even be feasible. Creating a new credible branded offering, for example, is not always possible for some organizations. Developing efficient brand-building programs that break through the clutter is also elusive. Addressing organizational competence gaps may require excessive resources or, worse, may compromise existing operations. Wanting and doing are very different things.

One way to overcome the constraints of resources, time, and capabilities is to explore brand alliances. *Brand alliances involve two or more firms that associate their brands together to create superior market offerings, or to engage in effective strategic or tactical brand-building programs.* Other firms or entities will have capabilities or assets that one's own firm lacks; by joining forces, new offerings and brand-building activities can emerge that otherwise would not be available in a timely manner. Instant relevance, credibility, differentiation, or energy is at least theoretically possible through brand alliances.

Ford conceivably could have developed its own brand instead of using the Eddie Bauer co-brand—creating, let's say, the Ford Explorer LeatherRide vehicle. Two problems become immediately apparent. First, Ford, with all its existing brand-building needs, would have difficulty finding an adequate budget to create the LeatherRide brand and imbue it with the self-expressive benefits that it needed to fill the target niche. Second, even with unlimited resources, the effort may not have been feasible or would have taken so long that it would not have been worthwhile. The Eddie Bauer brand, in contrast, comes with immediate awareness, expectations, and self-expressive benefits. The co-brand with the Eddie Bauer name instantly provides Ford with a differentiated entry that it realistically could not have developed on its own.

Similarly, Disney uses McDonald's restaurants in its theme parks rather than developing its own menus and food-retailing expertise, and McDonald's uses the Disney characters and films to make its own promotions more effective. Wendy's sponsors an ESPN promotion in which participants can go to the Wendy's or ESPN website and win a trip to the home of ESPN, where they can be an anchor on the popular SportsCenter show. All of these brand alliances have the potential to increase the cost-effectiveness and impact of the alliance programs.

Most assume that the brand portfolio is restricted to owned brands.

The liberating concept is that external alliance brands are part of the brand portfolio. Although alliance brands are controlled and managed by another organization, their selection as alliance brands, their portfolio role, and their linkage to the rest of the brand portfolio need to be actively managed.

There are a variety of ways that brand alliances can be employed. The four types explored here will serve to illustrate the potential and the issues. One alliance type involves co-master brands, in that both brands act in the master brand role for the offering or program. Another creates external branded differentiators, with an external brand not available to competitors supplying a point of differentiation. A third involves external branded energizers, in which a branded event or personality will enhance a target brand. Tactical brand alliances represent a fourth type. After each is described, issues associated with managing brand alliances will be presented.

CO-MASTER BRANDED OFFERINGS

With co-master brands, both brand partners play a concurrent master brand role, where both brands are prominent and have major driver roles in the offerings. Sony Ericsson, for example, is a joint venture that combines Ericsson's reputation in telecommunication technologies with Sony's passionate commitment to personal creativity and self-expression. Among the first products from this alliance are a mobile phone and a CommuniCam Mobile Camera, which draws on Sony credibility. Each brand would have trouble generating customer value in the presence of the market leader Nokia without a co-branded offering.

Among the most important co-master brands in terms of financial impact are in the credit card space. The pioneer was the American Airlines AAdvantage, developed as a co-brand with the Citibank Visa card (itself a co-brand of Citigroup and Visa) in 1986. Providing frequent flyer miles with all credit card purchases, this card grew to more than 2.5 million holders, over 5 percent of the AAdvantage program members. The card in essence augments the basic frequent flyer program to something beyond getting rewards for flying. Since then, a host of imitators have cluttered the co-brand credit card space, so that the challenge is to build the equity of a co-brand in the face of this confusion.

Co-master brands can be powerful strategic tools with several potential advantages, as outlined below.

Creating Relevant, Differentiated Offerings

Co-master brands have the potential to create offerings with points of differentiation, but only if the brand associations are complementary rather than redundant. The whole point is to create an offering that is greater than either firm could develop by itself.

Amazon and Toys "R" Us established a co-master branded offering that provides two complementary brands. Amazon has proven credibility with respect to Internet retailing, with a deserved reputation of providing an easy-to-use, stimulating online experience and delivering reliable, fast service. It also provides a huge customer base of Internet shoppers. Toys "R" Us has credibility in retailing, a set of quality products that include classic toys, and more current offerings.

The co-master brand can be compared to the efforts of each firm to go it alone during the holiday season of 1999. The Toys "R" Us Internet delivery system simply broke down, resulting in a very visible set of disappointed, angry customers and a tarnished brand. Amazon's amateurish effort to enter the toy business resulted in a $39 million writedown of unsold toys. The brand alliance provides a co-brand that is outstanding on two key dimensions, and it is unlikely that either firm working alone could have created the result, certainly not within a reasonable time frame. The results in terms of both sales and margins have been impressive.

The impact of co-branding can be more than expected when there is real synergy between the brands, when the associations of each are strong and complementary. A research study by Kodak showed that for a fictional entertainment device, 20 percent of prospects said they would buy the product under the Kodak name and 20 percent would buy it under the Sony name, but 80 percent would buy the product if it carried both names.[1] The implication was that the combination would represent an advance that could not credibly be claimed by either alone.

A successful co-master brand needs to involve visible customer benefits from each brand that collectively represent a point of differentiation. Just having similar customers or associations are not adequate if the benefit is not there. Fisher-Price and McDonald's, for instance, co-branded a line of play food and appliances for children that failed.[2] The

McDonald's brand simply did not provide any customer benefit over and beyond what the Fisher-Price brand offered. In fact, it probably decreased the credibility in the toy space.

Stretching the Brand

The co-master brand might also allow greater freedom to stretch—like tying two rubber bands together, the combination goes farther than one. Co-master brands thus represent a way to enter a new product-market that is an alternative to creating a new brand or extending an existing brand. A new brand, of course, is usually too expensive or simply not feasible. A brand extension risks stretching the brand beyond its product boundaries. In a co-brand situation, the risk can be minimal, because each brand can be true to its heritage and image. Neither Amazon nor Toys "R" Us had to compromise its brand in their alliance; the co-brand provides the augmented dimensions.

Both Braun and Oral B would find an extension into electric toothbrushes to be a stretch, but the co-brand Braun Oral-B toothbrush is a fit. The Braun brand brings credibility in building reliable electric personal-care devices, based in large part on its established background in razors. Oral-B brings credibility in dental care, with a strong association with dentists' endorsement. Together, they combine to offer a dominant position on these two key dimensions.

Reduce Brand-Building Investment

A co-master brand can draw on existing brand equities so that investments supporting the new brand can be minimal. For example, General Mills' Yoplait used the Trix brand to introduce Trix Yoplait yogurt, a product geared for children. No additional television advertising expenditures were applied to the new product beyond the $12 to 15 million already spent on Trix cereal. The company capitalized on the awareness level of Trix cereal and its identity among children. If Yoplait had tried to develop its own brand for children, however, the cost would have been prohibitive.

The combination of Dunkin' Donuts, Baskin Robbins, and Togo's brands in shared facilities created brand and operational synergy that led to an estimated sales bump of 50 percent for each of the brands.[3] Each brand drew customers, thereby creating visibility for the others.

And because the three brands have different time-of-day usage patterns the facilities and people could be used more efficiently. In contrast, an effort to combine Italian and Mexican brands failed because customers were attracted to both concepts at the same time, and both service and operations declined.

Playing Defense

A co-master brand alliance can be strategically defensive. If a competitor is on the verge of creating a strategically important position in response to a market trend, it can be critical to implement a response quickly with a high likelihood of success, and without a lengthy test and refinement period. For example, competitors have attempted to stake out positions in the healthy segment of the cereal industry, an important growth segment that has proved difficult to crack. There have been a stream of failures from Kellogg's and others. Kellogg's licensing of the brand Healthy Choice, however, provided instant credibility with the image of being relatively healthy and having good taste. Such a move provided a beachhead to block competitors and also prevented a competitor from exercising the Healthy Choice option.

Co-Master Brands Involve Three Brands

A co-master brand involves three brands, the two master brands (e.g., Amazon and Toys "R" Us) and the co-brand (e.g., Toys "R" Us on Amazon). The impact of the two master brands on the co-brand is, of course, important. The co-brand needs to succeed, and the associations and credibility of the two partner brands largely define its presence in the market.

This relationship was shown empirically in a study by Simonin and Ruth, who linked a car brand (Ford, Toyota, Volkswagen, or Hyundai) with a microprocessor brand (Motorola, Fujitsu, Siemens, or Samsung) in a print ad and measured the response to the co-branded offering.[4] They later replicated the study with Northwest Airlines and Visa, paired with Disney and retailers. The researchers found that the partner brands indeed affect the reaction to the co-brands. They also found that the stronger and more familiar of the two partner brands will have a greater impact, and that the fit of the two brands will also affect judgments about the co-brand.

Further, in any brand alliance, it is not only what I can do for you, but what our association will do to me and my image. Thus, in evaluating a co-brand it is important to consider what impact one partner brand and the co-brand will have on the other partner brand. The best case is when the partner brand and co-brand will have associations that enhance the brand image.

The study by Simonin and Ruth also showed that the perception of a co-brand affects the associations of the partner brands. Partner brands that are less familiar, however, experience stronger effects than partner brands that are more established. It is easier to influence attitudes toward less well-known brands. At the extreme, a brand unknown to a customer will be significantly impacted by the co-brand and the partner brand.

Thus, the Ford Explorer Eddie Bauer edition will have styling, features, and a feel that should enhance the Eddie Bauer brand if it is done well. In addition, the associations with Ford Explorer (and, to a lesser extent, to Ford) can also potentially impact the Eddie Bauer brand. So any negative publicity associated with the Ford Explorer, even though it may be unrelated to styling, could affect the Eddie Bauer brand. The influence of one partner brand on the other is particularly likely when one of the two brands is "above" or "below" the other brand in terms of perceived quality and/or prestige. In that case, hanging outside your caste can be risky.

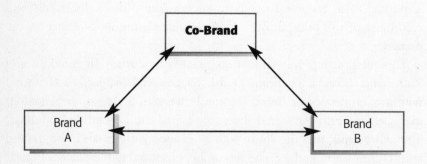

EXTERNAL BRANDED DIFFERENTIATORS

A branded differentiator, as the last chapter emphasized, is a way to create differentiation even in mature product categories where involvement and interest is low. It can help communicate and make visible points of difference that, properly managed over time, can create a basis for choice, loyalty, and competitive advantage. The problem is that it is difficult to find suitable features, ingredients, services, or programs that merit a brand and the brand-building and brand management effort required. Creating and building a brand is costly and, often, simply not feasible. And attaching it to the target brand can also be a nontrivial task.

An alternative is to use a brand from another firm, a brand that already has traction, credibility, and strong associations as a branded differentiator. Because it comes from outside the organization, it can be termed an *external branded differentiator.* Assuming such a brand can be located, the problem is then reduced to creating an alliance and attaching it to the target brand, which can be considerably more feasible and economically justifiable than creating a new brand.

External branded differentiators can be branded features, services, programs, or ingredients. The most common are branded ingredients. Dreyer's, for example, has an agreement with Mars Inc. that allows it to use Twix, M&Ms, and Snickers candy as the basis for ice cream flavors.

To qualify as an external branded differentiator, competitors cannot have access to it. Thus, brands available to all competitors such as Dolby Systems, Gore-Tex, Lycra, Teflon, TetraPak, THX, Woolmark, Intel Inside, and GE engines would not qualify as branded differentiators. There must be an exclusive relationship or the appearance of one. An exclusive ingredient brand such as Hershey syrup potentially provides to its partner, Betty Crocker Cake Mixes, a sustainable point of differentiation. In the mature and competitive cake mix world with three strong but weakly differentiated brands, the Hershey ingredient brand provides some distinction. Differentiation, however, only occurs because competitors such as Duncan Hines and Pillsbury do not have access to the Hershey ingredient brand.

One way to make an external branded differentiator exclusive is to create a long-term contract specifying that competitors cannot get access to it. Thus, Giant bicycles, as part of their arrangement with Eddie Bauer, knows that no other bicycle firm will have access to the Eddie Bauer brand.

There are other ways to create the appearance of exclusivity that can be nearly as effective. One is to use first-mover advantage and heavy co-brand-building to become so dominant that others are either discouraged from a similar strategy or lack adequate visibility to the customer. Another is to create and own or have exclusive access to a complementary ingredient or technology. The combination will come to be the point of differentiation and the combination may be ownable. Still another is to pick a co-brand that would not be attractive to competitors. For example, a value brand may use a premium ingredient brand as a branded differentiator. A competitor with a premium or superpremium brand may not find it useful to be associated with the same premium ingredient brand, even if it is available.

To understand how external branded differentiators can be effectively created and employed, it is helpful to look at the motivation of each party.

The Branded Differentiator's Motivation to Co-Brand

An ingredient brand has several motivations to partner with a master brand firm, with the importance of each motivation depending on the context. Besides creating a synergistic co-branded offering with appeal to customers, there is also a desire to:

- *Obtain visibility and association reinforcement.* Becoming an external branded differentiator can be a great brand builder. KC Masterpiece barbeque sauce obtains visibility and credibility as a category leader by its attachment to Lay's potato chips.
- *Build a relationship with a customer that will generate revenue over time.* When a firm commits to promoting an external branded differentiator, it also commits to buying and using that brand. When Poulan Lawn Tractors emphasize that they are powered by Briggs & Stratton engines, that makes a statement to customers about their product. As a result, Poulan is much less likely to go elsewhere for engines.
- *Create licensing revenue.* Simply licensing a brand to be used as a branded differentiator is a significant revenue source for brands

such as Sun-Maid. The Sun-Maid brand is worth more than the raisins the firm supplies.

The Master Brand Motivation to Use an External Branded Differentiator

The motivation to use an external branded differentiator is usually to gain relevance or differentiation more efficiently, more effectively, and in a more timely fashion than using an alternative strategy.

The basic role of a branded differentiator is to provide the brand with an edge in a salient dimension. This edge can potentially be sustainable when the level of exclusivity is high. Thus, Snickers-flavored ice cream could obtain a worthwhile following among Snickers devotees, and the ice cream brand involved would have a point of differentiation.

To be an effective differentiator, the ingredient brand needs to augment or buttress the product with something that is meaningful to the customer and capable of influencing choice and loyalty. KC Masterpiece brand, when applied to snacks, clearly adds a flavor perceived to be tasty and unique. In contrast, Pizza Hut Doritos and Taco Bell Doritos failed because they offered no flavor or customer connection that could be leveraged.

A branded differentiator can also create relevance by moving a brand with an inferior quality reputation into the consideration set. Poulan Lawn Tractors, less expensive and established than their competitors, visibly communicate that Briggs & Stratton engines are used in their equipment in order to reduce the perception of inferiority. Since Briggs & Stratton engines can be assumed to be of good quality, a natural implication is that the other Poulan components would be as well, in part because Briggs & Stratton would not be associated with inferior equipment. In contrast, more established competitors such as John Deere and Craftsman are already assumed to have excellent components, and so they have no incentive to use such a brand. In fact, such a use could detract from their offering by suggesting that customers need reassurance about their components.

The perceived quality of the master brand can be affected by a branded differentiator only when its reputation exceeds that of the master brand. Private studies of chocolate morsels in packaged cookies and of a well-known nonstick surface for cooking equipment both show that branded components are valued and help the perceived quality of the master brand *unless* they are placed on brands with an already very strong image. For example, the branded chocolate morsels helped Nabisco but did nothing for Pepperidge Farm, a superpremium brand (presumably because consumers assumed that Pepperidge Farm used only the best ingredients anyway).

A decision that has to be made, given the presence of a potentially influential ingredient brand, is the extent to which the branded differentiator is emphasized in the positioning and in the brand's long-term strategy. The answer will depend on its ability to deliver meaningful differentiation and/or relevance, and the likelihood of sustaining an exclusive relationship. At one extreme, the brand could drive the position; at the other, it could be a visible attribute but secondary to the positioning strategy. For example, the fact that a Mark Levinson audio system is in Lexus automobiles is noted in Lexus brochures and on its website to impress audiophiles, but will not be salient for the balance of the customer base.

Lease or Own?

When a branded differentiator is enough of a factor in the perception or evaluation of an offering that it merits a brand name, there are two choices. The first, discussed in Chapter 5, is to own and control the brand. If the owned branded differentiator gets traction and equity because of its unique value or because the firm has invested behind it, there is the potential to use that equity to support a sustainable point of differentiation.

The alternative, the focus of this chapter, is co-branding the offering using an established brand from another firm as an external branded differentiator. The result will combine the existing associations and credibility of the two firms. The use of the co-brand going forward will, of course, depend on the two firms continuing to have the motivation and organizational ability to implement the co-brand.

Should an established brand be "leased"? The decision will depend in part on the power of the established external branded differentiator, and the feasibility of creating an ownable internal alternative. Leasing was the answer in the case of Heinz, which struggled when attempting to market a hot ketchup with its own "hot sauce" brand. However, the co-brand Heinz Ketchup Kick'rs with Tabasco brand pepper sauce did

Nonexclusive Ingredient Brands

Many prominent and powerful ingredient brands (such as Intel Inside, Microsoft Windows, Dolby, and Gore-Tex) are not exclusive, in that multiple competitors can use them. Indeed, the objective of the firms owning these brands is to have *all* competitors sign on to use the brands. The problem is that the differentiating power of the ingredient brand is reduced or eliminated. At the extreme, the customer will look for the branded ingredient, and the partner brand will be little more than a commodity.

The question then becomes why anyone should partner with a nonexclusive ingredient brand. There are three reasons. First, an ingredient brand may have to be used because of the technology and related patents. This is the situation that Dolby has created in many of its contexts, as has Microsoft; co-brand partners cooperate because they have little choice. The branded ingredients in essence have a monopoly on a key ingredient, every strategist's dream.

Although a monopoly position is enviable, it can also make the partnership unequal and authoritative. A partner forced to participate may look for ways to get out from under the power structure, and this can make the partnership unhealthy and vulnerable. The partner can look for options and even support legal efforts stimulated by the ingredient brand's market power. Thus, there can be considerable long-term value for the powerful ingredient brand to make sure that the relationship remains healthy and that incentives outside the power structure are created for the co-brand partner.

Second, as we have seen in the Intel case from Chapter 1, there are financial reasons for master brands to accept nonexclusive ingredient brands. Intel provides a 6 percent discount to be used to pay up to 50 percent of a partner's advertising costs as long as the Intel Inside logo is on the product and in the ads. In a competitive low-margin business, that is indeed compelling.

Third, if an ingredient brand like Intel or Dolby has developed significant equity, an offering that omits them might be at a signif-

(continued on next page)

icant disadvantage. An omitted ingredient brand, if it is sufficiently established, can cause customers to drop the master brand from their consideration set. Recall that the strength of the Intel Inside brand resulted for many years in a 10 percent price premium for computers that bore the Intel Inside logo.

If an ingredient brand is to be nonexclusive, there is still the option to private-label it—that is, to allow the user to develop its own name. GM developed the OnStar navigation, communication, and safety system that allows motorists to know where they are, get directions to an address, and get help when they are in trouble. The innovation provided a point of differentiation to Cadillac, and then other brands in the GM family. When licensing the innovation to Lexus, GM allowed the firm to rebrand it as Lexus Link, thereby undercutting the differentiating power of the OnStar brand. From a branding point of view, this may seem to be a blunder, but branding does not operate in a vacuum. In fact, Lexus would not adopt the innovation without the private-label option. Moreover, GM had made an economic decision to establish OnStar as an industry standard, and to achieve this goal it was necessary to accommodate licensees like Lexus.

much better. The Tabasco brand communicated the nature of the product and gave it both credibility and differentiation.

The leasing answer was not optimal in the case of GE, who marketed a water filtration system to their upscale refrigerators using a "Water by Culligan" brand. Culligan, the top name in water conditioners, seemed like an ideal co-brand partner, and the concept tested well. However, GE also has a line of stand-alone water filters for the kitchen, with the GE-owned brand SmartWater. It turned out that the Culligan brand did not offer enough of a marginal benefit in the refrigerator context compared to SmartWater, so it was dropped.

A study by Desai and Keller showed the power of an established branded differentiator.[5] In their experiment, they compared the reaction to extension concepts using an established ingredient brand (LifeSavers with DayQuil) with a self-branded ingredient brand (LifeSavers with ClearCold). The established brand was superior in both the line extension and brand extension contexts in part because of its credibility in the extension space. Of course, this was a laboratory test, and it may be that with a compelling story and brilliant execution ClearCold could have eventually been accepted.

EXTERNAL BRANDED ENERGIZERS

A branded energizer, as the last chapter emphasized, can be used to create energy, visibility, interest, associations, and/or emotional and self-expressive benefits, especially in mature product categories where involvement and interest are low. There are a host of internal branded energizer sources, including products (Audi TT), promotions (the Oscar Mayer Wienermobiles), internally owned sponsorships (the Adidas Streetball Challenge), programs (the Avon Breast Cancer Crusade), symbols (the Pillsbury Doughboy), a CEO (Bill Gates), or even a lifestyle (mLife). These can be powerful devices to build or revitalize a brand when its energy level is low and it is struggling in a competitive marketplace.

As the last chapter made clear, branded energizers that resonate with target segments and will enhance the target brand are difficult to find and expensive to develop. Building and managing an internal branded energizer not only can be costly in resources, it can take years when action is needed in months. Indeed, it may not be feasible at all in a marketplace where competitors have strong brands and active energizers of their own.

The problems of finding and managing internal branded energizers leads firms to look to brands external to the organization. There is practically an infinite supply of brands outside the organization that have enormous strength, are linked into the lifestyle of customers, will have the needed associations to enhance the brand, are not tied to competitors, and can be linked to the target brand. With discipline and creativity, candidates can be located. The challenge, then, is to create and manage a co-brand alliance.

An external branded energizer will have a variety of sources. In each case, however, there are commonalities among the most effective. They will be a source of energy, be interesting to customers, be visible, have on-brand associations, and provide ways to generate brand links. Among the most important are sponsorships, endorsers, products, countries or regions, and symbols, each of which are discussed below.

Sponsorships

The right sponsorship, handled well, can transform a brand. Consider a rather utilitarian product like motor oil and a venerable brand like Valvoline. Such a brand would normally have trouble generating interest and energy, much less becoming an important part of a person's life. Few people would be motivated to read ads about motor oil, which is perceived by many to be an undifferentiated product. Through sponsorship activities, however, Valvoline becomes part of the NASCAR scene, and everything changes.

The Valvoline racing program is multidimensional. Valvoline is not just a sponsor of NASCAR but has a NASCAR racing team as well. At the Valvoline website, a destination site for those involved with racing, a visitor can access the schedule for NASCAR and other racing circuits and learn the results of the most recent races (complete with pictures and interviews). A "Behind Closed Garage Doors" section provides information and analyses from an insider. The visitor can adopt the Valvoline NASCAR racing team and learn about the team's current activities and recent finishes. In addition, it is possible to send Valvoline racing greeting cards, buy Valvoline racing gear, download a Valvoline racing screensaver, and sign up for a weekly newsletter (TrackTalk) that provides updates on the racing circuits. Valvoline thus becomes closely associated with the racing experience, much more than simply being a logo on a car.

The core segment for Valvoline consists of customers who change their own oil, are very involved in cars, and live for NASCAR races. The Valvoline racing program has the potential to influence this group in several ways. At the most basic level, it provides credibility and associations of being a leader in motor oil technology. Top teams would not use it if it were not superior; there is too much riding on the engine's performance. But there are more subtle possibilities. By choosing Valvoline, a customer can receive self-expressive benefits, as it is a way to tangentially associate oneself with the top drivers and teams. Research shows that this association pays off for the brand. In 1998, a study indicated that 47 percent of the U.S. public had an interest in watching NASCAR racing. In another study, 60 percent of NASCAR fans said they trusted sponsors' products (as compared to 30 percent of NFL fans), and more than 40 percent switch brands when a company becomes a sponsor.[6]

A sponsorship can provide the ultimate in relevance, the movement of a brand upward into an acceptable or even leadership position. A software firm trying unsuccessfully to make a dent into the European market became a perceived leader in a few months when it sponsored one of the top three bicycle racing teams. Part of the Samsung breakthrough from being just another Korean price brand to a real player in the U.S. market was its sponsorship of the Olympics. Such sponsorships communicate more about the brand than product advertising could ever say. Tracking data confirms that well-conceived and well-managed sponsorships can make a difference. The Visa lead in perceived credit card superiority went from 15 percentage points prior to the Olympics to 30 percentage points during and 20 points one month after—huge movements in what are normally very stable attitudes.[7]

A significant problem with sponsorship, indeed with any external branded energizer, is linking it to the brand. DDB Needham's Sponsor-Watch, which measures the linkage, has shown that sponsorship confusion is common.[8] Of the 102 official Olympic sponsors tracked since 1984, only about half have achieved sponsor awareness of at least 15 percent and at least 10 percent higher than that of a competitor who was not a sponsor (hardly a demanding standard). Those successful at creating links, such as Visa and Samsung, surround the sponsorship with a host of brand-driven activities, including promotions, publicity events, website content, newsletters, and advertising over an extended time period. The Valvoline NASCAR program is a model. The potential of a sponsorship will not automatically be realized.

Some guidelines in using sponsorships include the following:

- **Reach.** Does the sponsorship reach the target audience? Or is it too narrow? Consider the spillover audience, not just those who are directly exposed.
- **Involvement.** Look at the target customer's interests and activities. If a sponsorship reaches into the customer's interest and activities, the brand has a chance to become a part of or associated with an important part of a customer's life—like NASCAR racing for Valvoline, and a local car agency for a college football team.

- **Associations.** Know the objectives. What elements of the brand identity are to be dialed up by the sponsorship? Then proactively find a sponsorship that has the right associations.
- **Programmatic potential.** Are there ways to leverage the sponsorship around programs, as in the case of Valvoline? Is there the potential to have a long-term brand relationship with the sponsorship?

Endorsers

A brand may lack energy, but there are plenty of personalities who are contemporary, on-brand, energetic, and interesting. Buick has struggled to maintain relevance as its owner base became the oldest among all car brands, even older than Cadillac and Lincoln in 2001.[9] They needed to become acceptable, if not cool, to those who would turn to Japanese or European options and who view successful young professionals as their reference group. Turning a brand like Buick around though, especially among the target market of younger buyers, is just about impossible with products or advertising. Enter Tiger Woods, who entered into a long-term Buick relationship in 1999 and since then has been using a Buick bag, appearing in commercials, supporting Buick promotional events, and playing in Buick tournaments. The association with Tiger Woods and his endorsement of Buick made new products like the Rendezvous truck more credible and started a decline in the age of the user base.

The connection to the brand and the resulting leverage for any celebrity endorser will be more effective if it is part of a larger program. The association of Buick with Tiger Woods is embedded in an extensive involvement with golf that dates back to 1958, when the Buick Open was created; there are now four Buick-sponsored tour events. In addition, there is the amateur Buick Scramble (formerly the Oldsmobile Scramble), an amateur event started in the mid-1980s that attracts more than 100,000 participants and holds a highly visible finals in Orlando. Tiger Woods is the honorary chairman. The website has links to a Buick Pro Shop selling Buick golf bags, Buick-labeled sportswear, and Tiger Nike balls. So Tiger Woods is the centerpiece of a brand portfolio involving golf tournaments and supporting activities, websites, and programs.

Selecting and engaging an endorser is a critical first step in creating a strategic brand energizer. There are a host of considerations. An endorser target should:

- Be appealing
  - Visible among the target audience (Low visibility will limit the impact.)
  - Attractive, liked (Simple liking can and does get transferred to the endorsed brand.)
  - Sincere (Will there be a feeling that the endorser is doing it for money and lacks a sincere belief in the product?)
  - Fresh, not overexposed (An endorser's impact can be diluted by overexposure as an endorser.)
- Have the right associations
  - Reinforcing the brand identity goals of the brand
  - Forging a natural link to the brand itself
  - Instilling confidence that the positive associations can be leveraged, and the negative ones managed
- Have potential for a long-term relationship
  - A compatible relationship that is likely to endure
  - Endorser associations that will wear well, not just some that are hot for the day
  - An endorser that is unlikely to develop negative associations
- Have potential to create programs surrounding the endorser
- Be cost-effective and available (Tiger Woods cost Buick $25 million over five years, but the real cost will be the programs surrounding the endorser.)

Products

Exciting new products such as the Heinz EZ Squirt or iMac are much less of an option with external branded energizers, but there are exceptions. Target has used a branded architect, Michael Graves, to create a host of products for them, from bedding to games to houseware items. They also got the trendy Southern California designer Mossimo (Mossimo Giannulli) to design an extensive line of clothing and shoes. As a result, the products created by Graves and Mossimo have been branded energizers for Target.

Dreyer's Ice Cream Limited Edition is an energy source for Dreyer's. The idea is to introduce ice cream flavors for a limited time around themes like Scooby Doo, a professional football team like the Oakland Raiders, and Girl Scout Cookies (which makes an annual appearance). These special flavors attract attention, creating bursts of energy and sales. The only problem is that Limited Edition flavors have so much energy, the big sellers—vanilla and chocolate—tend to get a bit lost on the shelf.

Creating a home run co-brand product involves thinking outside the box to find creative, new ideas. There should also be an insistence that the result resonates with customers. Target's designer-quality items at discount prices and Oakland Raiders ice cream each hit a sweet spot with a meaningful segment. Finally, the execution needs to be flawless. While Dreyer's licensed the co-brand and controls execution, Target has faced an execution challenge because two firms are involved in delivering the product promise.

Symbols

One of the problems with an endorser is that even if a good selection is made, things can go wrong. Any real person is fallible and gets older. Even Michael Jordan eventually retired for good, reducing his impact, and Nike had to phase in new endorsers such as LeBron James. And other endorsers, some by no fault of their own, attract negative publicity that limits their effectiveness and, at worse, damages the brand. A symbol does not have this risk. Bart Simpson created energy, a personality, and significant sales gains for Butterfinger in the early 1990s, and Snoopy has been a symbol of MetLife for nearly twenty years.

MetLife adopted the Charlie Brown characters in 1985. Its goal was to provide a warm, light, nonthreatening approach to insurance—a tough sell in the context of an industry perceived by many to be boring, money-grubbing, and bureaucratic. Snoopy provides a vehicle toward those objectives. He is familiar, lovable, and associated with humor, warm feelings, and the rest of the Charlie Brown characters. Snoopy's image on the MetLife website, on a blimp in ads, and even on the MetLife logo acts to prevent what psychologists call counterarguing. The natural tendency to be cynical toward an insurance company's ad or claim is reduced for MetLife due to the presence of the likable Snoopy, in part because it would make no sense to argue with a likable cartoon character.

It is important to understand the role of the symbol. Is it to create a personality? To suggest or reinforce associations? To inject humor and likability into an otherwise bland and uninteresting message? With the role in mind, it is possible to proactively look for the right one.

Countries or Regions

A country or region can have a strong brand that can provide interest, energy, and differentiation to a target brand. For example, Chanel and L'Oréal mean Paris; Beck's beer and Mercedes are German; Stolichnaya vodka means Russian; Volvo is from Sweden; Bloomingdale's is New York; McDonald's, Coca-Cola, and Levi's are American; Sony is Japanese; Buitoni has Italian authenticity; and Dewar's is Scottish. In each case, the brand's association with a country or region implies higher quality because the country or region has a heritage of making the best within that product class. A host of studies have confirmed that brand credibility within a certain product class will be influenced by the country of origin.

A country or regional brand can do more than create credibility; it can also provide emotional and self-expressive benefits. Connecting a brand to the West has for decades created self-expressive benefits within the Japanese market and accounts in part for the high regard Western brands have in Japan, from Starbucks and McDonald's to Rolex and Mercedes. Bloomingdale's has drawn on the energy of Manhattan to create a destination store that would be difficult to establish on functional benefits alone. And a region or country can usually be counted on not to fade like an endorser. There are risks, however, because political and cultural forces can affect the image and personality of a country, turning an association into a liability.

Several considerations go into deciding whether to dial up an association with a region or country. Is the region or country relevant to the product category? Does the brand have a legitimate link to the area? Will this link be ownable and represent a meaningful point of differentiation? Can the link be leveraged into a series of effective brand-building activities? The link of Buitoni to Italy, for example, provides authenticity and a host of activities around the house of Buitoni, with its kitchens and heritage.

TACTICAL BRAND ALLIANCES

Brand alliances can also be employed in tactical brand building, where the task is to create relevance, differentiation, and energy quickly in an effort that is not expected to have a long life. Tactical programs can take many forms, including advertising, publicity, guerrilla marketing, and promotions. Promotions, a particularly powerful use of tactical brand alliances, will be used here as a vehicle to introduce the issues involved.

Promotions are usually perceived as tactical devices to create short-term sales or other customer activity. As such, rather than being brand builders, they can detract or damage the brand. Thus, financial incentives such as a $3,000 rebate for a car purchase or a fifty-cent coupon for a food item suggest that the brand should be discounted, since they shift attention away from the brand to price. Dialing up price implies that the purchase involves a commodity, exactly the opposite of creating differentiation and energy. Brand alliances can help generate promotions that are cost-effective, unique, and involving, however, while still enhancing and reinforcing brand values.

An alliance brand can add or reinforce associations. For example, Volkswagen offered a Trek mountain bike and bike rack with the VW Jetta in a summer promotion that resulted in some 16,000 cars being sold. The Trek bike was in sharp contrast to the rebate wars that pervaded the automobile marketplace and represented a lifestyle statement to the Jetta brand and its customers. Pepsi offered a free bottle of Diet Pepsi or Pepsi One when three Weight Watchers Smart Ones (meal components) were purchased. The association with Weight Watchers provided a subtle reinforcement of the low-calorie attribute of the Pepsi drinks, and Weight Watchers received some of the Pepsi energy. Nouvelle recycled toilet tissue, for example, appeals to a "green" segment that has an intense interest in the environment and conserving resources. Nouvelle ran an on-pack promotion that featured chances to win one of 100 active family holidays at CenterParcs, a network of five large parks in Europe, and ten thousand Meadow Flower Kits.[10] Both promotion brands were compatible with being sensitive to environmental issues.

To be effective, promotions need to break out of the clutter with novel, involving content that will appeal to a broad target segment. This is not easy in a cluttered marketplace. The use of a partner brand, though, can bring a twist that will help the promotion stand out. The use of Trek bicycles was new to the car industry and provided the basis for a differentiated promotion. The Nouvelle promotion was a novel way to combine three brands with common values.

An alliance of two or more firms to support a promotion means that the cost of the promotion will be shared. This often completely changes the economics of the promotion. In fact, one danger is that shared cost becomes the driver of the promotion and so other facets of an effective promotion are ignored, creating brand risks and lost opportunities. An alliance also makes more resources available; each firm will bring certain capabilities and customer bases that can contribute. In particular, more websites and more website traffic will become available to support the promotion when multiple firms are involved.

The good alliance partner will thus have several characteristics. First, it will have associations that support the brand identity and positioning strategy. Second, it will lead to a promotion that will be interesting, involving, and apart from the clutter. Third, a partner will contribute resources or capabilities that will make the promotion more cost-effective.

DEVELOPING EFFECTIVE BRAND ALLIANCES

An effective brand alliance should offer a compelling customer proposition that can become an ongoing competitive advantage and/or helps to build the brand effectively or efficiently. It should support both the business strategy and the brand building needed to implement that strategy. It should at least have the potential of supporting an ongoing relationship, rather than being an ad hoc effort. The experience of those who have successfully developed and managed brand alliances suggests some guidelines worth considering, which are outlined below.

Cast a Wide Net
One advantage of a brand alliance is the unlimited number of possibilities. Explore a lot of options to make sure that the alliance selected has the best chance of making a difference. Too many firms consider

brand alliances opportunistically, screening alternatives that come to the firm rather than proactively looking for the best possibilities. A home run is much more likely if the right alliance is actively guided by the business, marketing, and brand strategies.

A potential brand alliance partner needs to be compatible along several dimensions. What brands from other firms have your brand's aspirational associations? Which of these brands are connected to the same customer base or are involved in the same applications? The perfect mate is elusive in any quest, whether it be for friends, spouses, or firms. The key is to cast a wide net and be persistent.

Create Customer-Driven Alliances

Let the customer drive the brand alliance strategy at two levels. First, how does the customer relate to the product class? What is relevant, what motivates him or her? What are the trends? Look to committed customers. Why do those people have such a strong attachment to the brand? What is the linkage? How can the offering be made more relevant? Second, more broadly, what are the interests, values, and activities of the customer? How can the brand be linked to customers' lives?

The home run is to link to meaningful parts of customers' lives. Valvoline target customers are involved in cars and NASCAR racing. Buick's target customers will connect or can relate to golf. The Olympics have a broad-based upscale audience that is highly interested in travel, an ideal market for Visa. MetLife customers in general value humor and have a love for the Peanuts characters.

Think Long-Term

A brand alliance that creates a co-master brand, branded differentiator, or a branded energizer is by definition a program with a long-term perspective. Success will rarely occur without a long-term brand-building program, in part because it takes time to create associations between brands. Further, the full economic impact will usually build over time. The alliances between Ford Explorer and Eddie Bauer, Buick and golf, Snoopy and MetLife, and Visa and the Olympics are based on relationships that span decades, and the longevity has contributed to the strength of associations and the impact.

In 2001 National Car Rental, a premium business traveler–oriented brand, and Alamo Rent-a-Car, a value leisure traveler–oriented brand, merged their operations under a co-brand badge. The result was enormous cost savings—one set of buses, one counter with a single set of employees, one lot, and so on all under a co-brand. However, the consequences were extremely damaging—especially to National, whose share in some top cities fell by 5 to 15 percent. What was remarkable was the effect on perceptions. Even though the shuttle frequency improved some 35 percent, customers felt that the buses were slower. They also believed that lines were longer and the service worse. Two years later, the brands were bought by Vanguard Car Rental, who immediately began undoing the brand merger. As the brands became separated, customer dissatisfaction went down.

Even tactical brand alliances around promotions could benefit from a long-term perspective. A co-branded promotion that is truly a one-shot event wastes not only the equity of the promotion itself but the learning about how the two firms work together. Building a promotion franchise by giving it a longer life spreads costs over years and exploits equities that have been built up. Compare an ongoing promotion involving a theme park with the involvement of a one-time event.

Surround the Brand Alliance with a Portfolio of Brands and Programs

Embedding a brand alliance in a set of brands and programs can potentially strengthen both the impact of the alliance and its value over time. Finding co-brand partners is challenging because brand fit is needed, and in many cases organizational structures and processes must be created so that the programs are implemented successfully. So, when a suitable partner is found, it makes sense to look for a family of co-branded programs instead of one and to move to a long-term partnership.

Disney has relationships with several brands, including McDonald's and Kellogg's, that involve multiple joint brand-building efforts and have a long-term perspective. For example, Kellogg's licenses such Disney characters as the Pooh Bear for use on a line of cereals with the co-branded endorsement of Disney. Kellogg's role as the official sponsor of breakfast at the Disney theme parks is one of several partner programs.

Beware of the Downside

An alliance, particularly if it involves strong brands, has significant risks. Committing to a portfolio of programs and a long-term perspective increases those risks. If one partner should falter, the other could fail to receive the expected benefits and, in the worst case, could be damaged. For example, the long-term commitment between McDonald's and Disney assumes a flow of successful Disney movies to support McDonald's promotions, as well as continued reputation and energy of McDonald's among kids and families. If either assumption falters, the alliance could become a burden rather than an asset.

As the programs and time frame increase, so does the possibility that one of the alliance brands or the market will change so that the benefits are less than expected or, worse, one of the brands will be tainted by the other. Further, there is the risk that the business strategy of one of the partners will change, making the alliance less of a priority. The challenge is to pick the right partner and to actively manage the alliance to detect emerging problems and deal with them.

Aligning Organizations

The fact that brand alliances involve multiple organizations with their own structures, systems, and strategies creates challenges, especially for alliances that require active collaboration over time. Debilitating tensions and inefficiencies can too easily surface. Key people move on, requiring the relationship to be reestablished over time. And perhaps most troublesome, changing priorities can affect organizational commitment.

A good example of a brand alliance in which the strategic goals of the parties diverged and the cultures of the firms made implementation difficult occurred between Swatch and Mercedes-Benz in the mid-1990s.[11] The alliance was formed to make and market the Swatchmobile, conceived by the Swatch folks as a "disposable" fashion-statement car with changeable colored body panels to be manufactured and distributed by Mercedes-Benz. Mercedes-Benz grew to realize that any car associated with it would have to be seen as safe, environmentally friendly, and of high quality, which was not the thrust of the Swatch concept. As a result, Mercedes-Benz ended up taking over the partnership, buying out Swatch, and ultimately renaming the car Smart.

Studies of alliances by students of management have generated some insights to help avoid such situations. First, it is important that the alliance provide value to both parties on an ongoing basis, so a solid, enduring basis of value contribution needs to be identified going in. Second, the alliance needs a strategic home within both organizations so that it receives sufficient priority. Many alliances fail not because of disappointing results but, rather, because other priorities and strategic directions distract one of the firms. At one extreme, the alliance can become an orphan initiative with no real champion. Third, there needs to be a good working cross-firm team, which means assigning first-rate people who can work together.

The problem is simplified if one brand is licensed to another organization, who then will control the implementation of the co-brand. Hershey's licenses the use of its brand to signal the cocoa ingredient in Betty Crocker cake mix and other products. The involvement in cake mix production and marketing by Hershey's is minimal. However, the licensor (Hershey's, in this case) needs to have procedures in place to ensure that its brand is always presented in a consistent way and that the end product supports the perceived quality of Hershey's. To develop and enforce such an agreement can create tension. So even a licensing-based alliance can require management of cross-firm issues.

Think Portfolio

The insight that external brands are part of the brand portfolio and can be assigned roles is indeed liberating. A portfolio view means that the external brands and their relationships will be actively managed. This, in turn, means that information should be obtained as to the external brand's image, personality, product attributes, and organizational associations. If the alliance is truly strategic and long-term, its future brand directions should also be known. The brand alliance strategy can then be adjusted to reflect the strengths and prospects of the partner brand.

A portfolio view of external brands further means that budget allocation involving brand development and enhancement activities can be made across the portfolio, including both internal and external brands. The external brand set should then not be treated in an ad hoc manner.

Creating, implementing, and leveraging brand alliances is not easy. Brand strategy issues, difficult enough on their own, are overlaid with organizational challenges when alliances become involved. However, when the environment requires rapid, efficient, and compelling responses to fast-emerging threats and opportunities, the ability to successfully use brand alliances as an option can be critical.

QUESTIONS FOR DISCUSSION

1. Select one or two brand alliances, preferably avoiding those mentioned in the chapter. For each specific co-brand:
   a. What impact will the two brands have on the co-brand offering?
   b. What will be the impact on Brand A from its association with Brand B and the co-brand offering? How will this be affected by the co-brand position and brand-building programs?
   c. Answer the preceding questions for Brand B.

2. Select a brand and a product-market context for that brand. Develop potential brand alliances that would bring about each one of the following, develop criteria to evaluate each choice, and discuss implementation problems:
   a. A co-master branded offering
   b. An external branded differentiator
   c. An external branded energizer
   d. A tactical alliance generating a promotion or advertising campaign

PART III

Leveraging Brand Assets

CHAPTER 7

LEVERAGING THE BRAND INTO NEW PRODUCT-MARKETS

Brands have become the barrier to entry, but they are also the means to entry.

—EDWARD TAUBER

Three things I never lends—my 'oss, my wife, and my name.

—ROBERT SMITH SURTEES

DOVE

In 1955, Unilever (then Lever Brothers) introduced the Dove "beauty bar."* The product contained a patented mild cleansing ingredient that generated a noticeably different "feel" to the skin when used regularly. It was positioned then and now as a beauty bar composed of one-fourth cleansing cream that "creams" skin while washing (as opposed to a traditional soap, which would dry your skin while removing dirt and grease). The cleansing cream was shown being poured into the beauty bar. In 1979, the phrase "cleansing cream" was replaced with "moisturizer cream."

That same year, a University of Pennsylvania dermatologist showed that Dove dried and irritated skin significantly less than other soaps. Based on this study, Dove began aggressively marketing to doctors. As a result, about 25 percent of Dove users bought the soap because a doctor

---

* Information in this section was drawn from Julian E. Barnes, "The Making (Or Possible Breaking) of a Megabrand," *New York Times,* July 22, 2001, Business section, p. 1; Times & Trends, Information Resources, June, 2002; Dove and Unilever websites, 2003; "Unilever to Expand Two Billion Dollar Global Dove Brand with Launch of Dove Hair Care in North America," *Business Wire,* January 28, 2003; and Lavel Wentz, "On the Wings of Dove, Exec Extends Reach," *Advertising Age,* June 2, 2003.

recommended it, which greatly enhanced the brand's credibility as a moisturizer. By the mid-1980s, Dove had become the best-selling soap brand and commanded a price premium. Today, Unilever sells $330 million of Dove bar soap or more than 24 percent of the market, far ahead of its nearest competitor.

The first effort to extend the Dove brand occurred in 1965. The extension, into dishwashing detergent, survives but has to be regarded as disappointing. The leading competitor at the time was Palmolive, which promised a product that "softens hands while you do dishes." The hope was that the Dove cleansing-cream message would translate into a benefit competitive with Palmolive. Instead, customers felt no reason to change from the well-positioned Palmolive—and because the creamy Dove message did not imply clean dishes, there was simply no benefit. After receiving weak market acceptance for the extension, Dove lowered the price, which created another source of strain on the brand. Fifteen years after its launch, the brand was a rather poor seventh in the U.S. market, with a share of around 3 percent. The Dove dishwashing detergent not only failed to enhance the Dove brand, it also undoubtedly inhibited Dove from extending its franchise further for decades.

In 1990, the Dove soap patent ran out, and arch-competitor P&G was soon testing an Olay beauty bar with moisturizing properties, a product that rolled out in 1993. One year later, Olay body wash appeared and soon garnered over 25 percent market share in a high-margin product category. The Dove brand team, who recognized that Dove was the natural brand to own the moisturizer body wash position, was blindsided. They apparently missed the chance to be a leader in this new subcategory.

In response to Olay, the Dove organization rushed the Dove Moisturizing Body Wash product into stores. The product was based on the traditional European body wash model, but did not live up to the Dove promise. A reformulation in 1996 was an improvement, but it wasn't until 1999 that Dove really got it right with the innovative Dove Nutrium line, which used a technology that deposited lipids, Vitamin E, and other ingredients onto the skin. The advanced skin-nourishing properties provided enough of a lift to allow Dove to charge a 50 percent premium over its regular Dove body wash. Later Dove introduced an age-defying version of Nutrium Body Wash with anti-oxidants (linked to reduced

FIGURE 7-1
A DOVE AD

Nutrition Pack

signs of aging), which helped Dove to pull even with Olay in the body wash category. By leveraging strong brand equity, pursuing innovative technology, and being persistent, Dove was able to overcome being late into the category.

The Dove body wash efforts influenced the Dove soap business, which was flat until the mid-1990s and in fact declined in 1996. The introduction of the body wash corresponded to a 30 percent growth surge in Dove soap from the mid-1990s to 2001, evidence that the energy and exposure of the Dove body wash helped even when the product was somewhat wanting. Once it was established in the body wash category, the Nutrium subbrand was employed to help the soap business. In 2001, Unilever introduced a Dove Nutrium soap that would replenish the skin's nutrients, priced about 30 percent higher than regular Dove.

Another battlefield was the rather mature category of deodorants, where dryness (the key benefit) seemed contradictory to the Dove promise of moisturizing and the target segment was younger than the typical Dove customer. Despite the apparent risks, in 2000 Dove introduced a deodorant line with some un-Dove-like advertising, blaring lines such as "Next stop, armpit heaven." As it turned out, Dove deodorant was named as one of the top ten non-food new products in 2001, garnering over 70 million in sales with a share point close to 5 percent, making it the number two brand among female deodorants. The mild "one-quarter moisturizing lotion" positioning platform, coupled with communicating the fact that underarm skin needs protection, generated a Dove spin on dryness that turned out to be differentiating.

In spite of this win, P&G's Olay again beat Dove to the market in mid-2000, this time with "daily facials"—disposable face cloths infused with moisturizers. It took Dove about a year to respond with its Dove Daily Hydrating Cleansing Cloths. With the body wash success behind it, however, the Dove brand was well suited to compete in this category, and initial results were promising.

The next product was Dove Hair Care, with a branded differentiation (Weightless Moisturizers) that was directly responsive to moisturization, one of the top two unmet needs in the category. (Weightless Moisturizers are a set of fifteen ingredients designed to make the hair softer, smoother, and more vibrant without adding any extra weight.) The product achieved number one status in Japan and Taiwan, then was introduced in the U.S. in early 2003 with a massive promotional campaign. Dove Hair Care joins a Dove family that is used by nearly one in three families in the United States. In 2002, after several years at 20 to 30 percent sales growth, the Dove franchise exceeded 2 billion.

There are a host of insights from this case study:

- The potential to turn a narrow brand into a power brand exists and, when well executed, can result in a substantial payoff. One key is a strong position on a valued attribute that has legs—in this case, the moisturizing qualities of Dove.
- Successful extensions provide the basis for future extensions. It seems likely that the deodorant entry would not have done as well had it been introduced with only bar soap behind it.
- Extensions that struggle are worse than those that fail, in part because they are a drag on the brand and inhibit future extensions.
- Competition can be healthy. Dove was pushed into the power-brand strategy by Olay, which applied intense pressure. Dove had to respond or face a gloomy strategic picture going forward. Per-

haps Dove should have made up an imaginary aggressive Olay if one had not existed.

- Subbrands and branded differentiators can make the difference. The subbrand Nutrium played a key role in helping to create a high-margin, differentiated body wash offering, and then new soap offering; the Dove brand could not have done it alone. And the branded differentiator, Weightless Moisturizers, was critical to the Dove Hair Care story.

- First-mover advantages are real, but they can be overcome. Not being first to market can be a steep barrier (as Dove found when it attempted to take on Palmolive in the dishwashing detergent market), but a follower can also win with the right stuff, and Dove found it in body wash and deodorants.

One recipe for strategic success is to create, enhance, and leverage assets; in fact, that might be the essence of strategy. In most firms, one of the most powerful assets is the brand. A strategic question, addressed in this and the following chapter, is how, then, can a brand asset be leveraged to create larger and stronger business entities? The brand could be employed on new offerings that might be internally developed, acquired from others, or developed by firms who would license the brand. In any case, the brand can potentially play a key role in the new product-market business.

A key brand portfolio dimension is defining the brand scope. For what product categories and subcategories can the brand play a role? How far should a brand be stretched as a driver brand, or as an endorser brand? Does the brand have permission to extend? If not, does the brand need to be redefined in order to support the business strategy? Is a new brand needed to support a new product-market?

The major motivation to leverage the brand portfolio into new product-markets is simply to grow the business by finding areas of unmet customer needs that will provide incremental sales and profit. Growth is not only financially desirable, it is also central to organizational vitality. Opening up new product-markets is a way to create opportunities for organizational members and partners. It is easier to hire and retain good people when growth is present.

There are, however, other strategic reasons to extend the brand that can be equally important in some contexts. In particular, an extension of a brand into a new product-market context can do the following:

- Enhance a brand's visibility and image. Placing the brand in another setting can be a more effective and efficient brand-building approach than spending money on advertising.
- Create communication efficiencies, in part by having a larger brand-building budget. This is especially true when the extensions will have the same markets and when cross-product brand building (such as a World Cup sponsorship) is used.
- Change a brand image. If a brand needs to broaden or shift its associations in order to support strategic initiatives, moving the brand into a new area may be the most convincing way to do that.
- Provide a way (as noted in Chapter 4) to maintain relevance by creating competitive entries in emerging product-markets that would be difficult or impossible to enter without an existing brand asset.
- Inhibit a competitor from gaining or exploiting a foothold in the market. Thus, an extension can be strategically defensive and be worthwhile even though it might struggle. Microsoft has entered a variety of arenas with the prime objective of limiting the ability of competitors to encroach on core business areas.
- Provide a source of energy for a brand (as described in Chapter 5), especially a brand that is established and a bit tired.

Entering a new product-market may require a new brand, or at least a new endorsed brand. New brands are risky and expensive, however, so leveraging existing brands is the preferred route. And we know that, in general, brand leverage pays off. A McKinsey study involving 130 firms found that firms with strong brands that span product-markets earn 5 percent more than their industry counterparts, whereas firms with strong but focused brands earn 1.9 percent more than the industry average.[1]

There are two related approaches to brand extensions. The first is to engage in sequential brand extensions in an ad hoc manner. The challenge is to make sure that each extension has a maximum chance of achieving its objectives and that the risks to the brand are minimized. Ideally, an extension would be placed in the product-market in which the brand's associations will be most likely to add value and in a setting in which the brand will be enhanced rather than tarnished.

The second, a more strategic perspective, is to develop range brand platforms that are intended to support businesses in multiple product-markets, a *range brand* being a brand that ranges over product classes. The range brand platform perspective involves managing the brand for the long term, with a vision of the ultimate product scope of the brand after a series of extensions have been introduced. With this ultimate goal in mind, a firm must create associations that will drive the brand in all of those product classes. The sequential brand extensions are then introduced in a way that allows the desired vision to emerge.

The range brand platform perspective, where a program of strategic brand extensions is implemented, will be described in more detail later in this chapter. First, however, the dimensions of a brand extension decision will be examined. In doing so, the central issues that should be considered in any brand leverage context will be detailed. These issues are relevant to establishing the scope of a brand platform and developing a sequence of extensions to implement the brand platform vision.

The extension of a brand into a new product-market is the focus of this chapter. Two other types of extensions involve the existing brand market and a similar set of issues. One is a vertical brand extension, discussed in Chapter 8, where the brand is used to access a market either above (premium) or below (value) its current position. Another is a line extension, where the brand is extended into different variants of the same product-market through alternative flavors, models, packages, or sizes. One danger, addressed in Chapter 10, is that incremental line extensions that are each sensible in isolation can cumulatively create excessive options that confuse customers, actually reducing profitability and brand impact.

Several levels of brand extensions can exist in combination, as suggested by Figure 7-2. The first level is where the brand plays the primary driver role in the extensions, coupled with either descriptors or weak subbrands. Mercedes, Dove, Weight Watchers, Healthy Choice, Virgin, IBM, and Newman's Own are examples of a single brand leveraging its core associations to enter new product classes. The second level is where the brand is extended with strong subbrands. Sony, as was seen in Chapter 5, has extended its brand widely but with strong subbrands

FIGURE 7-2
THE BRAND SCOPE

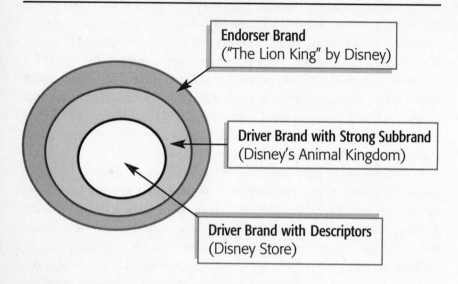

Endorser Brand
("The Lion King" by Disney)

Driver Brand with Strong Subbrand
(Disney's Animal Kingdom)

Driver Brand with Descriptors
(Disney Store)

such as VAIO, Handycam, and Walkman. The third level is where extensions use an endorsed brand. Microsoft, as was described in Chapter 3, has extended widely as an endorser brand, supporting such brands as Word, Office, .NET, and MSN.

The scope of the brand will be the greatest when it is used as an endorser, and the least when it is the primary driver. Figure 7-2 illustrates graphically the differences in scope, with Disney demonstrating how a brand can be a driver with a descriptor on one set of products, have a strong subbrand on others, and still play an endorser role elsewhere. When Disney is used as an endorser, the target categories can be very broad.

LEVERAGING THE BRAND INTO NEW OFFERINGS

The first part of the brand extension decision involves the judgment of where to extend. What product offerings would both leverage and reinforce the brand? The second decision is what brand strategy to use. The options developed in the discussion of the brand relationship spectrum in Chapter 2 apply. As Figure 7-2 suggests, a brand extension can involve a strong subbrand or an endorsed brand. Ultimately, there is also the option of creating a new brand for a proposed offering if it is concluded that the existing brand simply doesn't fit.

Where to Extend?

Finding the most promising extension direction will involve first determining where the brand can add value. Extension customer research can help. A first step is to understand the associations. Which are leveragable? A second is to identify candidate product categories for which there would be a fit. A third is to evaluate the category as to its business attractiveness. Are there unmet needs? What is the competitive climate? What barriers to success are there? The fourth is to consider some product offering and positioning options. What is available to the firm given its strengths and weaknesses? Will that be likely to be successful?

EXTENSION RESEARCH—FINDING LEVERAGABLE ASSOCIATIONS

Extension research identifies those product categories for which the brand fits and adds value. The first step is to determine the existing brand associations and the brand identity—that is, the vision of the associations going forward. Clearly, there can be many sources of a common association, including user types (for example, babies), location (France), ingredients (contains oats), and symbols (an umbrella). In addition to its banking associations, Wells Fargo generates associations of a stagecoach, Old West, safes, and pioneers. McDonald's is associated with Ronald McDonald and his friends, as well as fun times for kids. In each case, the issue is what associations are strong and likely to be helpful as the brand moves beyond its home.

One research approach developed by Gillian Gakenfull and colleagues provides insight into a brand's extension potential. Respondents are asked to identify from a broad set of forty products (ranging from automobiles to jewelry to lawnmowers to yogurt) the ten that represent the best fit and the ten that represent the worst fit. They are then asked to pick the single best-fitting product and explain the logic of that choice. This is followed by the second best, the third best, and so on. The respondent is then asked to identify two products not on the list that would have a good fit and explain why. Attention then turns to the ill-fitting products. Respondents are then asked to rank order the worst-fitting products and to explain the reasons for the choices. One output is a feel that the brand associations are not the same across customers—there are different patterns. For example, Pennzoil to some has primarily associations of automobiles and to others it is motor oil. Some think of Kraft as dairy while for others it is easy preparation. Another output is insights into brand characteristics that can lead to the prediction of fit issues for brand extension concepts.[2]

EXTENSION RESEARCH—IDENTIFYING CATEGORIES

The second step is to identify related product category opportunities for each of the brand's major associations or sets of associations. At this stage, the screening should be limited; the goal is to get extensions options on the table. Thus, the Wells Fargo stagecoach and Western associations might suggest a line of Western clothing or a Western theme park. The safe association might suggest burglar alarm systems or cash transfer services. Thus, McDonald's could build on the association with children to have a line of toys, clothing, or games, or even a theme park directed at kids. The efficient, low-cost service association might allow it to enter any service in which those qualities might be valued. Thus, a McDonald's clothing store would be expected to sell items at a relatively low price in an efficient manner.

Vaseline Intensive Care is associated with moisturizers, which might suggest extensions for soap, face cream, and skin cream, all with a moisturizer position.[3] Another Vaseline Intensive Care association is medicinal, which could suggest products such as antiseptic, first aid cream, and hemorrhoid cream. Still another is lotion, which leads to products like sunscreen, aftershave, or baby lotion. Vaseline's actual extensions into Vaseline Lip Therapy, Vaseline Intensive Care Foam Bath, and Vaseline Intensive Care Renewal and Protection lotion were built on the lotion and moisturizer associations, but positioned the brand as medicinal/therapeutic. All have done well in the market, as has Vaseline Baby Oil, a close competitor to Johnson & Johnson. Not so successful, however, is Vaseline Hair Tonic. The brand's association with greasiness from the original Intensive Care product was undoubtedly a liability.

Extension research at Clorox revealed that consumers associated the brand with cleaning in general, not just laundry. As a result, Clorox expanded its focus from the laundry room to the rest of the home. A series of successful products were introduced, including Clorox Disinfecting Wipes and the Clorox ReadyMop mopping system.

EVALUATING THE CATEGORY

The categories suggested by extension research need to be evaluated. Is the category attractive, and will it remain so? Is it growing? Are margins healthy or deteriorating? What is the competitive landscape now and in the future? Are the existing competitors strong and committed, or vulnerable and looking elsewhere for future growth? Will other players enter? Is there overcapacity? Are there pockets of unmet customer needs? Are there opportunities defined by segments that might fit the brand? Would a new entry become a platform for future business opportunities? Are there other strategic objectives of the extension besides entering a new product-market?

The firm also needs to ask whether it has the necessary assets and competences to compete in that category. Among the assets and skills that could be strategically necessary are R&D, manufacturing, marketing, finance, global sourcing, distribution, or customer relationships. If the needed assets are not in place, can they be created or acquired in a timely and cost-effective manner?

THE EXTENSION CONCEPT

Ultimately, the firm will need to go to market with a particular offering and positioning strategy. The biggest mistake is introducing a me-too product with no differential advantage. Dozens of studies over the years have found that the most significant predictor of success of a new product is the degree to which it is different from existing options. It pays to be patient and persistent in developing products with superior benefits and points of differentiation.

An extension concept, like any new offering concept, can come from a variety of sources. The new concept can be developed internally. When Intel developed a new line of microprocessors or Disney conceived of a new theme park in China, a potential extension of an existing brand becomes available. It also can be acquired from another firm, either by itself or as part of a portfolio of product and service offerings. In fact, obtaining a product offering that can be used to extend a brand into a new category is one motivation for acquisitions. Thus, when HP acquired Compaq, the merger provided products and services that allowed the footprint of HP to be expanded. Whatever the source, a strong entry is needed. Brand strength can enable a good product to succeed; it rarely can make the difference for a weak product.

The concept then needs to be tested. Conventional concept testing techniques are normally used. The key is to create a concept that is as close as possible to how the customer will ultimately be exposed to it. If actual ads and packaging are not feasible, the concept should be described in detail. The branding options should be tested at the same time.

Customers are usually capable of directly appraising the fit and credibility of a brand option. They can even assess the brand's ability to add value. A good tactic is to expose prospective customers to the concept and the brand name, then ask whether they would buy it and why. If they can articulate a reason that the branded new product concept would be attractive, then the brand is adding value. If they are unable to provide a specific reason, however, it is unlikely that the brand name will add significant value.

Developing a Viable Brand Strategy

The extension offering needs to have a brand strategy (which, of course, is the focus of this book). Basically, the options are drawn from the brand relationship spectrum introduced in Chapter 2. While there are many variants in the brand relationship spectrum, four major brand options exist, three of which leverage existing brands:

- An existing master brand with a descriptive subbrands (a branded house)
- An existing master brand with a subbrand
- A new brand endorsed by an existing brand

The fourth option in the brand relationship spectrum, a new brand unrelated to an existing brand (also known as a house of brands), should be kept in mind when considering possible extensions. When evaluating the brand extension options, the most accurate conclusion might be that none of them will be desirable and feasible. Comparing them to a new brand option may keep the process from being channeled toward a suboptimal decision.

These four options (and their variants) represent the key points on the brand relationship spectrum. In Chapter 2, the choice among these options for any new offering was judged to be based on three questions, the analysis of which was postponed. It is now time to address them. The three questions upon which the optimal extension branding choice depends are as follows:

- Will the brand enhance the extension?
- Will the extension enhance the brand?
- Is there a compelling reason to generate a new brand (whether it be a stand-alone brand, an endorsed brand, or a subbrand)?

The first two of these questions focus on what happens when a brand is leveraged. Figure 7-3 suggests that brand equity (in the form of its visibility, trust/perceived quality, associations, and loyalty) can affect the

FIGURE 7-3
BRAND EQUITY AND THE BRAND EXTENSION

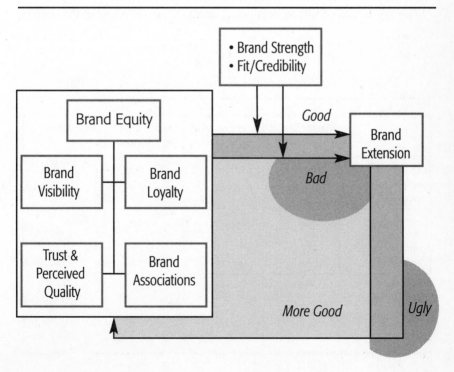

extensions both positively and negatively. The figure also indicates that the extension in turn can affect these brand equity dimensions both positively (more good) and negatively (the ugly). Too often the impact of the extension on the brand is not given enough weight, but in the long run, it can be the most important result of an extension. The nature and size of the effect in both directions will depend on the strength of the brand equity, as well as the brand fit and credibility in the new context.

The third question reiterates that a new brand option needs to be on the table when an extension is considered. In general, though, a new brand (even in a subbrand role) is inherently costly and risky. The default strategy should always be to minimize the number of brand-related mouths to feed, and to have the most parsimonious brand portfolio possible.

These three questions will direct the branding strategy, as suggested by Figure 7-4. Positive answers to the first two questions and a negative answer to the third will move the needle to the left side of the spectrum, toward a branded house. Conversely, negative answers to the first two questions and positive ones to the third suggest that the optimal branding strategy will be found to the right side of the spectrum.

The sections that follow explore each of these three questions in turn.

FIGURE 7-4
PLACING STRATEGIES ON THE BRAND RELATIONSHIP SPECTRUM

	Master Brand Descriptor	Master Brand Subbrand	Master Brand as Endorser	New Brand
Will the brand enhance the extension?	Yes			No
Will the extension enhance the brand?	Yes			No
Is there a compelling reason to generate a new brand?	No			Yes

WILL THE BRAND ENHANCE THE EXTENSION?

A brand can affect the extension positively or negatively. First, the good news.

The Good

An established brand name can help a new offering by creating or enhancing awareness, quality/trust associations, and a customer base. As a result, there is the potential to save go-to-market time and resources, thereby enhancing the chances of success.

AWARENESS/PRESENCE

A very basic task when entering a new product-market is simply to become relevant, as described in Chapter 4. When Crest extended from toothpaste into toothbrushes, it needed to make customers aware that it made toothbrushes and, ideally, encourage them to consider Crest for a toothbrush need. When Black & Decker, an established name in home power tools, extended to kitchen appliances, it needed to make itself relevant in this very different context. Without some level of brand relevance, an offering will be excluded from consideration by much of the market.

To achieve relevance, the brand needs to gain awareness and be linked to the product class. The use of a recognized brand name such as Crest or Black & Decker on a new product means that name recognition has been accomplished, and the communication task is reduced to the more manageable one of associating the name with the new product class. It is easier to communicate the fact that Virgin is an option for a cola drink than to establish a new brand name, such as Walker's Cola.

Name familiarity also provides in itself a basis for customer affinity. People have been shown to like the familiar in many settings, even when there is nothing to back it up. (Experiments have shown that nonsense words to which a subject has been previously exposed are preferred to others.) Further, customers often assume that because a brand is familiar, it has achieved market acceptance at some level. Certainly the success of Intel Inside is partly due to people's assumption that there must be a reason why a computer maker would put the Intel logo on its products.

Even for an established brand, however, building an association with a new product class is not a trivial task. Black & Decker spent more than $100 million dollars to make consumers aware that it was in the small appliance business, having bought that business from GE. The campaign achieved a 57 percent awareness level—which was good, but still lower that what GE retained even without making or distributing products in the category.

PERCEIVED QUALITY AND TRUST

An established brand can potentially bring to the extension perceived quality, an organizational intangible that is often pivotal to getting into the consideration set and can even become a key influence on the purchase decision, especially when sharp differentiation is lacking. In a study by Aaker and Keller, perceived quality was shown to be a predictor of the evaluation of eighteen proposed extensions of six brand names (McDonald's, Vuarnet, Crest, Vidal Sassoon, Häagen-Dazs, and Heineken).[4] This study has been replicated eight times over five countries, and the impact of perceived quality is very consistent.[5] There is little point in extending mediocrity.

A related organizational intangible is trust, where the organization can be trusted to deliver whatever is promised. It reduces buyer risk and means that the firm is established, is unlikely to promote a flawed product, and is likely to be around to support it in the future. Thus, a GE or Marriott name on a product or service has credibility, while an unknown brand may have little chance even with a good product or service behind it. In concept tests for consumer products, the use of a brand name such as Pillsbury, Kellogg's, Toshiba, or Sony will nearly always result in a dramatic improvement in the evaluation of a new offering.

The use of established brand names is an efficient way to build on organizational associations such as perceived quality and trust. American Express earned a reputation for quality over many years and products. The IBM name provides thousands of products with an umbrella quality reputation that usually means far more than specifications of individual products. In fact, some corporate names such as HP, Kraft, GE, or Ford are on so many products that they lack strong specific associations. Their value, then, is primarily to provide a sense of perceived quality and a related feeling that the product will be around for some time to come.

BRAND ASSOCIATIONS

Brand awareness and even a high level of perceived quality and trust will often be inadequate to carry the day. There usually needs to be a point of differentiation that is relevant to buyers in order to stimulate purchase and loyalty. Pillsbury Microwave Popcorn initially benefited from the Pillsbury name, but it was vulnerable to the entry of an established name with an equal or superior product. Orville Redenbacher entered the category late but with significant category authority, and it ended up winning with a perceived point of differentiation. Pillsbury had a similar experience in microwave frozen pizza, where it saw its early gains attacked by established pizza names with Italian heritage.

A sustainable point of differentiation with respect to a key attribute can be difficult to create, especially if one's competitors are established. Drawing on the association of an existing brand—whether it is a functional association, a brand personality, a lifestyle association, or some other basis for a customer relationship—can provide or support a point of differentiation efficiently, credibly, and economically.

A strong association can help the communication task as well as positioning of a brand. Consider the problem of communicating the qualities of a line of snow chains, power air pumps, and halogen spotlights. Giving them the brand name Michelin Equip means that the line will likely gain from the safety that is associated with the Michelin brand. The communication task is reduced to exposing customers to the brand name and symbol.

A host of other brand associations can provide credibility and a point of differentiation for an extension. Most fall into one of the following leverage points:

- *Product category*—Mercedes in vehicles, IBM in computers, and British Air in global air service
- *Product attribute/functional benefits*—Volvo's safety, the taste of Hershey's, the dealer experience at Saturn
- *Application*—Duracell Durabeam flashlights, Samsonite clothes for travelers
- *Technology*—Honda's experience in small motors helped its lawn mowers, while Bic's razors were aided by a competence in making disposable, inexpensive plastic items
- *Channel*—Amazon and e-commerce, Avon and in-home selling

- *User*—Visa travelers checks, Sears Savings Bank, Gerber baby clothes
- *Brand personality/self-expressive benefits*—Virgin luggage, Harley-Davidson clothing, Tiffany watches, Caterpillar boots

When the brand has associations that are strongly tied to a product class, the extension potential is limited. However, when a brand's equity is based on more abstract associations—such as the user imagery, brand personality, or self-expressive benefits—it will travel farther. Such bases for identity as prestige (Jaguar), personality (Virgin), fashion (Pierre Cardin), lifestyle (Sharper Image), technology (HP), and health (Healthy Choice) are not associated with a specific product class, and will be capable of casting a wider shadow than a brand that is tied to a product-specific attribute.

BRAND LOYALTY

Existing customers have an affinity for the brand, a deeper understanding and relationship that can be tapped by the extension. Kraft Philadelphia Cream Cheese is a $1 billion-plus business that has extremely committed users. In late 1999, Kraft introduced Philly Snack Bars, a sweet snack with a cheese base as a key ingredient. One of the most successful new products ever launched by Kraft, it drew on the Philadelphia Cream Cheese customer base for its core user segment.

Of course, not all extensions draw on the brand's customer base. If Honda were to extend its brands to private planes (as it is actively exploring), it would move beyond the base for Honda motorcycles and cars. But relevance to the customer base can be a significant asset to the extension.

FIT/CREDIBILITY OF THE BRAND AND THE EXTENSION

Several studies have shown that the success of the extension will depend on the fit and credibility of the brand with the product context of the extension. The fit relates to whether the customer is comfortable with the brand in the new context, while the credibility relates to the brand's perceived ability to deliver in the space. Each are important.

The Aaker and Keller study of six extensions, cited earlier, showed that on average, fit and credibility, in addition to perceived quality, affected customer response to extensions.[6] A credibility measure was whether the brand's firm had the assets and skills needed to make a superior extension product. A fit measure was whether there existed a complementary relationship (a hiking-boot company making camping equipment, or a golf club maker introducing golf clothing). Fit and credibility each influenced success, a finding that was replicated across eight studies in five countries.[7]

Sometimes, though, the evaluation of fit and credibility can be tricky. Close-Up has a breath-freshening association that works for mouthwash and breath mints but is much less effective for dental floss and toothbrushes, according to a study by Broniarczyk and Alba.[8] In contrast, because of its dental protection associations, Crest works with dental floss and toothbrushes, but less so with mouthwash and breath mints. And Aaker and Keller found that, for example, the Crest taste was a problem in chewing gum but not in mouthwash, although both had positive associations of good teeth care and oral hygiene.[9] Good taste may not be important in mouthwash; indeed, Listerine has associated unpleasant taste with effective freshening action.

Fit and credibility also can depend on the context. Milberg and colleagues compared extensions for Timex, a watch with strong functional associations, with those for Rolex, a prestige brand.[10] The extensions were for products that also were oriented toward either prestige (bracelet, necktie, cufflinks) or function (flashlight, calculator, batteries). The Rolex name was significantly more helpful for the prestige products than was the Timex name, but the reverse was true for the functionally oriented products. The same study found that Timex had fit problems when it was extended into garage door openers, smoke detectors, and cologne; clearly, the distance from watches and timepiece technology was an issue.

A low fit or credibility rating is not necessarily fatal. Some products with an apparent problem may actually work if positioned in such a way as to accentuate a link between the brand and the product class. McDonald's photo processing, for instance, might be acceptable if the convenience and efficiency can be dialed up. Thus, an attractive extension (one that involves a desirable market, for example) may merit a more extensive concept test even if there appears to be a problem. A study by Klink and Smith showed that fit and credibility would improve when the extension concept was elaborated more, and also when the prospective customer was exposed to the concept multiple times.[11] Also, a successful extension can change perceptions of the brand. If Timex could create a winning garage door opener, that success would change perceptions of its fit in the smoke detector category.

The Bad: The Brand Fails to Help or Even Inhibits the Extension

As suggested by Figure 7-2, a brand's ability to help an extension depends on its strength as well as fit and credibility in the new context. A brand lacking strength will not help an extension. However, strong brands can become a liability if there are fit and/or credibility issues.

The following extensions all had some supporting logic. However, they each lacked fit or credibility and thus were not perceived to add value or, even worse, inhibited the extension. Some were in the worst case scenario when the incongruity was bad enough to stimulate ridicule.

- The Levi Strauss Tailored Classics line of suits failed in large part because Levi's associations with casual living, rugged material, and the outdoors were not a fit with suits. The brand also lacked credibility in the new context; Levi Strauss was perceived as a firm with proven skills around casual clothing.
- The Swatch car suffered because the brand's flare in colorful watches did not transfer to automobiles.
- The Corn Flakes name reduced the expectation that Honey Nut Corn Flakes would deliver sweetened cereal taste. The product failed and was only successful under the Nuts and Honey name without the Corn Flakes association.
- Bausch & Lomb, the eye care specialist, decided to leverage its R&D, distribution channels, and perceived quality into the mouthwash market—and failed; the Bausch & Lomb brand delivered no customer benefit.
- Bic perfume offered convenience and disposability, but lacked standing in that arena.
- Clorox laundry detergent was perceived to fade clothing because of its association with bleach.
- Log Cabin was unable to extend its syrup brand to the pancake mix business; the association with a sticky, sweet syrup probably did not engender visions of a light and fluffy product. (In contrast,

Aunt Jemima, with links to the friendly namesake character, was successful in going the other way—from pancake mix to syrup.)

- Arm & Hammer succeeded in building on baking powder's odor-destroying associations to extend to toothpaste, detergent, and oven cleaners, but was unsuccessful in extending to a spray under-arm deodorant because of fit problems.

- Sony and Apple have struggled to extend into the business market, and IBM and HP have similarly found it difficult to move into the home market, in part because of the brand personality each has fostered.

- Even though Dole has associations with Hawaii, the introduction of Dole Hawaiian resorts or travel services might be too far a stretch.

Sometimes, if the extension is distanced from the brand's core products, credibility problems are actually reduced. If Coca-Cola or McDonald's were to extend into clothing, attributes such as taste could not be transferred. Thus, whereas Coca-Cola orange juice would not work, Coca-Cola sweatshirts might be acceptable. Of course, in this case the consumer is relying upon the manufacturer of the extension (such as Murjani for Coca-Cola) or the retailer (such as Sears for McKid's) rather than the licensed name to warrant the quality of the clothing.

WILL THE EXTENSION ENHANCE THE BRAND?

The focus of most extensions is on making sure that the extension is successful. Yet an equally or more important consideration should be how the extension affects the brand equity. The extension has the potential to contribute to all four dimensions of brand equity.

More Good

An extension provides visibility. Whether it is the Apple Xserver (the Apple entry in the server market) or Gillette Venus razors for women, there are additional advertisements, package placement, and people talking about the brand. All this exposure is a bonus for the brand, exposure that would not otherwise occur. Simple exposure also implies market acceptance and capability; studies have shown that customers are impressed with firms that can cross product classes successfully.

Loyal buyers will have a strengthened relationship with the brand because they will be able to use it in another context, and perhaps more important, will not be using a competitor's brand. Thus, Nike dialing up its golf equipment line with Tiger Woods's endorsement means that a user of Nike running shoes and tennis rackets will now have still another link to the brand, and another chance for Nike to build its perceived quality and trust.

Such associations are critical in that extensions can have an important influence on the brand image. Extensions can and should reinforce the brand image, thus providing a brand-building function instead of weakening the brand name and draining its goodwill.

Sometimes a brand needs to change its image in order to remain relevant or to adapt to a new strategic direction. The image change or augmentation may be the most important objective, and the sales success of the extension may be relatively unimportant. Because the extension of IBM into portable computers with the ThinkPad had significant impact on the IBM brand, its value was far more than its sales reflected. For Philips, a large electronics company, the opportunity to co-brand some electronic devices with Nike provides a unique opportunity to make its own brand more contemporary and relevant.

An extension can enhance the brand over all of the equity dimensions by introducing the brand to new segments that might, as a result, become buyers in the existing contexts. For example, when Slim-Fast extends its brand from shakes and bars to soups and pastas, new customers are exposed to it.

The Ugly: The Extension Damages the Brand

The brand name is often the key asset of the firm. It can be more important than bricks and mortar, or even the people in terms of replacement investment. So, however tempting it may be to evaluate the extension as a business decision on its own merits, firms should consider the possible damage it could cause by diluting the brand image, creating undesirable associations, failing to deliver on the brand promise, or predicting some visible disaster.

In fact, a failed extension is usually not nearly as problematic as one that succeeds (or at least survives) and damages the brand name by creating undesirable attribute associations, reducing the brand's perceived quality, or altering existing associations. A brand extension failure usually lacks visibility, which can be a saving grace. For example, Green Giant received no detectable damage from a six-year effort to establish a line of frozen dinners, in part because so few people were even aware of it. It is the "successes," such as the Dove dishwashing detergent that struggled, that are the problem.

DILUTING EXISTING BRAND ASSOCIATIONS

The brand associations created by an extension can fuzz a sharp image that had been a key asset, and at the same time reduce the brand's credibility within its original setting. Cadbury's association with fine chocolates and candy certainly weakened when it got into such mainstream food products as mashed potatoes, dried milk, soups, and beverages. The company risked that consumers would not be able to compartmentalize Cadbury chocolate and continue to evaluate it the same way, especially new consumers who lacked loyalty and a sense of Cadbury's heritage.

When a brand's self-expressive benefits are supported by the fact that it is not for or available to everyone, excessive extensions (particularly via licensing) could make the brand too commonplace. The Lacoste alligator became overused at one time and lost much of its appeal. The undisciplined use of the Gucci name—at one point there were 14,000 Gucci products—was one of the contributing factors in the fall of that brand.

UNDESIRABLE ATTRIBUTE ASSOCIATIONS ARE CREATED

An extension will usually create new brand associations, some of which can be potentially damaging to the brand in its original context. There is certainly a possibility that Sunkist fruit rolls hurt the Sunkist health image, that Black & Decker small appliances hurt its power-tool image, that the investment bank image of Solomon suffered when it combined with Shearson (a brokerage firm) and even more when it joined a bank (Citibank), that Carnation pet food hurt the brand's food items, or that Lipton soup at one time hurt the image of a purveyor of fine teas.

Under what conditions will an extension's potentially negative association(s) be transferred to the original brand context? The transfer should be less likely if (1) the original brand associations are very strong, (2) there is a distinct difference between the original brand context and the extensions, and (3) the difference between the original brand context and the extension is not so extreme as to appear incongruous. Thus, Cheerios has strong associations with oats, the doughnut shape, and nonsugar cereals. Honey Nut Cheerios, as a presweetened cereal, has a distinct difference that allows it to be categorized in consumers' memories separately. The two categories, while distinct, are not incongruous.

THE BRAND FAILS TO DELIVER ON ITS PROMISE

Any extension will risk brand equity if it does not deliver on the key brand promise. This is particularly true if the extension draws on the brand's loyal customer base. If Black & Decker appliances are not of the quality that has been established by the company's power tools, the brand will be risking its customer base, and the long-term result could be costly indeed. The brand is particularly vulnerable when it is vertically extended downward, as will be discussed in the next chapter.

A DISASTER OCCURS

A disaster out of a firm's control (such as the discovery that an Ivory model was a porn star, that Tylenol boxes were tampered with, that Firestone tires used on Ford Explorers were potentially unsafe, or that Rely products had a serious health hazard) can happen to almost any brand name. To the extent that the name is used on many products, the damage will be more extensive. The threat of a disaster to the Fisher-Price name has inhibited the company from going into the child-care business. Its brand has very positive associations of quality playthings for children that could very likely be transferred to child care. However, just one child molestation incident, or even an accusation, might cause serious damage to the whole Fisher-Price equity.

An alleged sudden-acceleration problem with Audi 5000 cars made from 1978 on created adverse publicity that culminated with a feature on CBS's "60 Minutes" in November 1986. Audi's response—to blame American drivers—did little to defuse the situation, and Audi U.S. sales plummeted from 74,000 in 1985 to around 23,000 in 1989. It took fifteen years before Audi was able to recover, despite putting a stream of excellent cars on the road. A study of the incident's impact on the depreciation rates of other Volkswagen products is illuminating.[12] The Audi 4000, which had no such problem, was impacted nearly as much as the Audi 5000 (7.3 vs. 9.6 percent) whereas the Audi Quattro had a smaller effect (4.6 percent) because it was less closely tied to Audi—the name Quattro was separated from Audi on the car, and Quattro ads often did not mention the parent brand. Further, other Volkswagen names such as Porsche and Volkswagen were not affected.

THE BRAND FRANCHISE IS CANNIBALIZED

An important part of the brand equity is a brand's customer base. If sales of a brand extension come at the expense of the original brand, the extension's sales may not compensate for the damage to the original brand's equity. Of course, it is better to cannibalize a brand's sales than to have a competitor erode a position. Thus, it was probably better for Miller's High Life to be cannibalized by Miller Lite than to have its market position lost to a competitor.

A key question is the degree of overlap between segments. If the extension appeals to a distinct segment, the cannibalization may be minimal. General Mills was reluctant to introduce a presweetened version of Cheerios because of the cannibalization potential, as well as the possibility of disturbing the Cheerios brand associations of being a nonsugar cereal. It tested Honey Nut Cheerios for a long time and even tested an adult cereal position to avoid the Cheerios core market. The extension did not damage the sales of Cheerios at all, however, in part because it was relevant to the presweetened segment (even though there was segment overlap, in that many people consumed both unsweetened and presweetened cereals). Further, Apple Cinnamon Cheerios was introduced, gaining a 1.5 percent share of the cold cereal market without affecting the share held by either Cheerios (4.8 percent) or Honey Nut Cheerios (3.1 percent). The Diet Coke story is similar.

IS THERE A COMPELLING NEED FOR A NEW BRAND?

The development of a new brand (or the continued support of an existing separate brand) is expensive and difficult. Multiple brands complicate the brand architecture for both the firm and the customer. Thus, a separate brand should be developed or supported only when a compelling need can be demonstrated.

Because of the enormous pressure to create new brands by those who believe (often wishfully) that the latest product improvement merits a new name, organizational discipline is required to make sure that any new brand is justified. This discipline might involve a top-level committee with sign-off authority. In making that judgment, one or more of the following rationales should be present:

- All existing brands have associations that are incompatible with the offering.
- The offering would damage the brand name.
- A new name is needed to realize the chance to create and own an association.
- Only a new name would signal the newness of the offering.
- An acquired brand has significant loyalty that would be at risk if a name change were to occur.
- A channel conflict requires a separate name.
- The business is of sufficient size and longevity to justify investing in a new brand.

The first two have already been discussed. The remaining five deserve elaboration, which is provided below.

Create and Own an Association

The potential to own a key association for a product class, particularly a newly introduced association, is one rationale for a new brand. Pantene ("for hair so healthy it shines") would not be successful under the Head & Shoulders or Pert brands, because the unique benefit of Pantene could not emerge from the shadow of the existing associations. When an offering has the potential to dominate a functional benefit (as is the case for many of the Procter & Gamble brands), a distinct brand is justifiable. However, a similar argument applied to General Motors turned out to be faulty. GM at one time aspired to be a house of nearly three dozen brands, but it could not create that many motivating value propositions or identify distinct segments.

Represent a New, Different Offering

A new brand name can help tell the story of a truly different offering or signal a breakthrough benefit. There is a temptation, however, for all new-product managers to believe that they are managing something dramatic. A larger perspective is needed. A minor evolution or an empty attempt to revitalize a product will rarely qualify. A new brand name should represent a significant advance in technology and function. For instance, the retro PT Cruiser merited a new subbrand name because its design and personality represented a radical departure from other Chrysler offerings, as well as for the industry.

Retain/Capture a Customer/Brand Bond

When a firm buys another brand, there is an issue as to whether the purchased brand name should be retained. In making that judgment, the strength of the acquired brand—its visibility, associations, and customer loyalty—should be considered, as well as the strength of the acquiring brand. The customer bond to the acquired brand name is often the key ingredient. If it is strong and difficult to transfer, keeping the acquired brand could be a sound decision. Several considerations, could make a brand equity transfer difficult:

- The resources required to transfer the brand equity may not be available (or may not be justified).
- The associations of the acquired brand may be strong and would be dissipated with a brand name change.
- There may be an emotional bond, perhaps created by the organizational associations of the acquired brand, that may be difficult to transfer.
- There could be a fit problem; the acquiring brand may not fit the context and position of the acquired brand.

There are circumstances, of course, when a name change is wise. Usually the rationale involves a strong branded house. HP has made hundreds of acquisitions over the years and has consistently changed the name to HP even when the previous brand name had substantial visibility, attractive associations, and a customer following. It is not clear that the HP policy generated the right decision in all cases, but the strong associations of HP and the advantages of a branded house strategy provided defensible reasons.

A Channel Conflict

Channel conflict can force new brands. The problem usually is twofold. First, an existing channel may be motivated to stock and promote a brand because it has some degree of exclusivity. When that is breached, their motivation falls. Second, an existing channel will support a higher price in part because it provides a higher level of service. If the brand became available in a value channel, the brand's ability to retain the high margin channel would be in jeopardy.

Fragrance and clothing brands, for example, need different brands to access upscale retailers, department stores, and drug/discount stores. Thus, L'Oréal has Lancôme, L'Oréal, and Maybelline cosmetics brands for different channels. The VF Corporation supports four distinct brands—Lee, Wrangler, Maverick, and Old Axe—in part to deal with channel conflict.

Will the Business Support a New Brand Name?

If the business is ultimately too small or short-lived to support necessary brand building, a new brand name will simply not be feasible, whatever the other arguments are. It is almost always much more costly and difficult than expected to establish and maintain a brand. Too often in the excitement of a new brand, unrealistic assumptions are made about the firm's ability and will to adequately fund it. The will is particularly important; many organizations have deep pockets but short arms. It is futile to plan brand building, only to fail to fund its construction and provide a maintenance budget.

PUTTING EXTENSION RISKS INTO PERSPECTIVE

The risks associated with brand extensions can fairly be described as scary. Some argue that these risks are often such that extensions should be avoided. In their classic and influential book on positioning, for example, Ries and Trout warn that strong brands will lose their focus.[13] They suggest that the meaning of the Scott name became confused when extensions such as ScotTowels, ScotTissue, Scotties, Scottkins, and Baby Scot were added; the names tended to confuse a shopping list and were in sharp contrast to the strong product class identity of Bounty, Pampers, or Kleenex. And Ries and Ries argue that the power of a brand is inversely proportional to its scope, observing that Chevrolet means nothing because it has been placed on ten models, some very disparate.[14] Certainly there *are* risks, and extensions should not be done without analysis and strategic thought. Several observations, however, will place that risk in perspective.

First, a brand extension decision can involve a business model issue. If McDonald's sees growth slowing and even going negative, it appropriately should look to using its assets—namely, its tens of thousands of retail locations and its brand—to enter new arenas, even non-food areas. It could, for example, sell Ronald McDonald toys in its outlets in order to gain growth in sales and profits. If Sony is not making money on consumer electronics, there might be a compelling business reason to enter financial services, even if that means stretching the brand. And the harsh reality is that it is not always feasible to establish a new brand (even an endorsed brand) in a cluttered marketplace, so that option may not be available. It does not make sense to neglect business considerations when making extension decisions.

Second, it is important to make a distinction between adding and diluting associations. If the original associations are strong, they are unlikely to be affected by an extension that simply adds other associations, as was exemplified by the Schwab story recounted in Chapter 4. Some names and symbols like the Pillsbury Doughboy and Hewlett-Packard are so strong that it is very difficult to damage or change existing associations. New associations are simply added and often restricted to a new context.

Third, as noted in Chapter 4, the issue is not what products are associated with the brand, but rather whether the brand is associated with a product arena. For there to be a product scope image problem, an extension would have create a reduced tendency for a customer to consider the brand relevant. It does not matter if the customer learns that Jack Daniel's makes barbeque sauce, as long as Jack Daniel's is in the consideration set when selecting a spirits option and the associations of Jack Daniel's in that context are preserved.

Fourth, as noted in Chapter 5, a brand that is tired might gain some much-needed energy and visibility from an extension. This boost can be particularly welcome when the brand is competing in a mature arena in which innovation is difficult. There is some validity to the old adage that it doesn't matter what you say about me, just get the name right, because it is only the name that registers.

Fifth, an extension can be managed to reduce the brand risk, being distanced from the original context through a subbrand or even an endorsed brand. The introduction of these brand portfolio tools provides a direct way to manage the risks. Further, the positioning can look for a spin that is compatible with the brand. The extension also can be kept on a short leash to make sure that incompatible brand building is avoided, and the offering itself will be pulled if it is not meeting goals and brand damage seems imminent.

Finally, an extension that is a stretch may still be successful because of a compelling value proposition and superb execution. After such success, the brand will then have a new set of credibility boundaries. For Virgin, an offbeat music company, to go into airlines was one of the dumbest brand decisions ever. When it pulled off the extension with flair and personality, however, its ability to extend further became very broad.

Clearly, extensions that enhance the brand by reinforcing its brand identity will always be the goal. But operating a business in a dynamic market over time can be challenging, and rigid rules of thumb are not realistic. To understand when brand risks might be acceptable, an in-depth analysis needs to be pursued in the context of a strategic vision, a topic to which we now turn.

CREATING RANGE BRAND PLATFORMS

An extension decision usually focuses on whether a brand can be leveraged by using it to support an offering in another product class, either directly or by an endorsement strategy. The problem with this mindset is that the decisions tend to be ad hoc, with a short-term perspective, and thus potentially suboptimal or even damaging with respect to a longer-term strategic view of the business.

A more strategic brand strategy should conceive of range brand platforms rather than brand extensions. A *range brand platform* is created by a range brand (that is, a brand that spans product categories) whose identity includes a differentiating association that is applicable across categories. Some illustrations are as follows:

- Dove's range brand platform uses the moisturizer association to create a point of differentiation in soap, detergent, body wash, facial cleaners, deodorant, and hair care.
- Nivea has based its range brand platform on mildness and caring.
- Healthy Choice's range brand platform leverages the "good taste and good for you" position across some three hundred products.
- Volvo leverages its safety position across a variety of vehicle types.
- Tylenol has leveraged its pain reliever (acetaminophen) into a host of products, including sore throat, cold, sinus, flu, and arthritis relief, as well as Tylenol for women.

Creating a point of differentiation that can be employed across a set of target product categories is very different from creating one that will resonate with a single candidate product category. The brand identity and position might be reflected in the initial offering, as it was in the case of Dove, or it can be initially aspirational and only achieved as the brand is attached to a widening set of product classes and offerings. A systems orientation for a software company may have to evolve as the firm introduces components of the systems offering. Many corporate brands span product categories and contribute associations such as size, financial assets, and even innovation but really lack differentiating associations that would be relevant in most of the categories in which they compete.

The range brand platform perspective also differs from ad hoc extensions in that the strategy involves a judgment about the composition of the ultimate product scope that will be driven by both a driver brand and an endorser brand. These specifications will evolve over time, but there should always be a target scope to guide decisions.

In implementing a range brand platform strategy, the order and timing of extensions becomes critical. The idea is to gradually enlarge the brand scope and perhaps the brand associations as well. Ultimately, extensions that at one point would be an excessive stretch become feasible as the brand evolves into its new portfolio strategy. For example, Gillette meant razors when it introduced Gillette Foamy, a shaving product. This subbrand, closely linked to razors, was a bridge to the line of toiletries for men introduced under the Gillette series brand. A series of toiletries would have been more of a stretch if Gillette had only been known for razors.

As suggested by Figure 7-5, a range brand platform is strategic, focusing on groupings of product categories, and has a long-term perspective. In contrast, the ad hoc extension decision is incremental, focusing on a single product category, and has a short-term orientation.

Adapting Platform Brand Identities

It should not be assumed that the range brand platform will have a brand identity and position that by itself will need to carry the day in all its contexts. Each product line can have its own identity and position as long as it does not introduce inconsistencies that confuse or detract. Competing in a product class setting will usually require additional associations that represent an augmentation of the basic brand identity.

Thus, while Healthy Choice has a clear identity (based on nutritious food, low in fat and sodium, that tastes good), Healthy Choice Generous Servings added a frozen dinner and portion-size dimension to the identity. The Calvin Klein range brand has associated fashion with a New York personality. Its product line identities, however, are distinct without being inconsistent. The fragrances emphasize sexuality and rebellion, whereas the suits and eyewear products are more conservative. Honda has a common identity involving associations such as competence, efficiency, few defects, and good engines, even across disparate products. However, the Honda motorcycle includes dimensions of being fun for young people while the Honda car line in the United States is more for families and dials up the resale attribute.

FIGURE 7-5
BRAND PLATFORMS

	Brand Extension	Range Brand Platforms
Decision Focus	Incremental	Strategic
Decision Scope	Product Class	Product Class Groupings
Time Frame	Short Term	Long Term

Why Brand Platforms?

There are several motivations for brand platforms. Strategically, the concept can provide coherence and structure to an organization's strategy. The essence of a business strategy is to address three questions: What business areas (product-markets) will be included, what value proposition will be offered, and what strategic assets will exist in each of these business areas? A range brand can provide answers. The brand scope of Virgin or Newman's Own defines the product-market scope, and the brand identity will provide the value proposition, and the brand strength will be a key asset.

A second motivation is simply to leverage strong brands. A brand platform strategy will often result in a larger business base and a stronger brand as well. Consider, for example, how Calvin Klein has leveraged its fashion credibility from designer jeans to a host of items, including not just clothing of all types (underwear, jeans, and men's suits) but also fragrances and eyewear. Braun leveraged its success in small personal care appliances to clocks and a wide range of household appliances, including food processors, hand blenders, coffeemakers, curling irons, and toothbrushes. Disney, which started out with cartoon shorts, is now also strongly associated with feature-length film production, theme parks, clothing, toy stores, a hockey team, and cruise lines.

The extendability of these range brands is particularly remarkable when one compares the brands to some of their competitors. What if suitmaker Brooks Brothers marketed perfume or hosiery? What if the Cuisinart kitchen appliance brand was placed on an electric razor? And what if the Montreal Canadiens hockey team wished to put its name on a theme park or a film company? Or Hallmark put its name on a cruise line?

A range brand platform will tend to be broader when the brand draws more heavily on associations that are not tied closely to a specific product. The wide scope of Virgin, for example, was driven by personality and style rather than a particular customer benefit. The Amazon platform is based on a way of interacting with customers and a distribution method that can be applied to a wide variety of products. In contrast, some brands are so closely tied to a product that their potential to play a large role is limited.

A third motivation is economic. A brand platform provides the opportunity to be cost-efficient in brand building. An economist would observe that a brand platform provides classic economics of scope (that is, the fixed cost of maintaining a brand name can be spread across different businesses). A business strategist would see a brand platform as providing synergy—a grouping of businesses is greater than the sum of its parts, because an investment in one will help the others. Both perspectives really capture the same efficiency potential. In addition, the awareness and image of a brand platform can reduce the costs and risks of new product efforts.

The reality is that creating or supporting a brand is very expensive in the modern era, especially with high advertising and promotional costs. A stand-alone brand competing with brand platforms can be at a big disadvantage because of the lack of scale economies (although a well-positioned niche brand can, of course, be a winner).

A fourth advantage of brand platforms is that being associated with multiple products can add visibility and reassure consumers that the firm is capable of success in different contexts. Dacin and Smith explored the impact of the number of products associated with a brand and the variation in quality across these products.[15] The number of products was either three (small kitchen appliances, garage door openers, and hand-held garden equipment) or seven (those three plus hair dryers, small power tools, carpet sweepers, and telephone answering machines). The quality of the products was also manipulated. In evaluating an extension of this product line (a sports watch or electric iron), the number of products affiliated with the brand enhanced both the evaluation of the extension and consumer confidence in the evaluation.

Finally, a brand platform can create a broader, richer relationship with customers based on exposures and use opportunities that span product classes. If Dove were only a soap, a customer would have a limited chance to know and use the product. However, those who use more than one of its half-dozen products will potentially have a deeper feeling about Dove as its associations come to be reinforced.

Range Brand Platform Configurations

A range brand platform can exist in a variety of brand portfolio configurations. At one extreme, if a range brand is blessed with points of differentiation that can travel broadly, a single range brand with descriptors or weak subbrands may carry a business with a broad scope. Dell (examined in more detail in Chapter 9) leverages the direct model and all that implies across a wide variety of computer equipment and services. Virgin leverages its personality and reputation for customer-pleasing innovations as it enters a host of product categories, including cola and train service. IBM draws on its credibility in large-scale systems to drive a wide variety of products and services. Most firms, not so blessed, however, can create strong subbrands, use multiple range brand platforms or use endorser range brands.

Sony, as we saw in Chapter 5, supports its range brand with strong subbrands such as VIAO, PlayStation, Handycam, and Walkman. The Sony brand leverages its associations with "astonishing technology" and digital entertainment to be a leader in a wide variety of consumer electronics arenas. Even so, Sony could not accomplish this without the subbrand equities. It is no accident that Sony is consistently the strongest brand in Japan and others that compete with a corporate brand covering many product categories are far behind.

Many of the most successful firms have multiple brand platforms, some of which are range brands. Procter & Gamble has eighty-plus brand platforms that contribute to its strength and strategic flexibility. Compare the current value of P&G with Ivory, Tide, Joy, Pampers, Crest, Secret, and Pringles to a firm that simply had a line of P&G bar soap, P&G detergent, P&G diapers, P&G toothpaste, P&G deodorant, and P&G potato snacks. Although the range of brands such as Crest, Tide, and Pampers is broad, it is also limited. There is no way that Crest or Tide, for example, could cover diaper products.

Other firms have developed a set of endorser range brand platforms. Microsoft, for example, as an endorser spans all its products. Endorsed brands such as Word, Office, .NET, and Xbox are themselves range brands, but all are sold under the umbrella endorsement of Microsoft, which signals that the product will be supported by a large, successful, and durable company.

Nestlé has several such endorser range brands, including Nestlé and Purina. Purina is now the umbrella endorser brand for all of the Nestlé pet food lines. The Purina endorsement indicates that the pet food has the credibility of a larger firm behind it, a firm that has experience in a variety of pet food lines. The brand Nestlé does the same for much of the Nestlé food lines, such as Good Start baby formula and the ice cream lines.

QUESTIONS FOR CONSIDERATION

1. For your major brands, what associations have the potential to be leveraged? For what products would they support an offering? Would the brand enhance the offering? Why? How might it inhibit the offering? Evaluate the impact of the extension on the brand. Consider worst-case scenarios regarding a new offering and its impact on the brand.

2. Identify a brand extension in your industry, and one outside of it. Evaluate the extension. What branding strategy was used? Why? Evaluate the strategy.

3. What are the existing brand platforms in your firm? Do they provide adequate growth and vitality? Are more needed? Which brand platforms would be feasible, given the organizational assets and culture? Address these questions for your major competitors.

PARTICIPATING IN UPSCALE AND VALUE MARKETS

It is awfully important to know what is and what is not your business.

—GERTRUDE STEIN

I may not know where I'm going, but I sure as hell know what I'm running away from.

—JACK NICHOLSON, IN *FIVE EASY PIECES*

GE APPLIANCES

While competing in the competitive premium appliance market, GE considered options to enter the super-premium market in order to capture margin dollars, create interest and energy for the brand, and become relevant to the growing "designer" appliance category.* One option, to create a new brand like Toyota did with Lexus, was not feasible because the required investment could not be justified in this market context. Another option, to stretch the GE brand up, would not provide the needed distinctiveness and impact.

GE instead decided to use subbrands to leverage its brand upward. To do so, it introduced two new appliance subbrands. The GE Profile line of appliances was positioned above the premium GE Appliances line. Its models had a bit of a design edge, had consistently higher price points, and were positioned as innovative, with products representing the latest technology. GE Monogram was a designer line aimed at ultra-high-income customers and the associated architect and designer market; its appliances had trim kits, custom handles, and other personal-

---

* Information for this section is drawn from GE websites; Mark Yost, "General Electric Income up 20%," *Courier Journal*, April 12, 2003, p. 1f.

ization options. Positioned as showcasing personal taste, confident style, and professional-chef quality equipment, the complete GE Monogram line included offerings such as wine chillers, beverage centers, and outdoor cooking centers. The website displayed designer homes with Monogram kitchens. The Monogram and Profile brands became the key to profitability at GE because of the substantial, sometimes breathtaking, prices and margins that they commanded.

The challenge of using a subbrand to move upscale is that the master brand may lack the credibility and prestige needed to compete in the super-premium market. In fact, the GE Monogram line, although well positioned, struggled initially because it stretched the GE brand. Over time, however, the line became more accepted as it expanded, gained acceptance and benefited from the growth of the subcategory.

The GE Profile line was successful from the outset, in part because it was positioned off the existing line rather than trying to symbolize prestige. It offered improved performance based on innovative technology. Separated from the premium GE Appliances line in both price and design, it was consistently priced higher and generally had a bolder design, with better components and features. It has been bolstered by the use of branded energizers such as the GE Profile Arctica, a refrigerator with a host of advanced, branded differentiators such as the TurboCool setting. If the product had been a difficult one to differentiate, like film or fertilizer or motor oil, a subbrand strategy would have been more challenging to implement.

GE also faced a challenge in the value market, which was experiencing substantial growth because of aggressive shoppers and value retailers like Circuit City. GE felt that it needed to participate in this market actively in order to retain its sales volume and associated scale economies. The use of the GE brand in the value market, though, even with a subbrand or an endorsed brand, would have risked both cannibalizing GE (by attracting buyers of the premium GE Appliances line to the value alternative) and damaging its image. A new brand for the value segment was deemed prudent, given these risks. Because cost parity is crucial in the value market and margins are slim, however, a new value brand cannot afford to conduct brand building. As a result, establishing a new brand is harder in the value context than in the super-premium market.

For GE, a strategy to use previously acquired brands successfully nav-

FIGURE 8-1
THE GE APPLIANCES VERTICAL BRAND PORTFOLIO

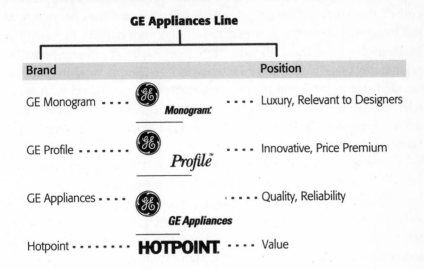

igated these challenges. GE had purchased the Hotpoint line, a premium appliance brand with substantial equity. Repositioned from a premium to a secondary or value line, Hotpoint provided the needed entry into discount retailers like Home Depot, Best Buy, and Sam's Club without risking the GE brand. Repositioning Hotpoint undoubtedly affected its perceived quality, making it unlikely that it could return to a premium status in the future, but the entry into the value segment created a stronger total appliance line for GE. The Hotpoint story illustrates the power of using an established brand (whether owned, bought, or licensed) when accessing a value segment.

The GE Appliances line thus resulted in a four-level coverage created by adding two subbrands and one distinct brand, as shown in Figure 8-1.

MARRIOTT

The Marriott brand started with a solid franchise in the premium downtown hotel market.[1] The Marriott organization, however, faced a vertical extension challenge similar to that of GE. Marriott's ultimate brand strategy, almost a mirror image of the GE route, provides additional insights into the vertical stretch problem.

Marriott, although a premium brand, did not participate at the highest end of the hotel industry. Because this market involved prestige and self-expressive benefits, it would have been very difficult to move the Marriott brand up. Thus, Marriott chose to move into the super-premium segment by buying a significant interest in Ritz-Carlton. Notably, Marriott decided not to associate the prestigious Ritz-Carlton brand with itself, even though it would have helped the Marriott brand and created operational synergies. Ritz-Carlton is not even connected to the Marriott Rewards program.

Marriott faced a very different challenge in the value segment. The size and growth of the value segment dwarfed that of the premium market in which Marriott was established. Further, having a more complete product line would provide operational synergies with respect to the reservation and reward systems. Entering that market successfully was therefore a strategic necessity for the Marriott organization.

The preferred choice would have been to enter the value market with a new brand or by acquiring an established one, as GE had done. However, the available established brands were a mess—with a hodgepodge of properties differing in quality, consistency, and geographic coverage. And creating a new brand would have been extremely difficult and expensive because of the clutter in the value end of the hospitality market. Thus, with considerable trepidation, Marriott decided to leverage the Marriott brand by endorsing three new value brands, Courtyard, Fairfield Inn, and SpringHill Suites.

With rooms and services designed for the business traveler, Courtyard by Marriott is a businessperson's hotel, usually located in the suburbs with no dining facilities. Fairfield Inn by Marriott is a family hotel that competes in the value segment. SpringHill Suites proves a simple suite-based offering. The Marriott endorsement of these value brands very likely does tarnish the Marriott brand, although there are so many forces driving the Marriott brand that it is hard to isolate the impact of the endorsement strategy.

The value of the Marriott brand endorsement is significant. Developers, hotel operators, and communities receive Courtyard, Fairfield Inn, and SpringHill proposals favorably because they realize that Marriott will stand behind the concept. Furthermore, the expensive and difficult task of attracting new travelers to try the hotels is reduced, because the Marriott brand reduces the risk of an unknown brand and the reward program is a driver for all the hotels visibly connected to Marriott. Even now, with the three brands well established, studies have shown that occupancy would be meaningfully reduced without the Marriott endorsement.

Three factors reduce the damage to the Marriott brand from its endorsement of "low-end" hotel brands. First, in each case, the endorsed offerings are distinct from the flagship Marriott hotels, so expectations are managed with different locations, amenities, and look and feel. Second, there are two Marriott brands—Marriott hotels and the Marriott organization. The endorsement by Marriott clearly indicates that the Marriott organization is standing behind Courtyard, Fairfield Inn, and SpringHill Suites, not the Marriott hotels. Third, the Marriott core identity elements of consistency and friendliness work in all the markets and provide a bridge between the brands.

The Marriott endorsement strategy can be contrasted to Holiday Inn's use of descriptors and subbrands to distinguish offerings: Holiday Inn Select (vs. Courtyard), Holiday Inn Express (vs. Fairfield Inn), and Holiday Family Suite Resorts (vs. SpringHill Suites). With less distance be-

FIGURE 8-2
A PARTIAL MARRIOTT BRAND ARCHITECTURE

A Partial Marriott Brand Architecture

Brand		Position
Ritz-Carlton	THE RITZ-CARLTON®	Personalized service, prestige
Marriott Hotels & Resorts	**Marriott.** HOTELS & RESORTS	Upscale, premium, fine dining
Courtyard by Marriott	COURTYARD® Marriott	For business travelers
Fairfield Inn by Marriott	FAIRFIELD INN® Marriott	Consistent quality, continental breakfast

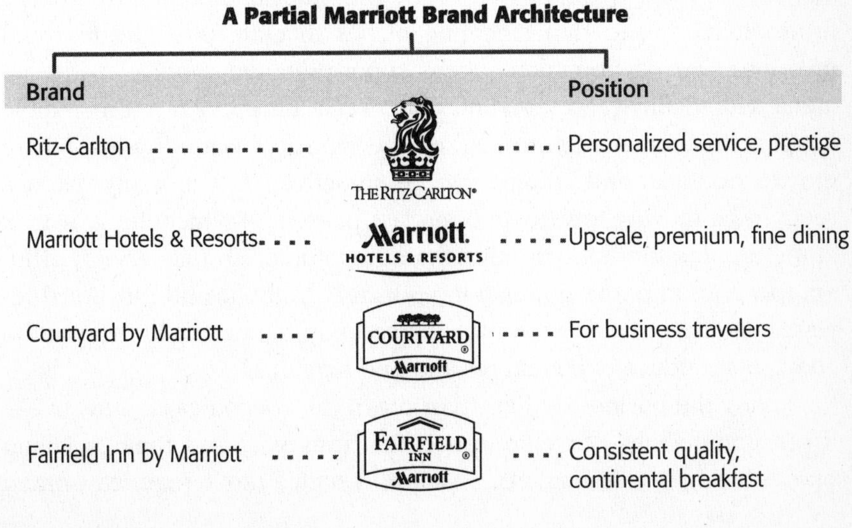

tween the Holiday Inn and value hotel brands than at Marriott, the tendency for confusion was far greater.

THE VERTICAL BRAND EXTENSION

Many mainstream, premium brands face hostile markets with debilitating overcapacity, shrinking margins, and dismal growth prospects. It occurs across industries from personal computers to airlines, banking, automobiles, telecommunications, canned soup, golf courses, and on and on. Competitors proliferate. Some enter from adjacent categories seeking to leverage their brand and others enter from different geographies seeking the scale of a regional or global player. Especially in the packaged goods arena, private-label brands—once a negligible niche player limited to low-priced, shoddy products—are now often competitive in quality.

Many of these competitors, from ambitious leaders wanting to dominate to struggling third- or fourth-place brands wanting to survive, begin to emphasize price promotions and sales events instead of product. As a result, brand loyalty erodes as customers focus on features and price. It becomes harder to maintain the historical brand price premium without seeing a fall, sometimes a dramatic one, in market share. The whole process is accentuated by customers and retailers who forcefully demand lower prices.

With the mainstream market of the premium brands turning hostile, firms often look to two emerging niches that are often healthy and growing. One is upmarket where super-premium brands reside, an arena with vitality (and sometimes buzz) plus attractive if not incredible margins. The other is downmarket, the world of value brands, where growth potential and volume can be attractive. In fact, many markets seem to be moving toward an hourglass pattern, in which the growth is at the top and the bottom rather than the middle. An increasingly affluent top portion of the population seeks the symbolic and functional rewards of their status, while an increasingly squeezed lower portion attempts to reduce expenditures and find bargains.

Moving the business either up or down thus becomes an attractive—if not compelling—strategic option for firms who see their premium brands facing hostile markets. To support such a move requires a brand strategy, and one obvious option is to vertically extend an existing brand. However, significant risks make vertical brand extensions one of the most difficult brand portfolio challenges. In this chapter, these risks will be detailed and strategies to reduce them will be discussed.

The Vertical Extension Decision

Moving a business into either a higher or lower market usually represents a critical strategic decision, one that should not be made casually. It is not just about a brand strategy; there are two other dimensions to consider. Figure 8-3, which draws on the credibility footprint introduced in Chapter 3, portrays the vertical extension decision dimensions.

The first dimension is the market opportunity. There needs to be a realistic appraisal of the market's attractiveness with a particular eye on customer trends; the quality, vitality, and commitment of competitors; and the likely margins that will emerge. Too many firms see strategic initiatives fail because they exaggerated customer trends, underestimated competition, or failed to anticipate margin pressures.

The second is the firm's ability to compete. To compete successfully in both upmarket and downmarket arenas often requires a certain organizational culture, systems, structure, and people. Can the firm develop the needed skills and assets and adapt its organization to be successful?

At the value end, the organization needs to develop a sustainable cost advantage, or the business will be vulnerable. Recall the efforts of airlines with a high cost structure and full-service culture to compete with the low-cost carriers such as Southwest. Shuttle by United was one of many that simply could not develop the cost structure and culture needed to compete.

At the super-premium end, it is necessary to deliver a sustainable point of differentiation. If one thing is known about business strategy, it is that offerings which are undifferentiated or lack customer relevance will probably fail, no matter how strong the market and the supporting brand strategy are. The firm must also be willing and able to deliver the expected quality level. The Maxwell House Private Collection, an effort to break into gourmet coffee in the late 1980s, failed after three years because the firm cut corners. It roasted the beans the same way it roasted its regular line, using large ovens, and did not keep them fresh on the shelf. The compromised quality that resulted was simply unacceptable.

The third dimension is the brand strategy. There needs to be brand

FIGURE 8-3
THE VERTICAL EXTENSION DECISION

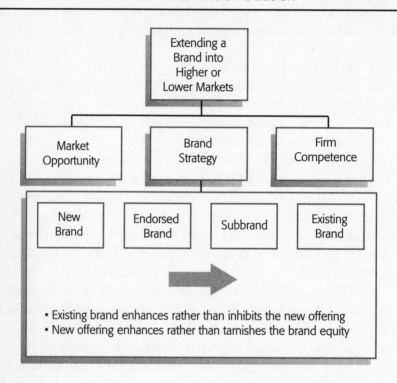

credibility in the new space. To achieve that goal there are usually four strategy options, which are modeled by the relationship spectrum introduced in Chapter 2. The use of an existing brand always requires the least investment. When the brand would be placed under risk or would not be successful in the new context, however, using a subbrand, endorsed brand, or new brand strategy can distance the new offering.

The selection among the four options will depend on the impact of the existing brand on the offering. If the existing brand will enhance the offering, and if it has no associations that will detract or inhibit, then the strategy can move to the right toward the existing brand option. The choice also depends on the impact of the offering on the brand equity. To the extent that the new offering will enhance the brand and not generate associations inconsistent with the brand identity, the pressure for separation will be less and the strategy can move left.

We will now take a closer look at both the opportunities and risks of vertical brand extensions, as summarized in Figure 8-4.

MOVING THE BRAND DOWN

In the face of maturing markets that exhibit anemic growth or even decline, there is a search for growth. Finding a source of growth can be an imperative if the scale of operations is threatened. When volume declines, manufacturing, distribution, and marketing may be in danger of becoming inefficient, and profitability thus is strained further. One source of growth is often the value market, whose frequently considerable vitality is driven by value-seeking customers, value retailers, and new technologies.

More and more markets, from tires to clothes to computers, are seeing a growing value segment. One driver is price-sensitive customers. In these markets, a significant number of buyers are turning from prestige and luxury to lower-cost brands that deliver acceptable quality and features. In part, this is caused in some contexts by the buyers being conditioned to price deals and promotions. As a result, perceived differentiation is reduced for the value-seeking segment, and the relevance of price is elevated. Another driver is simple economics. Especially when the economy becomes soft or worse, budget squeezes often make conserving money a family imperative.

A second and related contributor to the growth of value segments is a set of new channels that typically have a lower cost structure, use aggressive everyday pricing, and freely use private-label goods. Specialty superstores such as Home Depot, Circuit City, and Office Depot, in addition to chains like Target and Wal-Mart, have leveraged their singular buying power for consumers interested in an individual product category. Direct marketing from Dell and others has exploded in the past decade, in part because of the Internet, and these companies have consistently used their low cost structure to reduce prices. These retailers not only increase the saliency and availability of value merchandise but also put pressure on manufacturers to reduce prices.

A third driving force is technological change that creates a new generation of an offering with an inherently lower cost structure. Gillette

FIGURE 8-4
RISKS OF VERTICAL EXTENSIONS

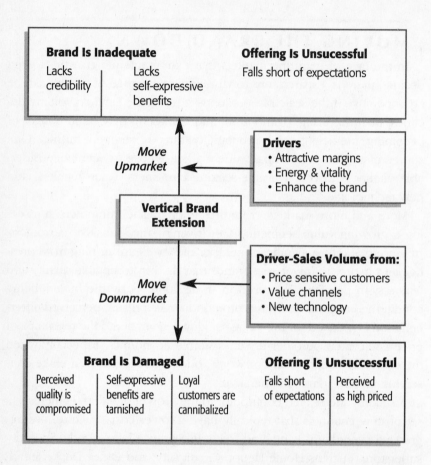

Good News disposable razor blades, Fuji Quicksnap disposable cameras, and Crest SpinBrush battery-powered toothbrushes each represent a value category with a price structure that is significantly less than the competing technologies they replaced.

These driving factors represent a major paradigm shift. The old assumptions do not hold any longer, and there is enormous pressure to participate at the low end. For example, John Deere makes a lawn tractor that it sells through full-service dealers. Although the price points in this channel have not eroded, volume retailers such as Home Depot are now serving a large and growing portion of the market, featuring products being sold at half the prices that John Deere commands. Thus, John Deere needs to find a way to participate in this new channel or accept a declining share of the market and a reduction in its scale economies. The problem that John Deere and many others face is how to do this without damaging the brand's accumulated brand equity. The approach in the case of John Deere is to offer Scott's, manufactured by John Deere, a brand with a weak endorsement in that "manufactured by" represents less of a commitment than "from John Deere."

Moving a Brand Down Is Easy, But Risky

Mountain bikers have discovered that although going down is much easier than going up, it usually creates a challenge of recapturing the vertical. Like mountain bikers, brands move down easily, sometimes inadvertently. And like mountain bikers, brands find that there are problems and challenges in returning to the top. The biggest challenge of accessing a value market is to avoid harming the brand, particularly by affecting its perceived quality associations, self-expressive benefits, and ability to retain existing premium customers in the face of a value entry.

The problem is that moving down affects perceptions of the brand—perhaps even more significantly than other brand management options. Psychologists have documented the fact that people are influenced much more by unfavorable information than by favorable information. Initial negative information about a person, for example, is resistant to subsequent positive information, whereas an initial good impression is much more likely to be altered by subsequent negative interactions. The use of negative political ads suggests that politicians are putting these findings to work.

Similar results have been found in more traditional marketing research contexts. For example, Motley and Reddy presented consumers with repositioning statements for Saks (a prestige department store) and for Kmart (a discount department store).[2] The statements described the store as either very upscale, very downscale, or in between. Results indicated that attitudes toward Kmart were not affected by the statements, even when the store was described as very upscale. However, attitudes toward Saks were influenced when it was associated not only with the downscale depiction, but also with the in-between portrayal. In another study, Arndt found that negative word of mouth had twice the impact on purchase intentions than did positive word of mouth.[3]

A companion risk is that the brand's ability to deliver self-expressive benefits may be reduced. Whether the product is water, high-end resorts, cars, or banking services, self-expressive brands are usually tied not only to quality products but also to exclusivity. When the brand is used in a downscale setting and more people (common folk if not the riff-raff) are using it, the prestige will fade. If Tiffany allowed the blue box to be used by department stores, for example, the symbol of giving a Tiffany gift would be tarnished.

A value entry can also create a cannibalization problem. Kodak Funtime film was an effort to provide a value entry to compete with alternatives to the Kodak line of film products. The problem was that its volume came not from the price brands, but from Kodak film loyalists. Because it was virtually impossible for a price brand to avoid staying at a price below any Kodak product, price buyers were not attracted to the Kodak Funtime product. Instead of attacking competitors, it ended up attacking Kodak and was quickly killed off. Gillette wanted a value entry in shaving cream and considered extending the Gillette Good News disposable razor line, but feared similar cannibalization.

Another challenge is the failure risk. A value offering may fail because customers expect that it may be relatively high priced. If Marriott were to enter the value market with the Marriott brand instead of the Marriott-endorsed Fairfield Inn brand, customers may have suspected (probably correctly) that the offering would be more expensive than its competitors. If price is a key driver in this value market, that would be a problem. With a Marriott endorsement the perception may still be there, but its impact would likely be reduced.

There can also be an expectation problem when the value entry is perceived to be inconsistent with the quality expected from the brand. The Cadillac Cimarron value entry was a thinly disguised economy Chevrolet that bombed. Efforts by Porsche to go downscale with models such as the 914 (which used a Volkswagen engine) or the 924 (which put the engine in the front) met similar fates. Porsche finally succeeded with the Porsche Boxster, which was perceived to be true to the Porsche heritage. This is another lesson, if one is needed, that the substance behind the brand cannot disappoint.

There are a variety of strategies to deal with these risks, as figure 8–5 suggests. One bypasses the risks by walking away from the premium

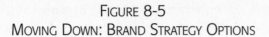

FIGURE 8-5
MOVING DOWN: BRAND STRATEGY OPTIONS

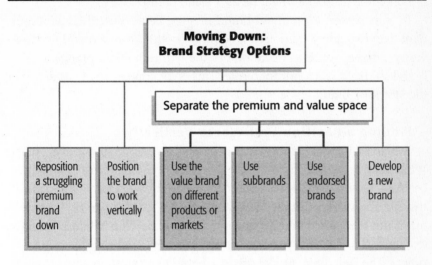

space and repositioning an existing struggling brand as a value brand—the logic being that there is no significant brand equity to be lost. Another approach is to position the brand so it works across price points, because it does not involve products that have low quality.

Other options seek to separate the brand's entries in the value and premium spaces. Using the brand as a value brand but only in adjacent product classes or different markets, using subbrands and endorsed brands, creating different brand personalities are all ways to create this kind of separation. A new separate brand is the ultimate option and provides the maximum protection to the brand.

Repositioning a Struggling Premium Brand Down

If a premium brand is struggling, a better use of its equity may be to compete in the value market. If, for example, the brand is a weak third or fourth player in its market with few prospects of moving up, a value play may have a higher long-term potential. The same logic applies if a premium brand has suffered an image setback, like Schlitz beer did after a disastrous effort to reduce production costs resulted in a compromised perceived quality. Efforts to recover its premium image were unsuccessful, and the only option was to have Schlitz become a price brand. If resuscitating a damaged brand is excessively expensive or even infeasible, the only role available might be as a value brand.

In some cases, a premium brand may be better described as redundant than struggling (although it could be both). From a brand portfolio view, it makes sense to make one of the two redundant brands a value brand so that it has a portfolio role. This is, of course, what GE did with the Hotpoint brand.

Finding a Position that Works Vertically

A brand's image, identity, and position can help it span price points. What must be avoided is vertically extending a brand whose quality perceptions or self-expressive benefits are driven by exclusivity and price. Instead, the value position should represent a smaller size or fewer features, but the same inherent quality and essence. The Virgin brand, for example, is based on a personality that can be effective at different price points. The Dell direct model drives a brand that can span a wide variety of equipment and services. BMW also works over a wide vertical span because its identity of being the ultimate driving machine (a car that is responsive and fun to drive) applies to all of its models.

Sony is able to span price points in part because its position on digital convergence, innovation, and fun (the kid in all of us) can be applied at multiple price points. Sony makes relatively high-end television sets and relatively low-end audio equipment; its Walkmans alone span an enormous price range. Yet, as noted in Chapter 5, one reason why Sony is still one of the top brands in the world is that customers believe its philosophy can be applied at the premium and value levels. At the low-price end, Sony is given credit for having the best value offering. Clearly, the absence of a value brand or subbrand is a risk for Sony, but the fact that its brand has thrived is instructive. (Perhaps to be safe, Sony is dialing up the use of the Aiwa brand, in which it has a significant investment, to brand value categories.)

A compelling business model can also drive a firm to take some risks with the brand. Mercedes was criticized for introducing its 190 model, which costs around $30,000, because it might jeopardize the significant self-expressive benefits that the brand had delivered, especially in the U.S. marketplace. However, the hard reality was that Mercedes in the long run could not sell enough cars to support its advertising and dealer structure without venturing downscale. In addition, its customer profile was aging, and it needed to attract younger buyers. The business model dictated taking some risks—and it worked. Sales were robust, and the Mercedes brand was not damaged, in part because the brand was repositioned. The status dimension of the brand was dialed down in favor of emphasizing quality, an identity that worked at all price points.

Using the Value Entry for a Different Product Class or Market

One way to separate the value entry from the premium brand context is to use the branded value entry for a different product class. Another is to use it in a very different market.

The risk involved in using a premium brand in a value segment is reduced when multiple product classes are involved. GE, which no longer makes small appliances, has given Wal-Mart the exclusive right to put the GE name on small appliances within its stores, where the GE premium large appliance line is sold. The risk that appearing in Wal-Mart at a relatively low price with conventional products will tarnish the GE large appliance brand is reduced by the fact that it is in a different (albeit adjacent) category. Also, because the exposure is limited to Wal-Mart, an important GE customer, some controls over its presentation may exist. It is still a case of drawing down some brand equity in order to achieve marginal sales and profits and to strengthen a relationship with a key retailer.

There is some experimental evidence that value extensions in different product classes reduce the risks to the brand. For example, Keller and Aaker found that the perceived quality of a brand of potato chips was not affected by its extension to cookies or ice cream, even when the extension was described as not well accepted because of taste and texture.[4] Loken and John found that an extension of a shampoo brand to an inferior tissue product did not affect the perceived quality of the shampoo, but only if respondents were first asked if the extension was representative of the brand.[5] The implication is that customers can separate the brand's identity in two product classes but may need help doing so, perhaps through careful positioning efforts. If the extension is far afield (for example, Coca-Cola clothes), the risk of transferring a quality impression is reduced, but there is also the danger that the brand will not contribute anything in the new context and may even make customers feel uncomfortable.

Aiming at a different market will not only provide a point of distinction but reduce the image-tarnishing risk, because customers of the parent brand will be less likely to be exposed to the new offering. The mainstream offering of an upscale health chain, for example, could be for a younger clientele or focus on a small city market, leaving the large cities for the parent brand. In either case, the core loyal customers will be unlikely to be exposed to the extension.

Using Subbrands

Subbrands have the potential to permit a brand's entry into an emerging low-end market while reducing the threat of cannibalization and image damage. The job of the subbrand is to reduce these dangers by distinguishing the downscale subbrand from the parent brand. This job is more feasible when the value offering itself is very distinctive and when the subbrand is given its own personality.

There is evidence that subbrands do help to insulate the value offering. In one study, Aaker and Markey explored a toilet paper extension from Kleenex and a low-calorie orange juice from Snapple fruit drinks.[6] In each case, an inferior extension (a hard, coarse toilet paper and a watery orange juice) affected attitudes toward the parent brands *unless* a subbrand was used. The subbrand served to protect the parent brand from the inferior performance of the extension.

The separation between the premium brand and the subbrand is enhanced when the latter offering is qualitatively different or is designed for a different segment. Sainsbury, the UK retailer, launched its Savacentre format to emphasize a value position. Martha Stewart Everyday provides a separation for the Kmart line of merchandise from the other Martha Stewart offerings and activities. Masterlock has a "Lockers and Bikes" line of lighter locks; by clearly reflecting a restricted application for which a different design would be appropriate, the subbrand helps create a separation and manages expectations. Fender makes high-quality electric guitars that sell at premium prices, but it also sells a "starter" electric guitar through its Squier Mini subbrand for much less. In this case, the subbrand reflects a clearly defined market segment for which a value product is appropriate.

The absence of size or features can be suggested by a descriptor. For example, a convenience store whose expansive offering includes a bakery, fast food, and specialty coffee has a need for an offering on small sites. A solution would be to add Express or Junior or Mini to denote that it is in the family, but is not the complete offering. Pizza Hut uses the brand Pizza Hut Express for its outlets with limited menus and no table service.

The goal of the value descriptor is to manage expectations and to position the offering within the value spectrum. If an offering is clearly positioned with a subbrand as a value product, it will be evaluated with respect to other value products and has the potential to be the best of this group of products. Gillette Good News disposable razors may be far from "the best a man can get" (the promise of Gillette), but they are positioned to be the best of the disposable subcategory.

The challenge is to protect and separate the premium position while introducing a value subbrand. One strategy is to simultaneously elevate the premium brand or create a super-premium subbrand by introducing an enhanced offering, perhaps with a branded differentiator. The value entry could actually help in this effort by providing a reference point that flatters the new premium position. A line of tools, for example, might be upgraded and given a subbrand name such as ProChoice while the firm also introduces a thrifty subbrand, the HomeMaster. In essence, the tactic is to simultaneously move the brand up *and* down. The down-level subbrand Gillette Good News works in part because the rest of the razor line is positioned with a Gillette Mach3 that elevates the Gillette brand; it is easier to separate Good News from Mach3 than from Gillette.

Using Endorsed Brands

An endorsed brand provides more separation from the parent brand than does a subbrand. Marriott, for example, was able to use an endorsed brand strategy to help it move into value arenas. But this approach still involves risks to the brand due to the visible connection between the parent brand and the value entry, which can lead to both cannibalization and image erosion.

The separation options (whether they use endorsed brands or subbrands) will work best when there can be physical, tangible differences between the brands. When the product is more difficult to distinguish because key product characteristics are not visible, the problem is more severe. For products like motor oil, film, or detergents, it can be helpful to create different personalities supported by logos, color, and brand-building efforts to provide the necessary separation. In contrast, Court-yard by Marriott has a consistent, differentiated offering. Similarly, the MINI Cooper from BMW (a retro-looking, funky, tiny car) is visually and functionally so different from the mainstream BMW line that the risk is reduced.

Creating a Different Personality: The Parent-Child Relationship

Especially when a value offering is not visibly different from the pre-mium offering, the separation can be made or reinforced by the brand personality. In that regard, conceptualizing a parent-child relationship as a metaphor for the positioning of the value brand can be extremely powerful as a way to reduce the risks of cannibalization and image tar-nishing. The endorsed brand or subbrand could be a child (either son or daughter) of the parent brand (the father or mother), one who cannot yet afford or appreciate the better version.

A parent brand such as John Deere might have a personality charac-terized as genuine, real, caring, honest, and hardworking with small-town values. Perhaps it is also competent and successful. The son of this brand (such as Scott by John Deere) could have many of these same characteristics. He could be hardworking, honest, and genuine. Further, he will have the potential to be competent and successful—after all, he is a chip off the old block.

The son, a different generation, could also be different in many re-spects from the father. He would likely be drawn to simpler, less expen-sive options, perhaps looking to move up as he accumulated money over time. With respect to a personality profile, the son is likely to have more youth, vitality, and interest in fun times. The son of a motorcycle brand, for example, might be expected to be cuter, more fun, and less expensive than that of the father. For clothes, a son might be sponta-neous and fun loving, someone with whom you would enjoy spending time, perhaps similar to the personality of the Jolly Green Giant "Little Sprout" character. For a sports car or mountaineering line, the son might have a reckless, living-on-the-edge element to him that might fit the line and the user imagery. In any case, the personality of the son offers a point of distinction from the parent brand and a way to connect with a target market.

In an effort to make Prada (upscale apparel, shoes, and accessories for men and women, from the designer Miuccia Prada) more accessible to a wider customer base, a youthful line, Miu Miu (the designer's nickname), was launched in 1993. Prada stands for a membership in an exclusive, cool, and affluent society. Miu Miu, in contrast, represents a youthful "bad girl" personality with fashions that are whimsical—sometimes saucy and sometimes innocent. The connection is a linked brand, as everyone interested in fashion knows that they are strongly tied through the brand name.

A New Brand

The ultimate separation and thus protection of the parent premium brand is to create an entirely new stand-alone brand. Gap stores, the retailer of distinctive casual clothing, faced competitors who were targeting value-conscious customers by offering Gaplike fashions for 20 to 30 percent less. To compete against this threat, in 1993 Gap tested warehouse-style outlets, called Gap Warehouse, selling a broad array of casual clothing at competitive prices. The problem was that the clothing was too similar to what was being sold at the Gap and cannibalization and image dilution became serious risks. As a result, a decision was made a year later to change the name to Old Navy, which then became one of the fastest-growing retail concepts in history.

Few organizations, though, can afford to introduce a truly new brand—particularly at the value end, where cost considerations make it difficult to support a brand-building effort. It is simply too difficult and too costly. If the organization has an established brand that is either dormant, redundant, or underused, however, it could be drafted as the value brand. Recall that GE in its appliance business took the brand Hotpoint (which GE owned) off the shelf and made it their value brand. The Hotpoint brand was redundant because GE was the flagship premium brand, but it had enough recognition, credibility, and positive feelings in the durable space that it was viable with minimal brand-building support.

MOVING A BRAND UP

Growth at the top of the market as suggested by Figure 8-4 is driven in part by increasing affluence in the developed countries during the last few decades. Even with economies struggling, the top statistical echelon has prospered and has money to spend. Further, these top wealth holders have the luxury of looking to emotional and self-expressive benefits that fuel the super-premium purchases in most markets. To focus only on functional options becomes unrewarding and boring.

Paradoxically, even those customers who are being squeezed financially seek out opportunities for indulgence. Those who cannot afford a large home or a fancy car can go to Starbucks, visit Disneyland, or buy an upscale piece of carpentry equipment, even though rationally such purchases might be extravagant. Many super-premium offerings, though very highly priced relative to their product options, are small parts of a customer's monthly or annual budget.

While the motivation for a firm to move into the value market is to obtain volume, the motivation to move up is very different. Although growth in sales might be welcome, the primary attraction is to access higher margins, provide vitality to the brand and the business, and enhance the brand by associating it with a higher-quality, more prestigious offering. Microbreweries, designer coffees, upscale waters, luxury cars, decorator appliances, and specialty magazines all represent attractive target niches that are less price sensitive than the larger market center and are capable of injecting interest into a tired category or brand.

Enhanced Margins

Firms are willing to invest in the super-premium market because too often, their core premium business faces a squeeze on its price and margins. At the same time, margins in a super-premium sector where there is real innovation, differentation, and energy can be breathtaking. One oil company's super-premium lubricant brand was responsible for roughly 5 percent of sales, but more than 90 percent of the profits of the business. Accessing this source of margins often can be more than attractive; it can be an imperative.

Consider the Whirlpool experience.[7] Whirlpool introduced the Whirlpool Duet washer and dryer set with rounded styling, room for nearly two dozen bath towels, and a computer that optimizes the washing and drying process to save time, save energy, protect fabrics, and improve the cleaning. Priced at a breathtaking three times as much as the average Whirlpool washer and dryer set, it got off to a fast start, doing twice the hoped-for sales. And the buyers were not the wealthy fringe, but solid middle-class customers. This high end became the point of attack for Whirlpool.

Energy and Vitality

Customers and firms are attracted to the very high end of the market because that is where all the interest and vitality of the category resides. Premium brands usually reside in mature, boring contexts that lack not only energy but also points of differentiation. Canned coffees in the supermarket, even the premium brands, are perceived as mundane, mature, and uninteresting. Designer roasted coffee and Starbucks stores, in contrast, are offerings that touch people's values and lifestyles and offer significant self-expressive benefits.

The fact is that in many categories, innovation and quality "so high it gets noticed" occur at the high end. With margins squeezed, the premium brands in the mature categories tend to avoid meaningful innovation and value-added branded differentiators, seeking instead to watch costs and protect the margins that remain. However, super-premium products such as the GE Profile or Whirlpool Duet often become hotbeds of innovation, fueling new avenues of brand personality, customer relationships, and differentiation. The innovation is stimulated in part by the fact that small organizations (sometimes within large firms) are involved, and in part because the large margins help pay for creating and marketing new products.

Enhancing the Brand

Another key motivation for creating an upscale brand entry is to enhance the credibility and prestige of the brand in the premium marketplace. When the super-premium entry can play a branded energizer or even a silver bullet role, the potential profitability of the new brand may be of secondary importance or even irrelevant.

Gallo is a rare example of a brand that has moved itself sharply upward. Subbrands and endorsed brands played a key role. To break out of the jug wine category in the United States, it introduced the Ernest and Julio Gallo Varietals, a line of moderately priced, corked wines. This served to strengthen Gallo's position in the value end of the market and started its effort to become a respected winemaker, a goal of the Gallo family. Acquiring a competitor in the jug wine business allowed the family to withdraw the Gallo brand from that market. The firm then relentlessly put out better and better wines, under brands such as Ernest & Julio Gallo Coastal Vineyard, Gallo of Sonoma, and the shadow-endorsed Turning Leaf and Sycamore Canyon. Gallo of Sonoma and Sycamore Canyon are primarily sold to restaurants, where objective quality and awards are valued more than brand legacy. Restaurant exposure to the Gallo brand added credibility to help the tough transition to a top-rated wine.

Consider the role that ultra-luxury cars play for their corporate brands who play a shadow endorser role. Both BMW with its new Rolls-Royce design and DaimlerChrysler with its Maybach are demonstrating their ability to design a car with incredible features and performance that can compete at the most prestigious levels. Both represent opportunities to interject news and buzz into a corporate brand that exists in a cluttered category.

The Risks of Moving Upscale

There are some risks of damaging the core brand when moving up, although much less than when moving it down. One is that the offering may fail because the firm lacks the capability of delivering a high-end experience, in part because it lacks the needed assets and supporting organizational culture. A failed effort that is noticed and remembered can damage the brand. Success also has risks in that the super-premium version can, by comparison, make the core brand look more ordinary than it was previously perceived as being. The scotch drinker may be less likely to believe that Johnnie Walker Red represents the best experience with Johnnie Walker Black Label available.

A more serious risk, noted in Figure 8-4, is that the brand trying to move upscale simply cannot pull it off even with a suitable offering. The brand may lack credibility in its ability to deliver the necessary perceived quality or functional benefits. The organization behind the brand is not perceived to have a commitment to the super-premium quality level. Even the use of visible subbrands and brand differentiators may not be enough to counter the brand's legacy position.

In most cases, it is difficult for the brand to deliver self-expressive benefits, which often drive the super-premium arena. Consider Holiday Inn's effort to create a high-end hotel, the Crowne Plaza endorsed by Holiday Inn. The strong image of Holiday Inn as being a familiar, comfortable, unpretentious hotel was a real handicap. Despite years of effort and considerable resources, Holiday Inn finally had to give up, drop the Holiday Inn connection, and let Crowne Plaza go on its own. Gallo showed that a brand can be moved up, but the fact that the largest winery with enormous resources had to struggle over decades (and that some buyers will never be won over) also illustrates the difficulty of the task.

Moving Up Brand Options

How can brands "move up" to take advantage of growth and get out from under oppressive margin pressures? The list of options is shorter when moving up than when moving down. In particular, while repositioning a brand down is nearly always feasible, repositioning a brand up is "a huff and a puff" (as a noted mountain biker once said about a steep climb). The legacy of an established position with respect to perceived quality and self-expressive benefits is nearly impossible to overcome.

An endorsed brand is rarely a viable option when attempting to brand an upscale offering. Endorsed brands do provide a greater degree of separation, so they have the advantage of having a weaker link to the offering. However, the nature of an endorsement is a problem. An endorsement identifies the organization behind the offering—its values, programs, and people. It affirms that the offering will live up to the standards of the organization. The endorsement then will usually become a liability, because it will inhibit the realization of self-expressive benefits and will not reassure customers that the super-premium quality level will be achieved. This was certainly true in the case of Crowne Plaza by Holiday Inn.

An endorsement may be more viable if it is a shadow endorsement, which will not get in the way of self-expressive benefits, or if it is a delayed endorsement. For example, Coleman, a leading camping equipment brand, had an image of being heavy and cumbersome that inhibited its desire to move upmarket to backpacking equipment.[8] Coleman launched the stand-alone Peak 1 brand, which was more successful in part because it did not have the Coleman associations. A few years

FIGURE 8-6
MOVING UP: BRAND STRATEGY OPTIONS

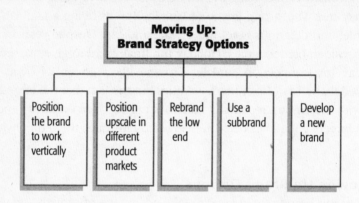

later, after the new brand had been established, the Coleman name was added to Peak 1 in order to enhance the Coleman brand.

The most viable strategies to consider for moving a brand upscale are as follows:

- Position the brand to work vertically
- Position the brand as a super-premium one with different products or in different markets
- Rebranding the low end
- Use a subbrand
- Develop a new brand

Finding a Position that Works Vertically

A brand can have or develop a position that can work vertically as noted above. The essence needs to work across premium, super-premium, and value markets. The brands mentioned above, such as BMW (the ultimate driving machine), Virgin (facing up to industry leaders like British Air with over-the-top features and service), Dell (the direct model), Sony (the digital dream kids) all have this quality. Of course, moving up is still a challenge, but it would be nearly impossible if the position was not compatible with the highest quality.

A brand will tend to have the ability to stretch vertically if its credibility is tied to the entire product class. Uncle Ben's rice, for example, is perceived to be a brand associated with a basic product that can participate in gourmet recipes. Thus, Uncle Ben's was successful with its Uncle Ben's Country Inn rice dishes, which include Rice Alfredo Homestyle Pilaf and Herbal Rice Au Gratin. The Country Inn subbrand indicates that the recipes are inspired by the finest inns and may even suggest a relative who is associated with interesting country restaurants. In contrast, Rice-A-Roni is a product used in everyday meals; in fact, it is often the core part of the meal, with a variety of flavors. Thus the effort to participate in an upscale product with Rice-A-Roni Savory Classics was not successful, because the Rice-A-Roni name was too much of a drag.

Involving a Different Product Class or Market

A brand can sometimes be leveraged into a super-premium arena more easily if a different product class or market is used. The fact that the brand is moving up is not so obvious, and the original product class can become an asset in another context.

Branding New-Generation Products

A brand portfolio problem that has similarities to those encountered when moving into an upscale space occurs when a new version of an offering involves a new technology or significant new features or benefits. Because existing brands might have credibility issues with a dramatic product advance, it might be necessary to signal the advance with a new subbrand, an endorsed brand, or even a new master brand. The Gillette Mach3 represented such a significant technological advance over the then premium subbrand, Gillette Sensor, that a completely new subbrand was justified. To turn itself around, the struggling Tampax introduced Tampax Pearl, a brand with significant advances that was expected to sell at a 40 percent premium.

Several branding options are relevant to the new-generation context. One is to use the existing brand with a "new and improved" story added to it. Another is to use a branded differentiator to give credibility to something new, like the Pentium with MMX. Another is to use a subbrand that can be adapted to reflect

(continued on next page)

---

a new generation without creating a new name (Intel has rolled out the Pentium Pro, Pentium II, III, IV, and so on). The Air Jordan XVII comes in a metallic briefcase along with a CD and costs over $200 a pair. When the Gillette Mach3 was improved, the brand became the Gillette Mach3 Turbo.

A series of questions can help structure the brand portfolio issues associated with the creation of new-generation technology:

- How new is the technology? Intel's Itanium, which went from a 32-bit device to a 64-bit device, clearly was a significant change and warranted a new name.
- Will the next-generation technology be around long enough to justify the brand-building effort and investment?
- How ownable is the new technology or a version of it? There is a danger that a new technology can become generic, like personal computers or personal video recorders, and a brand is needed to own the technology or at least a version of it. Intel's Pentium was not such a major technological change, but a new name was justified because Intel needed a more ownable and controllable name than the Intel 586.

Positive answers to these questions would tend to justify movement to the right side of the (chapter 2) relationship spectrum, toward a new brand. The rule of parsimony should apply to this context; the fewer brands, the better. There should be a good reason to march down the relationship spectrum by creating and dialing up new brand names.

Samsonite, a premium brand that is the global leader in luggage, needed to create more visibility, expand its domain from luggage to travel, and enhance its image to be more of an upscale, prestigious, fashion-forward brand.[9] This task was difficult within the confines of luggage, so Samsonite stretched its brand to include travel-friendly, fashionable clothing and accessories—where fashion meets function. This "designer travelwear" was branded Samsonite Black Label, a subbrand that provided enough space from the hard luggage business in order to give Samsonite credibility in fashion clothing.

While Gallo is a value brand in the United States, Europe (where it does not have the jug wine legacy) is another story. Drawing on the three generations of the Gallo family, its California connection, and award-winning wines, Gallo has developed a solid mid- to high-end European position. The brands dial up the heritage with names like Ernest & Julio Gallo Wine Cellars and Ernest & Julio Gallo Coastal Vineyards.

Rebranding the Low End

When entering a premium space, the chances may improve if the lower end is rebranded, thus removing one driver of a value brand image. Gallo used the acquired Carlo Rossi brand for its low-end wines and phased out the Gallo name in that market. Samsonite used the acquired American Tourister brand to serve low-end, discount stores, and mass merchants; Samsonite was then reserved for channels associated with higher-end merchandise. Sony similarly has plans to transfer some of its value products to the Aiwa brand.

The Role of a Subbrand

Using a subbrand such as Coors Extra Gold or GE Profile to penetrate the high end has several advantages. First, it will almost always help the parent brand by associating it with higher-quality offerings and the prestige and credibility that go with them. The only danger is when the high-end brand implies that the parent premium brand is inferior by neglecting to provide a logical reason why the former is better than the latter. The easiest way to get around this is to have a visible point of difference or a branded differentiator. The original premium offering then becomes something less, not something of lower quality.

Second, the use of an existing brand, even with a subbrand, makes the brand-building task more feasible and less costly. Much of the expense of creating visibility and associations for a new brand name is reduced or avoided. It is potentially easier to associate Coors with a super-premium beer or GE with an upscale appliance than to start with a new name that must be established in the midst of the marketplace clutter.

A third advantage of an established brand is that its applicable associations and programs can help provide a value proposition. Customers of GE Profile know that they can access the GE customer service system, and Coors Gold customers recognize that the beer is manufactured by a major firm (and may know that it is connected to High Priority, the Coors program to fight breast cancer).

The basic problem with using a subbrand to move up is that the brand lacks credibility at the higher end. How can a credible claim be made that a premium subbrand under the sponsorship of a middle-tier brand can really meet the standards of a high-end market? This fundamental inconsistency makes moving a brand up very difficult. But it is not impossible. There are approaches that can work.

Create a silver bullet. The move up can be made more palatable when there is a silver bullet, either in the form of a branded differentiator or energizer, within the higher-end line to credibly make the case that the product can deliver. A visible flagship hotel in New York or London could conceivably have helped the Holiday Inn Crowne Plaza become a viable brand, for example. As noted in Chapter 6, Target has branded energizers in the form of architect Michael Graves and Mossimo Giannulli, who both have designed lines of branded products that have given Target a perceptual lift in the marketplace. A branded feature can be a vehicle to lift the upscale entry.

Use an upscale descriptor. A descriptor can signal an upscale offering in a way that is easy to remember and yet clearly separates it from the brand offering against which it is positioned. Upscale descriptive subbrands include names such as Special Edition, Premium, Select, Professional, Gold, or Platinum. Wineries use names like Private Reserve or Library Reserve or Limited Edition to capture the higher end, while airlines have labels like Connoisseur Class and the Red Carpet Club.

Position as the "value super-premium." In any well-established super-premium market, there can be room for one positioned at the bottom of the subcategory. There will be customers who would like the functional benefits of the product or service, but would take satisfaction from getting those benefits at a reduced price. In the case of 100 percent Arabica coffee beans, one option is to buy Safeway Select Estate whole coffee beans. They may not have the reliable quality of Starbucks or Peet's, but they will clearly have a price advantage. The challenge is to build a following so that the brand is viable. In the case of Safeway Select, getting on the shelf is not an issue, because Safeway controls the shelves.

Co-brand with a prestige brand. One way to credibly signal a high-end offering is to co-brand with a brand that already has prestige. For example, Philips created an upscale line of appliances working closely with the trendy designer tableware firm Alessi, which is itself associated with such top Italian designers as Alessandro Mendini. The line included a coffeemaker, a toaster, a kettle, and a juicer all with bold designs in vivid colors and priced at three times normal levels. The products were sold under the brand Philips-Alessi through exclusive interior channels.

Creating a New Brand

When the existing brand name is too much of a drag, the only feasible alternative is likely to be the creation of a stand-alone brand. For example, when Black & Decker created a line of tools for construction professionals, there was no mention of the Black & Decker brand because of the latter's association with do-it-yourself homeowners and, worse, with kitchen appliances. (A professional carpenter was not going to be attracted to or comfortable with a tool with the same brand name as a kitchen toaster, no matter how good it was.) Thus, the DeWalt brand was created. The DeWalt equipment is a cut above in terms of performance, bright yellow in contrast to the green of the Black & Decker line, and not visibly connected at all with Black & Decker.

Consider also Toyota's Lexus, Honda's Acura, and Nissan's Infiniti. In each case, the core brand—which signaled economy and simplicity rather than prestige, handling, and comfort—had the potential of preventing the new products from credibly occupying the upscale position.

The option of successfully introducing a new brand, however, is often either too costly or simply not feasible. Although the super-premium category will enjoy high margins, the sales volume is likely to be low, especially when there are several competing established brands. There is a considerable incentive, therefore, to look to alternatives that leverage existing brands.

Vertical brand extensions are, above all else, a strategic decision and need to be supported by a strategic analysis within the context of other options for the organization. Brand strategy is only one component of the decision, albeit a key one. It is difficult and risky to extend a brand vertically, but similar challenges apply to developing a new brand. Thus, the leveraging of existing brands using a vertical brand extension strategy should be explored, and there are role models of brands that have done it successfully.

QUESTIONS FOR DISCUSSION

1. Evaluate the health of your brand's market with respect to its future growth and margin. Would the future be more attractive and less threatening with an entry in the super-premium or value arenas?

2. Evaluate the super-premium or upscale markets by doing a customer and competitor analysis. How could a new entry be differentiated? How could existing brands be leveraged to enter that market?

3. Evaluate the value markets by doing a customer and competitor analysis. How could a new entry be differentiated? How could existing brands be leveraged to enter that market?

PART IV

Bringing Focus and Clarity to the Brand Portfolio

CHAPTER 9

LEVERAGING THE CORPORATE BRAND

Be distinct or extinct.

—TOM PETERS

If you cannot get rid of the family skeleton, you may as well make it dance.

—GEORGE BERNARD SHAW

DELL

Dell was founded in 1984 by Michael Dell on a simple concept—selling computers based on industry standards, assembled to order, directly to customers.* Never the only firm selling computers direct, Dell did emerge as superior on key components of the business model. Dell always seemed to be ahead in terms of efficiencies in logistics, distribution, and manufacturing, especially after it developed a volume advantage over its direct competitors.

A significant part of Dell's success was its ability to maintain leadership in sales and service systems. The absence of frustration in the Dell buying experience has led to the "Simple as Dell" promise. The service system, which features the next-day, on-site service pioneered by Dell in 1987, had periodic problems due to growth strains but generally has been exceptional over the years; Dell has won more than three hundred awards for its customer service and product quality. The net result has

---

* Information for this section was drawn from Dell annual reports, 2000, 2001, and 2002; "Dell Online," HBS Case 596-058; "Matching Dell," HBS Case 9-799-158; Andy Serwer, "Dell Does Dominating," *Fortune,* January 21, 2002, p. 71; Brad Stond, "Dell's New Toy," *Newsweek,* November 18, 2002; and an interview with Dell's global brand team, April 2003. Thanks to Scott Helbing, global brand manager of Dell, for helpful comments.

been 2002 sales of over $31 billion, up from $5 billion only six years earlier.

The direct-selling business model provides significant, visible advantages to the customer. First, because the computer is assembled after the order is received, it can be customized to exactly what the customer wants. Second, the firm can offer a value proposition based on the direct model; the mark-ups of retailers and other resellers are eliminated. Customers, especially business customers, understand that Dell's cost structure benefits from minimal inventory and warehousing costs—Dell turns inventory every four days. Third, because finished computers do not sit in warehouses or on retail shelves, the latest technology can be applied to each computer as it becomes available. Finally, in the direct model the customer interacts with the company, thereby allowing Dell's customer service values to be experienced. Roughly 90 percent of Dell's employees have some customer contact.

The Dell brand plays the major driver role in nearly all of the firm's offerings, in that it drives the purchase decisions and defines the use experience. The major Dell subbrands (Dimension and OptiFlex desktop computers, Inspiron and Latitude notebook computers, the Precision Workstation and Precision Mobile Workstation, and the PowerEdge Servers and the Power Vault Storage line) largely play a descriptive role, serving to define the scope of the Dell product footprint. At the end of the day, the customers are still buying Dell and its implementation of the direct model. As a result, these subbrands have received little brand-building attention.

To help address branding decisions going forward, Dell has conducted research about the power of subbrands in the space of computers and related products.[1] It found that the equity of subbrands in the high-tech space are remarkably weak in comparison to corporate brands. In fact, fewer that 12 percent of respondents even knew that VAIO was made by Sony, even though by attitude measures VAIO is one of the strongest notebook brands. (That does not mean that VAIO does not have worthwhile equity, of course, because Sony VAIO might be more impactful than a generic Sony notebook, but it still gives pause.) This finding is consistent with a much earlier Compaq study that found its Presario brand had far less equity than expected.[2]

Why should subbrands in the high-tech arena have low equity? First, corporate brands—such as Dell, HP, Sony, Canon, IBM, and Toshiba—

are so strong and extensively supported, especially during the early days of a category. The fact that Dell was going into notebooks was news—the Latitude brand was not. Second, the subbrands generally failed to develop a point of sustainable differentiation and lacked a brand personality. Branded features like TrackPoint from IBM and the personality of Apple's iMac were exceptions. Thus, there was really no reason for subbrands to get traction. It is not at all like the Doritos brand from Frito-Lay, a brand that has a personality and a point of difference from other snacks.

Organizationally, the central brand group at Dell took control of the proliferation of new brands. A business unit had to demonstrate to the brand group that a new subbrand had reason to exist. In Asia, for example, there was a need to provide a less expensive off-the-shelf offering that would not have the customized features associated with Dell. To protect the Dell brand, the SmartStep brand was introduced and applied across product lines. The name justification process was aided by an internal website that set forth new name criteria so managers could conclude for themselves whether their new brand would pass the role test.

The Dell brand worked for both business and individual clients. While Gateway and Apple both had colorful brand personalities that made some corporate buyers and users uncomfortable, the Dell persona was approachable but also serious, competent, and successful—very compatible with the corporate world, but also appealing to individuals.

While Dell has few brands or subbrands with equity or driver roles, there are branded differentiators in some markets. Substantial business customers could give their employees customized pages on the Dell website, called "Dell Premier Pages." There an employee could place orders (for models approved by his or her IT department), get discounted prices, track orders and inventory, and access contact information for the Dell account team. Further, companies with mission-critical computing environments could tap Dell's Premier Enterprise Services for advanced service competitive with that of IBM and others. The Dell Premier service program offered four service tiers (Platinum, Gold, Silver, and Bronze) so that customers could get the service level appropriate for them. The Premier service brand played a key role in providing a branded differentiator for an important market. Over time it was still useful, but got to be overused as it was stretched and lost some of its exclusivity and capacity of delivering self-expressive benefits. There is a question as to whether it was managed with discipline and strategic vision.

The Dell brand is both a corporate brand and a master product brand; thus, it represents both the corporation and its products and services. The role of the Dell corporate brand, like many corporate brands, is to provide trust and credibility to the Dell offerings based on the size, capability, heritage, and success of the organization over time. Certainly, trust and credibility are important, and this brand role is worthwhile. By reflecting the direct model, however, the Dell corporate brand does more—it provides a point of differentiation to the Dell product brand.

UNITED PARCEL SERVICE (UPS)

UPS was founded in 1907 as a messenger service in Seattle.[3] Twelve years later it became the United Parcel Service, and soon afterward it was serving the western United States with its now-familiar brown delivery trucks. However, it was not until the mid-1970s that UPS became a national delivery service. It was then positioned as a value option, with the goal of providing the "Best Service and Lowest Rates." In the mid-1980s, UPS entered the overnight air delivery business and, with a series of foreign acquisitions, improved its ability to offer international service.

In the mid-1990s, despite its expanded capabilities, UPS for many still stood for a U.S.-based, small-package ground delivery company. These boundaries increasingly restricted its ability to participate in important, growing market segments. Further, it was difficult to create customer partner relationships with such a narrowly defined product scope at a time when FedEx and DHS were perceived to be more of a global systems solutions alternative. Moreover, the signature solid brown trucks did not signal a global, contemporary firm.

UPS needed to radically energize and expand the corporate brand. Its goal was to become a global provider of distribution, logistics, and financial services, and to be a firm that companies looked to for global supply chain management. Toward that end, it introduced a host of new product brands, services, and programs that served to provide substance and branded energizers behind the new UPS.

The centerpiece of these new product brands was UPS Supply Chain Solutions, an umbrella product brand that includes a portfolio of branded

FIGURE 9-1
UPS ADVERTISEMENT

services designed to address customers' supply chain problems globally. This service group includes UPS Logistics, UPS Capital, and UPS Mail Innovations. UPS Logistics, founded in 1995, helps design and implement specialized supply chain systems that can include product labeling, product returns, and product repair. It can also provide warehouse and processing systems to deliver critical parts with time windows as short as one hour. UPS Capital offers financing solutions that include financing associated with export/import transactions, inventory, and working capital. UPS Mail Innovations helps use the U.S. postal services to reduce costs and improve service. These initiatives not only drove relatively high-margin service revenues but rather dramatically influenced the UPS brand.

UPS also needed to change its perception from that of a domestic company to that of a global one. Gaining credibility in the global space represents a real opportunity for UPS, because its major competitors have struggled and are far from owning it. Again, some branded initiatives and services have helped. One is the technology-driven UPS Worldport, a $1 billion expansion of the UPS hub in Louisville, Kentucky. With cameras reading UPS "smart labels," packages can be sorted and routed through the 122 miles of conveyers in minutes. In addition, there are branded package delivery services (such as UPS Worldwide Express and UPS SonicAir) that capture the firm's global service capability.

The challenge for UPS, like that facing many major heritage corporations, is to create energy and to appear contemporary while retaining the solid, reliable, comfortable familiar associations it has always enjoyed. In addressing that challenge, the UPS solid brown color was a liability. A temptation would be to make the traditional brown an accent in a contemporary colorful design. Instead, UPS turned it into a positive signal by associating it with the new expanded UPS organization, as exemplified by a series of advertising campaigns under the tagline, "What Can Brown Do for You?" Figure 9-1 shows a typical ad. Included in the campaign were some lighthearted commercials, such as one highlighting UPS's NASCAR sponsorship by suggesting that a driver race the "big, brown truck." In fact, "Brown" became an important brand as well as a symbol, and thus a liability was spun into an asset.

The redefinition of UPS is a business and branding success story. The firm in 2002 had sales of over $30 billion (up from around $20 billion in 1995), delivering about 6 percent of the U.S. gross national product. The nonpackage delivery portion of the company's business was well over $2 billion and growing sharply. UPS is a good example of the power of a corporate brand that serves as a master product brand.

This book so far has largely been about using brands in the context of brand portfolio strategy to achieve a business strategy goal. Strategic moves into new product-markets need to be supported by a branding strategy, which can involve new brands or subbrands or both. The use of new brands or subbrands can help a firm create or maintain relevance. Brands can increase their equity and health with branded differentiators or energizers. Or a firm can acquire branded customer franchises from other businesses, believing that internal growth may be slow or difficult.

In this chapter and the one that follows, the theme will instead be on generating focus and clarity in the brand portfolio, in part by supporting and leveraging a few brands. We here consider leverage of the corporate brand as a vehicle toward that end.

The corporate brand can play one of three roles. Of most significance is its potential in some contexts to be a master brand with a significant driver role. In fact, in the case of Dell, UPS, and others, it can been seen as the ultimate branded house, where the product brands consist largely of the corporate brand plus a descriptor. In the case of Sony, the corporate brand also serves as a master brand, spanning product classes but with the aid of strong subbrands. In both cases, the use of a corporate brand as a master brand maximizes such brand portfolio goals as generating leverage, synergy, and clarity. It also evokes the power and uniqueness of the corporation as an organization thereby creating differentiation for the product brand.

Another role for which the corporate brand is ideally suited is that of an endorser. Because it represents an organization that stands behind its products in spirit and substance, it can be a credible endorser that works at both a functional and emotional level. As an endorser, the corporate brand can still have a driver role, as it does in the case of Microsoft.

A third role is to represent a holding company, primarily to the financial community. Berkshire Hathaway (the investment vehicle of the legendary investor Warren Buffett), for example, is the corporate entity behind companies like Geico, Dairy Queen, Fruit of the Loom, Justin Brands, and many more. Viacom is the corporation that owns CBS, Paramount Pictures, Blockbuster, and Nickelodeon, among others. In that case, although not a visible endorser, it can be a shadow endorser in that many people know and take some comfort from the fact that Berkshire Hathaway has an investment in Geico, or that Blockbuster is part of the Viacom media family.

For the corporate brand to be developed, enhanced, and leveraged to reach its potential, it needs to be actively managed and supported. Active management starts with understanding the nature of the corporate brand, its potential power, and the roles it can play. The various roles assigned to it need to be clear, understood, and accepted by those charged with implementing them.

We start below by describing more precisely what the corporate brand is. The discussion then turns to why the corporate brand is potentially powerful. The third section turns to the challenges facing those who would mange and use the corporate brand. The fourth considers the corporate brand in an endorser role. The final section looks at changing a corporate brand name when an existing name becomes a liability or when a merger or acquisition happens.

THE CORPORATE BRAND

The corporate brand defines the firm that will deliver and stand behind the product or service defined by a product (or service) brand, the brand that the customer will buy and use. The corporate brand may be the same as the product brands, as it is for most of the products of Dell Computers, Toshiba, Mitsubishi, GE, and Motorola. As we shall see, however, it may be useful to actively manage the corporate brand separate from the product brand, even when they use the same name. The fact is that customers buying a GE Aircraft engine will receive a product that the GE organization stands behind. Thus, it is helpful to recognize that a GE product brand and a GE corporate brand are both involved, and both should be actively managed.

When the corporate brand is used in the endorser role, it will usually be different than the product brand, as it is for Courtyard (by Marriott), MSN (by Microsoft), or "The Lion King" (by Disney). As such, it provides credibility that can reassure the buyer, especially if a new technology is involved.

The unique and potentially powerful characteristic of a corporate brand is that it reflects an organization and thus can develop and leverage organizational characteristics, as well as product and service attributes. Most of the concepts, challenges, and opportunities facing a corporate brand apply as well to organizational brands, which define distinct organizational entities rather than corporate entities. For example, Saturn is an organizational brand in that it reflects a distinct organization with its own culture and style, even though in fact it is part of the

GM corporate brand. Sheraton is both an organization brand and a service brand but not a corporate brand, as Sheraton is one of several hospitality brands owned by the Starwood corporation.

Of course, many organizational associations will be relevant to product brands (such as Marriott, Betty Crocker, or Chevrolet), but the number, power, and credibility of organizational associations will be greater for a brand that visibly represents a corporate organization. In particular, a corporate brand will potentially have a host of organizational elements, including a rich heritage, assets and capabilities, values and priorities, citizenship programs, a performance record, and a local or global frame of reference.

Heritage

Any brand, but especially those that are struggling, can benefit from going back to its roots and identifying what made it special and successful in the first place. A corporate brand usually has roots that are richer and more relevant than product brands. L.L. Bean has a New England hunting and fishing background that has evolved into an outdoor/casual living lifestyle brand. The stories about the early roots and the Bean family help add authenticity and differentiation to the brand. The HP garage, the Wells Fargo stagecoach roots, GE tracing itself back to the days of Thomas Edison, Nike's early advances in track shoes, and Honda's engine development going back to the 1940s and 1950s all help define these brands today and add value, especially when they are interpreted in a contemporary light.

Assets and Capabilities

A firm brings to a market a perception of having assets and capabilities that influence its ability to deliver innovative products and value to customers. Shisheido has knowledge and expertise around skin care. Wal-Mart has the technology needed to deliver a wide variety of merchandise at low prices. Singapore Airlines can deliver exceptional service. Prudential has financial assets behind it. LeapFrog has the ability to understand the educational needs of children and translate them into engaging, effective products.

People

The people of an organization, especially for a firm with a heavy service component, provide the basis for the corporate brand image. If they appear engaged, interested in customers, empowered, responsive, and competent, the corporate brand will tend to engender greater respect, liking, and ultimately loyalty. What is involved is not so much what is done, but the attitude and culture that drive those actions. The people of Avon, Four Seasons, and Home Depot, for example, all tend to express a distinct personality that helps to define the corporate brand. Of particular importance are the visible spokespeople—such as Bill Gates for Microsoft, Michael Dell for Dell, and Richard Branson for Virgin—who will tend to represent the people of the corporation.

Values and Priorities

The very essence of a company is its values and priorities, what it considers important. What is it that will not be compromised, no matter what? Where is the investment made? A host of values and priorities, and combinations thereof, underlie business strategies. Some firms have a cost-driven culture that supports a value position in the marketplace. Others place priority on delivering a prestige customer experience. Innovation, quality, and customer concern are three values and priorities that are worth highlighting because they are so frequently seen as drivers of corporate brands. In fact, it is hard to find corporations that do not espouse one or two of these.

INNOVATION

Has the firm provided customer benefits by being innovative? A reputation for innovation enhances credibility. In particular, experimental studies have shown that innovation has made the acceptance of new product offerings more likely. However, it is not easy achieving an innovative reputation. In fact most firms, especially in Japan, aspire to be perceived as innovative, but few really break out of the clutter. R&D spending and a host of patents that do not result in branded products and services will not enhance the brand; innovation needs to be relevant and visible. Sony has benefited from being able to capture its innovation from a variety of categories within its corporate brand. Others, such as Home Depot and Dell, have visibly innovated to bring products to customers in different and superior ways.

PERCEIVED QUALITY

Does the firm deliver on its brand promise with reliability? Is it perceived to have quality that is high relative to its brand promise? Is it trustworthy? Does it stand behind its offering? Perceived quality, which requires a commitment to quality by the organization, has been shown to influence ROI and stock return.[4] However, perceived quality is even more difficult to achieve than perceived innovation. Delivering actual quality is not enough; perceptions need to be managed as well. Quality cues such as the thickness of the ketchup, the dress of the airline cabin attendants, or the appearance of a bank statement need to be understood and actively managed.

CONCERN FOR CUSTOMERS

Is the firm really concerned about customers? Is it seen as caring? Are customers treated with respect? Is the customer experience a high priority? Firms like Nordstrom's and Southwest Airlines have created significant loyalty based on a visible, enthusiastic effort to please customers. Customer concern is another value that nearly all firms aspire to have. They talk the good talk, but to gain the desired reputation, some visible, over-the-top programs (preferably branded) are often needed. Some legendary stories can also help—such as how Nordstrom's once took back a defective tire, even though it never sold tires, or how a FedEx employee once hired a helicopter to maintain service quality.

Local vs. Global Orientation

A characteristic of the organization that can affect the customer relationship is whether the corporate brand has either a local or global orientation. Although some corporate brands (notably Sony) attempt to do both, the more feasible route if geographic orientation is to be dialed up is to position on one or the other.

Being local—that is, striving to connect in tangible and intangible ways to the local environment and customers—provides at least two benefits. First, it allows customers to take pride in successful local companies and express that pride in their purchasing patterns. It can be rewarding for an American to buy an American car, or for a Kansas City native to bank with a firm intimately involved in the community. Second, such firms can relate to the customer by providing a look and feel and brand position that is attuned to the local culture. Lone Star Beer is unambiguously a Texas beer and built its brand around that concept.

Being global—that is, having global visibility, aspirations, and reach—has several potential advantages. There is prestige attached to a brand that has made it globally. People everywhere are likely to recognize and respect the brand and, by extension, the customer using that brand. Further, there is an implication that if it is successful on a global stage, the brand must also deliver innovation and quality products and services. One challenge is to enjoy the benefits of a global image without appearing distant and bureaucratic.

Citizenship: Creating Good Company Vibes

What kind of people and values are behind this corporate brand? People and organizations prefer to do business with those they respect and admire. Is the organization "good people," with a perspective beyond merely enhancing shareholder value at all costs? Is the company concerned about its employees and the community? What about fighting and coping with disease, improving education, helping the disadvantaged, or addressing environmental issues? The respect that companies such as HP and Johnson & Johnson have engendered for their values has resulted in positive attitudes and loyalty even during times in which their products were challenged.

A visible dimension of citizenship is the environment, which can be important to a growing and influential segment, especially in Europe. Evidence from a U.K. study supports this conjecture, at least industry is visible and the corporate brands are differentiated.[5] Both Shell and BP developed environmentally friendly brands, in part due to their visible investment in renewable energy sources. Esso, in contrast, took the principled position that renewable energy was not a viable solution and, further, that the Kyoto accords on the environment were flawed and should be opposed. As a result, a high-profile "Stop Esso" campaign has been coordinated by Greenpeace. A subsequent poll done by Greenpeace found that the proportion of British gasoline buyers who say they regularly use Esso stations dropped by 7 percent during the year of the campaign, a rather dramatic shift in preferences in a homogenous category.

The citizenship dimensions of a corporate brand can be enhanced if it can package and brand its programs. For example, General Mills has an initiative branded as "Box Tops for Education," complete with a logo and a core program to give 10 cents for each redeemed boxtop coupon that is on some 800 General Mills products. Over \$23 million was raised by this program for the 2002–2003 school year. Clorox has the "Safe Steps Home," a joint product with ASPCA to fight feline homelessness with programs like the Adopt-A-Shelter-Cat month. Verizon collaborates with numerous literacy groups for their "Verizon Reads" program to raise awareness and funds to fight illiteracy.[6] As noted in Chapter 5, if a branded program becomes visible and brand reinforcing, it can be a brand energizer. A program that merits ongoing support will be more effective at enhancing the citizenship of a corporate brand if it is branded.

Corporate Performance and Size

Is the firm successful? Is there a buzz around it? Is there vitality, with new products and new programs? Do the new products and services click with the market by gaining visibility and word of mouth, or do they struggle? As noted in Chapter 7, a perception of an extension product's success will make it more likely that further extensions will be successful. If a firm delivers on visible programs such as introducing new IT interfaces or customer service programs, perceptions of reliability and trust will be enhanced. On the other hand, a reputation of being an organization that fails to deliver on promises is hard to overcome.

Especially for corporate brands concerned with influencing investors, financial performance can be important. Does the firm perform well in terms of sales growth, earnings, and stock return? Is there a pattern of success, or is it erratic? The corporate brand performance of GE over the two decades in which Jack Welch was CEO certainly affected the corporate brand and, by extension, the GE product brands. Conversely, firms that have visible and ongoing financial difficulties will find that their brand is affected. In a study of the *Fortune* corporate image data, Bob Jacobson and this author demonstrated that, for the *Fortune* reader, financial performance directly affects brand image. The *Fortune* reader is attuned to the stock market and tends to respect those brands whose stocks are performing well. Success breeds confidence and positive attitudes, whether one is talking about a football team or a corporation.

Does the organization behind the brand have substance and visibility? The size and scope of a firm can signal both competence and staying power. Customers often sense that a large, successful firm will be around to provide service and will have an incentive to design and make good products. Of course, size could also be a signal for an organization that is bureaucratic, slow, and expensive. The challenge is to make sure that the right spin is placed on the brand by dialing up innovation and success and creating an image of being dynamic and adaptive, rather than slow-moving and clumsy.

WHY LEVERAGE THE CORPORATE BRAND?

The corporate brand is special because it explicitly and unambiguously represents an organization as well as a product. As a driver or endorser brand, it will have a host of characteristics and programs that can help build the brand. It can help differentiate, create branded energizers, provide credibility, facilitate brand management, support internal brand-building, provide a basis for a relationship to augment that of the product brand, support communication to broad company constituencies, and provide the ultimate branded house.

First, a corporate brand can potentially find differentiation in the organizational associations. The reality that while products and services tend to become similar over time, organizations are inevitably very different, in part because there are so many ways a corporation can differ. Wells Fargo is very different from its competitor Bank of America in terms of style, personality, headquarters location, skills, citizenship programs, and heritage. A person may be more comfortable with one organization than another, particularly if the products are similar. The challenge is to identify those organizational characteristics and make them relevant to customers.

Second, a corporate brand can draw on organizational programs for branded energizers. Because citizenship programs and major sponsorships will usually span the organization, the corporate brand is in a much better position to exploit these than product brands whose link to them might be weak. In a way, this reflects pure efficiency; a corporate program that spans product classes will be more effective and efficient than one that reaches only one product class.

Third, corporate brand associations can also provide credibility based on trust, liking, and perceived expertise. Attitude research in psychology has shown that believability and persuasive power are enhanced when a spokesperson is perceived as being trustworthy, well-liked, and expert. These same characteristics should be relevant when evaluating whether a claim made by an organization is credible. An expert organization is seen as especially competent in making and selling its products. An organization could be liked because of its citizenship activities, which could lead to its product claims being treated with more respect and less cynicism. A trustworthy organization will be given the benefit of the doubt.

Trust is a particularly important attribute, and one that is easier for an organization than a product to develop. One study found that the leading attribute identified by consumers when asked to describe the "best brands" is "the brand that I trust."[7] Trust is related to authenticity. Firms like Williams-Sonoma or Boeing, who are seen as having a long history of delivering on a heritage-based philosophy, have an authenticity that is very powerful.

Fourth, leveraging the corporate brand across products and markets will make brand management easier and more effective. In part because the corporate brand will have the attention of top management, product line managers that are using the brand will have an incentive to know the identity and take it seriously. Off-brand programs and initiatives will be more visible. Further, it is more likely that good brand-building programs around the corporate brand can be leveraged across the organization.

Fifth, the translation of the brand internally to employees will be much easier when the corporate brand is involved, because its brand identity will support and be supported by the mission, goals, values, and culture of the organization. There is little doubt that it is important for employees to buy into organizational values and programs. The corporate brand identity should be the link between the organization and the customer. As such, it can play a key role in articulating these elements to employees, retailers, and others who must represent the corporate goals and values to customers. In the case of product brands, there will be no such supporting system.

Sixth, a corporate brand can provide a message and basis for a customer relationship apart from those of the product brand. This extra voice can be extremely valuable, particularly for large, established brands that are perceived as reliable but also boring. In those cases, the organization brand can represent the heritage and the significant equi-

272 BRAND PORTFOLIO STRATEGY

ties that surround the organization while allowing the product brand to be an energy source. If the product brand involves a strong subbrand, the subbrand can perform that function, but if the product brand is the same as the corporate brand (as it is for Virgin, Mitsubishi, and GE) then only a dual brand conceptualization gets you there.

For example, the Budweiser brand has a rich heritage and is the market leader within the beer category. The Budweiser corporate brand (not strictly a corporate brand, since that would be Anheuser-Busch) is assigned to carry the heritage, using such symbols as the Clydesdales and such programs as the campaign against drunk driving ("We all make a difference") and the beer school. The product brands, Budweiser and Bud Lite, are then freed to inject energy, finding new ways to be young and relevant and to break out of the media clutter with very different brand building. Thus we have had the lizards, the "Whassup" group of friends, and other colorful characters who have appeared in extremely humorous and contemporary advertising. Without the corporate brand presence, the products would have much less freedom to break out of the clutter.

Seventh, another reason to leverage the corporate brand is to support communication efforts to stakeholders such as prospective employees, retailers, and investors. All will be influenced by the name visibility, its strategy going forward, and its performance. Just being familiar with a brand provides comfort. Investors are often a particularly important group; one study showed that institutional investors based 35 percent of their judgments on intangible factors such as management quality, effectiveness of new product development, and strength of market position, versus 65 percent on financial information.[8] Communicating the intangibles in the absence of a strong corporate brand would be difficult.

Finally, a corporate brand provides the ultimate branded house and captures all the efficiencies of dialing up a single brand, even more so when descriptors are employed and the use of subbrands is limited. In that case, the brand will gain synergy and, hopefully, association reinforcement as well in the different contexts. Further, and more important, limited brand-building resources will be less diluted when there is a single mother brand, and the brand's voice in the marketplace will have more impact. Recall that the branded house is always the preferred strategy when it is feasible.

Schlumberger, a leading oil-field services company, is one of many firms that have dialed up the corporate brand and dialed down product subbrands. Schlumberger over the years acquired some firms delivering specialized oil field services, each of which had extremely strong brands in their niche. The companies included Anadrill (a drilling services company), Dowell (oil well construction and stimulation), and GeoQuest (software and data management systems). These brands became en-

FIGURE 9-2
SCHLUMBERGER ADVERTISEMENT

dorsed brands that continued to drive customer relationships after the acquisition and support the traditions and cultures of the micro-organizations within Schlumberger.

One motivation to coalesce focus around the Schlumberger brand concerned achieving efficiency and synergy. The firm wanted to focus its brand-building efforts to create more impact on a single brand. Within the oil-field products, there were too many mouths to feed from a brand-building perspective. Further, the firm was in a position to leverage the Schlumberger name in other growth areas outside of oil-field services. The strategic direction of the firm, however, provided an even more compelling reason.

Schlumberger needed to change the way it operated and was perceived. The company had always stood for innovation and value creation for customers. However, it wanted to add teamwork to its brand, to be perceived as more of a team-oriented firm—one that was working closely across business units and with customers to provide integrated solutions. At it was, Schlumberger was not getting the synergy needed and expected from the strong organizations it had acquired, and its customer image was affected. The focus on a corporate brand was one way to signal the new direction both inside and outside the firm.

The brand strategy of the new Schlumberger involved making the Schlumberger brand the new driver brand, with descriptive subbrands indicating the business units. Schlumberger Oilfield Services became the brand for the major heritage services, which now included the following:

Schlumberger Data Delivery	Schlumberger Geology
Schlumberger Geophysics	Schlumberger Oilfield Software
Schlumberger Well Construction	Schlumberger Well Completion
Schlumberger Retrophysics—Formation Evaluation	Schlumberger Wireline Services

The former business brands (such as GeoQuest) appear as product brands where appropriate, but the attention is now without question centered on Schlumberger. Dialing up the corporate brand symbolized to the customers and employees alike that the firm is one entity implementing a set of values and programs.

CHALLENGES IN MANAGING THE CORPORATE BRAND

The corporate brand is indeed a powerful option to lead the charge, perhaps with the use of some subbrands and endorsed brands to handle situations where the corporate brand is stretched. Dell and UPS are both examples of firms that have been successful using this strategy. However, there are serious challenges to face—staying relevant, creating value propositions, managing negative associations, adapting the corporate brand to different contexts, and making the corporate brand identity happen.

Maintaining Relevance

What business is the firm in? What product scope is associated with the firm? In what product arenas does it have credibility? For what problems is the brand a solution? The brand boundaries, which directly affect the relevance span of the brand and its potential to extend into new product-markets, depend on the brand's heritage and business strategy going forward.

The heritage business associated with a brand will affect its effort to change. When a brand has strong category links, changing perceptions can be like turning a large ocean liner—it will turn slowly and require a lot of energy doing so. The difficulties that Xerox and Kodak have had in part rest on their strong associations with copiers and film-based cameras, respectively. Both have struggled to enter the broader world in which digital imaging systems are dominant. Clorox faces another kind of limitation; because of its close association with bleach, its corporate brand cannot be linked to any of the food products it makes.

Relevance is also determined by the business strategy. When it evolves or changes, the corporate brand itself needs to be altered, and accomplishing that task usually represents a significant challenge. UPS expanded from products to services and from being perceived as a U.S.-based, small-package ground delivery company to being a global provider of distribution, logistics, and financial services. Toward that end, new services and programs served to provide substance and branded differentiators behind the new UPS. IBM evolved from being an "e-business" company to eBusiness on Demand, a concept that information and technology should be available to the user "on demand" and computer resources should not stay idle when not being used. Some additional examples are as follows:

- *Hitachi.* In late 1999, unsatisfactory financial performance stimulated a rebranding of Hitachi. Whereas the future of the company was based on its computers and information electronics, its image was based upon a perception that it was largely an appliance and heavy machinery company. A program to change this image was led by the tagline, "Inspire the Next."
- *Sony.* Sony has long been a leading electronics brand but is less known for its participation in gaming (namely, PlayStation). Even less visible is the fact that Sony is one of the leading producers of movies (Columbia Pictures, Screen Gems, Sony Classics) and music (Sony Music), with a host of well-known films and celebrity singers. Sony has sought to expand its brand to include movies, music, and games as well as electronics so that it can become more relevant and powerful. After all, young people listen to music and play games, and creating a broad Sony brand among that group is important to the future of the brand.

Creating Value Propositions

Too many corporate brands in effect have no value proposition. They are simply large, stable firms that can be trusted to deliver adequate products and services, but with no point of distinction and sometimes with a hint of being bureaucratic and ponderous. Such brands are vulnerable. A strong corporate brand is one that will provide a value proposition that will help differentiate and support a customer relationship.

A corporate brand will work best when it delivers a functional benefit. The benefit could be based on its strategy; Dell's direct model generated explicit benefits that included customization and access to the latest technology. UPS, with its focus on service and systems, provided a value to any firm that needed to improve or outsource part of its logistics. The benefit can also be based on other elements of the corporate brand, such as its values. Nordstrom's concern for its customers provides a functional benefit to shoppers, who can be assured of a good experience. A firm with a reputation for high product quality provides a similar guarantee against unpleasant customer experiences.

A corporate brand can also deliver emotional or self-expressive benefits. The local connection by a bank can generate both emotional benefits from the experience and self-expressive benefits gained by supporting a local business. The purchase of an American-made Saturn has been shown to deliver significant self-expressive benefits both because it is built in the United States and also because the employees' commitment to customers is admired. Citizenship programs such as the political activism of Ben & Jerry's, the breast cancer campaign of Avon, and the environmental effort of Toyota's hybrid cars can all provide self-expressive benefits.

Avoiding Visible Negatives

The risk of leveraging the corporate brand is that the resulting brand equity and the businesses on which it rests are vulnerable to visible negatives. Thus, the water source contamination that Perrier faced, the Exxon Valdez oil spill, the cigarette health problem connected to Philip Morris, the Firestone tire crises, and the firms' responses affected the corporate brands. If the corporate brand is highly leveraged, as it is at Dell, Virgin, and Toshiba, then the whole organization needs to be sensitive to this risk in all of their decisions and actions. What would happen to the corporate brand if the worst happened?

When a controversy arises that endangers the brand, the accepted best practice when possible is to admit wrongdoing, or at least admit there is a problem and immediately provide a visible fix. But having a strong citizenship brand will be very helpful in such a crisis. In the now-classic case, for example, when faced with package tampering of its Tylenol brand, Johnson & Johnson immediately pulled the affected products and designed a tamperproof package. The positive impact of this action has lingered for well over a decade.

Managing the Brand in Different Contexts

A corporate brand may be involved in a host of product brands consisting of the corporate brand plus a descriptor or a subbrand in addition to representing the organization to various stakeholders. GE, for example, needs to fight the fight in aircraft engines, appliances, and in financial services. How can one brand, particularly a corporate brand, accomplish such multitasking? The answer is that the brand identity

FIGURE 9-3
THE CORPORATE BRAND: CHALLENGES AND POTENTIAL IMPACT

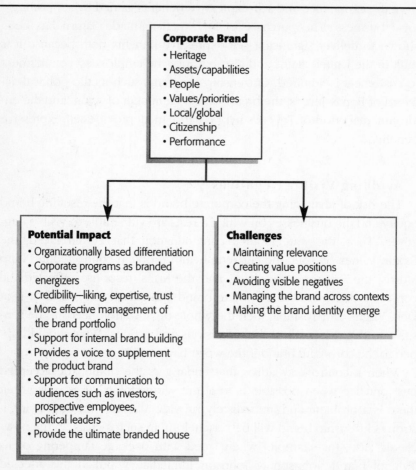

Corporate Brand
- Heritage
- Assets/capabilities
- People
- Values/priorities
- Local/global
- Citizenship
- Performance

Potential Impact
- Organizationally based differentiation
- Corporate programs as branded energizers
- Credibility—liking, expertise, trust
- More effective management of the brand portfolio
- Support for internal brand building
- Provides a voice to supplement the product brand
- Support for communication to audiences such as investors, prospective employees, political leaders
- Provide the ultimate branded house

Challenges
- Maintaining relevance
- Creating value positions
- Avoiding visible negatives
- Managing the brand across contexts
- Making the brand identity emerge

needs to be adapted to each context so it can win the day. This process is often not easy, though, because conflicting perspectives are involved.

There can and should be consistency across contexts; much of the core and extended identity should work everywhere. Some elements might be the same but need to have a different spin to work for a particular product or market, so innovation at GE Appliances might mean something different than it does at GE Capital. If that is not enough, it might be necessary to augment the identity for a context. Perhaps GE

Aircraft engines have a technology dimension not seen in the other GE business units.

Making the Corporate Brand Identity Emerge

The corporate brand will start with an image but will want to move that image toward a brand identity, a set of aspirational associations for the corporate brand to perform its assigned roles. For that to happen, the brand identity needs to be developed. The process for doing this is described elsewhere, but it involves setting priorities. Which of the aspirational associations are the most important in the short term and should be the basis of a positioning strategy, and which will be the most important in the long term and should guide strategic initiatives? The answers will depend in part on questions such as these:

- What can the corporation deliver? What will be credible given current market perceptions, as well as the firm's ability and motivation to develop and deliver meaningful programs?
- What will resonate with customers?
- What will support the business strategy and the roles that the corporate brand will be asked to play?

The identity and position of the corporate brand needs to be actively managed. For some firms, the corporate brand is somewhat of an orphan in part because it does not have a natural budget source from an active business unit. Thus, it is important to have a corporate brand manager with resources to build the brand, as well as authority to create consistency across the firm and to capture synergy.

The corporate brand will be based on substance. There needs to be both commitment and programs to make sure that the brand delivers on innovation, customer concern, or whatever the priorities are. It is wasteful to attempt to portray the corporation as being devoted to accomplishing a goal that it lacks the ability or will to make happen. Developing and delivering on strategic imperatives is not easy for any firm, however, especially when it faces economic strains.

Creating substance behind the brand is not enough, of course; the firm must also make sure that perceptions match the promise being delivered. Toward that end, each target association will require an actively managed communication program that should involve all stakeholder touch points.

Communicating an expanded scope or revised thrust can benefit from employing all of the assets in the brand portfolio. To what extent do subbrands affect the corporate brand? Which subbrands, if any, can play a silver bullet role? What subbrands can provide visibility and support to the corporate brand? What brand-building events can help? One software company generated nearly instant credibility as a major player in Europe by sponsoring one of the leading bicycle-racing teams.

When to Leverage the Corporate Brand

The corporate brand is the ultimate branded house and has all the advantages of any branded house, plus the fact that it represents an organization. In contexts involving service, such as retailing (Sears or Land's End) or financial services (Citigroup or Chase), corporate brands in driver roles will often be compelling. In these settings, such organizational associations as concern for customer service, being friendly, and being efficient are more likely to be the basis for customer loyalty. Customers will be more likely to relate to the people and programs of an organization than to its products.

The corporate brand, however, is not always well suited for being a product master brand with a driver role. In general, when the corporate brand has difficulty dealing with any of the five challenges, then its leverage potential will be limited, and other brand platforms will be needed. A realistic appraisal of the brand with respect to its ability to cope with the challenges is in order. Some examples are as follows:

- When the brand is too confining because of its product category associations, then its role will be limited. The Clorox corporate brand, for example, is confined to cleaning products and certainly cannot be associated with the food products like Hidden Valley Ranch Dressing or KC Masterpiece, both of which are Clorox brands.
- When the corporate brand lacks a relevant value proposition and thus its equity basically rests on being large and established, a strong subbrand or endorsed brand or even a new brand might be needed. Dell and UPS have such a value proposition embedded in their brand, but many corporate brands are not so blessed.

- When the brand has negative associations, there is no point in trying to leverage it until the associations are changed. In the wake of the rash of Ford Explorer accidents attributed by some to Firestone, Bridgestone dialed down the Firestone brand and dialed up the Bridgestone product brand.
- There is a context in which the corporate brand's equity and value proposition simply do not apply or become a liability, and therefore other brands might be needed.
- If the corporate brand identity will be a great asset but the organization cannot deliver against it because the necessary programs are not yet in place, there may be a credibility problem in relying on the corporate brand to play a product brand driver role prematurely.

ENDORSER ROLE

Because the corporate brand represents the organization and has credibility with some defined product space, it is well suited to playing endorser roles. An endorser brand will benefit from any of the general organizational associations. Some organizational brands, such as Microsoft, consistently play endorser roles. Others, such as Marriott or GE, can be an endorser in one context and a product brand in another.

An endorser role can provide more than trust and respect; it can also provide a service that spans the endorsed brands. The Starwood hotel chain, which includes Sheraton and the W chain, uses the Starwood brand as an endorser in part to provide a broad-based loyalty program to compete with the Marriott and Hilton loyalty programs. An endorsement of a value brand by an equipment manufacturer, such as John Deere, can signal to customers that they can access the parts and service program of the parent corporation.

Dialing Up the Endorser Role

The corporate brand can be leveraged through its endorser role. The corporate brand's authority may be limited and thus so may its ability to extend as a driver brand. It might be able to be leveraged aggressively, however, as an endorser brand. As an endorser used to provide trust and credibility rather than a product promise, the brand can travel further and still be effective. Some Kraft branding initiatives illustrate.

Kraft in the late 1990s elevated the role of its corporate brand across the brand portfolio. Until the late 1990s, Kraft was the master brand for cheese, barbeque sauce, salad dressing, and mayonnaise, and the endorser of Philadelphia, Cracker Barrel, Miracle Whip, and Velveeta. In addition, the Kraft brand portfolio contained over a dozen stand-alone brands (such as Minute Rice and Post, many of which were acquired when Kraft merged with General Foods in 1980) that were diffusing brand-building resources.

The decision was made to dial up the Kraft endorsement, making it more visible on some brands and adding it to others. As part of the strategy, Kraft-endorsed brands were expected to be compatible with the Kraft image of everyday, easy-to-prepare meal solutions for the American family and the Kraft personality of being wholesome, family oriented, and reliable. These brands were to evolve toward the Kraft image if there was a gap so that they would be comfortable under the Kraft umbrella. A major $50 million campaign to enhance the Kraft name supported the move to make Kraft a firmwide umbrella brand.

Thus, Kraft became a strong endorser for Stovetop Stuffing, Minute Rice, and Shake & Bake. In addition, it became a token endorser for Oscar Mayer, Tombstone, Post, Maxwell House, Breyer's, Cool Whip, and Jell-O. Interestingly, all these brands, especially the three that received a strong endorsement, are also everyday, All-American products, not that much of a stretch from Kraft. Others, such as DiGiorno Pizza and Bull's-Eye barbeque sauce, were left as stand-alone brands in part because they were positioned as upscale and in part because their companion brands, Tombstone Pizza and Kraft Barbeque sauce, were regarded as more "Kraft." Figure 9-4 summarizes the Kraft branding strategy.

The effort to extend the Kraft brand continues. When Cheese Nips was obtained in 2001 as a result of the Nabisco acquisition, it was given a strong Kraft endorsement that was considered a partial reason why a sales increase was observed. In addition, an ingredient brand ("made with real Kraft cheese") was added to Cheese Nips and other products. Kraft also endorsed the European chocolate brand Milka in an effort to enhance the Kraft presence in Europe and to provide a global spin to Milka. A net result of this ongoing program is to leverage the Kraft brand across a broad sales base in a coherent manner, providing the potential for synergistic cross-brand programs and promotions. The product

FIGURE 9-4
THE KRAFT BRAND STRATEGY

Brand	Brand Identity	Product Scope	Issues
Kraft as master brand with a driver role	Everyday, easy-to-prepare, good quality meal solutions for the American family. Personality is wholesome and reliable.	Cheese, mayonnaise, barbeque sauce, salad dressing	Weakness in non-creamy dressing. Weakness in upscale.
Kraft as strong endorser brand	Everyday, easy-to-prepare, good quality meal solutions for the American family. Personality is wholesome and reliable.	Stovetop Stuffing, Shake & Bake, Minute Rice	How to enhance and leverage the Kraft brand.
Kraft as token endorser brand	Everyday, easy-to-prepare, good quality, meal solutions for the American family. Personality is wholesome and reliable.	Oscar Mayer, Post, Maxwell House, Jell-O, Cool Whip, Tombstone, Breyer's	Will the Kraft endorsement help or hurt Kraft and the offerings?

brands don't have to work as hard, because the Kraft brand absorbs some of the driver role responsibility.

The elevation of the Kraft brand means that the Kraft endorsement is stronger and brand-building programs like the Kraft website and global sponsorships become more feasible because they can be leveraged over more sales. For example, a customer publication endorsed by Kraft called "Food & Family (What's Cooking in Canada)," with a circulation of over 3 million and growing, provides a relationship with the Kraft brand and its prime target.[9] Although an issue may contain features around healthy living and movies, the focus is on cooking with topics like dinner on hand, breakfast revisited, lunch leftovers, and delicious desserts. Over half of the readers report that they have tried a featured recipe and used a Kraft product in that recipe. The recipes leverage the research and aura surrounding Kraft Kitchen.

The energy company BP also decided to leverage its brand and brand-building programs through an endorsement program. The motivation was to scale the BP brand in order to exploit a new brand positioning strategy that was expected to gain a differentiated leadership position in the energy space. BP sought to change its image from being a stable, British petroleum firm that performed well to that of being an innovative, progressive, environmentally sensitive energy firm with a vision of "beyond petroleum." To help create and (more important) to leverage the new brand, the BP endorsement was added to many of the firm's consumer-facing businesses, including Arco, Aral, and Castrol.

CHANGING THE CORPORATE BRAND NAME

A corporate brand's image and customer relationship are captured in its brand, which in turn is indicated by a brand name. Changing the name of any brand is a dramatic and desperate move, and this is even more true for the mother brand. Even when the existing corporate brand name is inadequate or a liability, there are options such as subbrands, endorsed brands, or new brands for the context in question. Changing a corporate brand name is a last resort.

There must be compelling reasons to change the corporate brand name. In essence, three factors need to be present. First, a new direction for the corporation is so dramatic or so different from the existing corporate brand associations that the current name becomes a significant liability. Second, the existing associations cannot be modified to reduce that liability to acceptable levels. Third, resources and talent are available to create a new brand name.

Voluntary name changes have been found to be justified for some of the following reasons:

- **To reflect a new business focus.** Largely a pharmaceutical company, AHP leveraged its most visible and most strategic brand, Wyeth, to create a new corporate name. Clarity in the portfolio was achieved by dialing up the Wyeth name. For example, Wyeth-Ayerst Research became Wyeth Research, and Whitehall-Robins Healthcare became Wyeth Consumer Healthcare.
- **Stock market forces.** A change to a more familiar name or one that more correctly denotes the business can be helpful in attracting investors. Consolidated Foods changed its name to Sara Lee, its most

visible brand, and saw its stock price respond. The change from Prudential Insurance to Prudential Financial enabled the firm to signal to investors that it was no longer just in the insurance business.

- **Distancing from a demonized product.** In an effort to dial down tobacco associations and separate the corporate name from that portion of the firm, the division of Philip Morris involved with tobacco changed its name to Altria.

- **To overcome paralyzing organizational sensitivities in a merger.** The name Eg3, which had an energy connotation, was selected to represent the merger in the mid-1990s of three private petroleum companies in Argentina (Astra, Isaura, and Puma). Although each of the existing names had positive equity, a local connection, and a rich heritage, the families who controlled the firms were adamant that the merged entity's name could not be one of a rival. Logically, there are other organizational culture and structure levers that can address issues like this without creating a new name. But logic does not always win the day.

- **To overcome geographic limitations of existing brands.** Verizon was chosen as the name for the merger of GTE and Bell Atlantic, two brands with regional connotations. Similarly, the HSBC name was selected for a financial group created to capture global synergies and service global customers. It had been operating under brand names such as the Hong Kong and Shanghai Banking Corporation, Marine Midland Bank (New York), the Midland Bank (in the United Kingdom), and the British Bank of the Middle East. HSBC had some successes in its name change. In the fourth quarter of 1998, Marine Midland had an aided recall level of around 85 percent; the new HSBC brand name in that market grew from under 10 percent in early 1999 to over 60 percent in late 1999 and 80 percent by the end of 2001.[10]

A name change may seem tempting at times, but guard against three illusions that are all too common. The first illusion is that a name change will by itself change associations. Rather, the brand with all its associations will be driven by the new business strategy, how it is articulated, how it is implemented, and how it is related to the brand equities of the prior organizations. There must be substance underlying the name change, and that substance has to be communicated in order for it to work.

The second illusion is that a better name can be found. Available names, especially globally available names, that come close to being pronounceable, being memorable, and having acceptable associations are practically impossible to generate. After attempting to establish the name Consignia for two years, the postal service in the United Kingdom retreated to the name Royal Mail Group. Employees and customers alike never could get used to Consignia.

A final illusion is that equity can be evolved and transferred to a new name with a reasonable budget. In fact, this always costs much more than expected, and sometimes it is literally not feasible—in part because of name clutter as competitors also change names, and in part because target audiences lack motivation to learn a new name. Four years after $200 million was spent in the early 1980s (when $200 million was a lot of money) telling the Datsun-to-Nissan name change story, and after the Datsun brand had disappeared, it was still as strong a brand as Nissan. This is a sobering case indeed, especially considering that Nissan had several properties of a good name in that it was short, memorable, easy to spell, had no bad associations, and even had some equity going in.

When the rationale for a name change is compelling, it is important to make sure that competent teams have analyzed the problem with sufficient depth, alternatives have been thoroughly explored, and judgments are not clouded by these three illusions.

Mergers, Acquisitions, and Divestitures

There are circumstances brought on by divestitures or mergers/acquisitions in which a name change cannot be avoided. For example, a divestiture can force a name change because the corporate name may simply no longer be available. When the consulting arms of the large accounting firms were divested, they needed to have names not associated with their former parent. Thus Andersen Consulting became Accenture, a name change that was supported by a $175 million budget and fortuitously helped the firm avoid being caught up in the Andersen Enron scandal. DeLoitte Consulting become Braxton, choosing a name that it had owned.

When a corporate brand is acquired or merged with another, the stronger of the two should be retained, which means that the weaker experiences a name change. When the consulting arm of Price Waterhouse was acquired by IBM, it was renamed as IBM Business Consulting. When Norwest acquired Wells Fargo, the resulting brand chosen was Wells Fargo. The challenge is to transfer equity to the surviving corporate brand name; customers should feel that they are getting all the advantages of the prior brand (such as Norwest) coupled with the strengths that the new organization (Wells Fargo) contributes. The weaker brand name can be discarded or used as a product brand within the portfolio, as was the case with Compaq (acquired by HP) and Lotus (acquired by IBM).

If both brands in a merger have equities that are complementary and are expensive or impossible to transfer, an option is to have a composite corporate brand, such as Chevron/Texaco, DaimlerChrysler, or Mitsui-Sumotono. There can be an advantage, especially initially, in retaining the existing culture and values of the two organizations. Over time, however, they will need to be merged, and a composite name can end up inhibiting that process unless it is carefully managed.

The branding insight is that in divestitures, mergers, and acquisitions, the equity of the involved brands should be considered far more thoroughly than they are. Too often the three illusions exist, and time and resources are not made available to have people competent in branding and the markets involved analyze the tough brand issues and their associated risks and costs. Too often, market failures or organizational breakdowns are caused in part by defective brand strategies or their implementation.

QUESTIONS FOR DISCUSSION

1. Assess the corporate brand associations in your firm or in a reference firm. Are they capable of reflecting and supporting the business strategy going forward? If not, what other aspects of the brand portfolio can compensate?

2. What are the advantages of the corporate brand in your context?

3. Assess the challenges to the corporate brand being effective as a driver brand. Which are the most worrisome, and how are they being addressed?

4. Consider the current and potential uses of the corporate brand as an endorser. In each context, consider what the corporate brand gives and receives from the endorsement.

5. Inventory the ways that the organizational brands are used in the brand portfolio. Are they doing well in all contexts? What are their associations in each context? What roles do they undertake?

6. Consider a potential merger for your firm and develop a naming strategy. In doing so, consider questions such as the following: What are the equities of the existing entities? What are the customer relationships for each brand, and can they be transferred to the other brand? To a new brand? What would be the communication cost of transferring the equity of each brand to the other brand or a new brand?

CHAPTER 10

TOWARD FOCUS AND CLARITY

On how a block of stone could become a lion—it's easy, I simply get a chisel and chip away anything that doesn't look like a lion.

—PABLO PICASSO

An architect's most useful tools are an eraser at the drafting board and a wrecking bar at the site.

—FRANK LLOYD WRIGHT

We've learned that our big brands have broad shoulders.

—CHARLES STRAUSS, PRESIDENT OF UNILEVER

UNILEVER

Unilever in February 2000 announced a five-year strategic plan termed "Path to Growth," designed to accelerate sales growth and increase operating margins.* The plan included a focus on fewer, stronger brands. The goal was to reduce the 1,600 brands under its management to around one-quarter of that number and to focus on those leadership brands with enduring consumer appeal, plus worthwhile sales and growth prospects. At stake were resources such as brand-building budgets, people, and innovation initiatives that were spread too thin. The expectation was that the bulk of the resources would be devoted to 200 brands.

As part of the process, the brands at the local, regional, and global levels were evaluated with respect to three criteria:

---

* Information for this section was drawn from Unilever annual reports for 2000, 2001 and 2002; J. Rothenberg and J. Wilhelm, "HPC NA Mass Business Review Analyst Presentation," November 14, 2002; the Unilever website; and Matthew Arnold, "Unilever Names Brands for Growth," Haymarket Publishing Services, February 21, 2002.

- **The fit with corporate strategy.** Do the product-markets in which the brand participates fit with the strategic direction of the firm?
- **Media weight.** Does the brand have enough scale in the local market to achieve critical mass? Is the brand one of the market leaders? Brands that are too small to have a media or retail presence may not be worthwhile even if they have a strong customer following.
- **Portfolio balance.** With respect to the brand portfolio, does the brand have a unique position in the market, or does it overlap with other brands? It is inefficient to have multiple brands with excessive overlap.

At the top of the food chain were 40 core global brands that represented the heart of the Unilever business going forward. Global brands were defined as brands that were identical everywhere in all but brand name or would be evolving in that direction, guided by the same brand identity involving five components—the benefits it provides, its values and personality, the reasons to believe, its discriminators, and its brand essence. Of the 40 global brands, 18 were food brands such as Knorr, Lipton, Slim-Fast, and Bertolli. Twenty-two more were nonfood brands such as Axe, Cif (Jif in some markets), Vaseline, Snuggle, CloseUp, Lynx, Dove, All, Suave, Lux, and Comfort. Some of these brands (such as Knorr, Slim-Fast, All, Lynx, and Dove) were brand platforms that were targeted to expand their scope; see the Dove story in Chapter 7 for an illustration.

The 40 global brands were each managed by a global brand director (called SVP in the food division) who headed up a global brand team, which included regional brand leaders. Thus, the global brand team was made up of "local" people. The role of the global brand team was to create more coherent management of the global brand through a closer working relationship between global brand management and local brand activation. The global brand team was and is tasked to manage the brand equity and innovation stream, develop an agreed brand identity, plan the migration to that identity, and create and implement growth plans.

An additional 160 regional/local core brands that supported healthy and growing businesses were identified. The appeal of these brands was in part due to their heritage and customer relationships that could not easily be transferred to a global brand; examples include Elephant tea in France and Breyer's ice cream in North America.

Another, much smaller set of brands was considered as merge/migrate candidates. These brands occupied promising business areas but had the potential to have their equity transferred over time to a global or regional brand. An example is Surf, a twenty-year-old value laundry detergent brand in the declining powder category, with strength in the South of the U.S. and a fragrance heritage.[1] The decision was made to fold the Surf franchise into All, a detergent entry that had about twice the sales of Surf and was stronger in the liquid category. Several Surf market entries were co-branded with All as part of the transition to the latter brand. The All family was extended into fabric softeners and additives in order to create a platform brand. A similar example was the absorption of the Rave hair care line into the Suave brand family.

The remaining brands, those not in the core portfolio of 200 or so leading brands under management, could fall into one of three categories. The "delist" brands were simply to be phased out as soon as possible. As part of the brand culling, Unilever sold over a dozen brands, including Mazola cooking oil and Argo corn starch.[2] The "manage for value" brands would receive no resources but were expected to still generate cash flow. "On notice" brands would continue to be actively managed and supported, but unless they showed tangible signs of performance improvement, they would be downgraded.

After four years, Unilever expects its leading brands to represent at least 95 percent of the business, up from 75 percent at the outset of the program.

FORD VS. BMW

Ford has a brand portfolio strategy, summarized in Figure 10-1, in which a host of subbrands define offerings and potentially provide the basis for a customer relationship.[3] There are seven subbrands defining cars and minivans: ZX2, Focus, Mustang, Thunderbird, Taurus, Crown Victoria, and Windstar. Three more—Escape, Explorer, and Expedition—define SUV lines.

Most of these subbrands, such as Explorer and Windstar, play key driver roles, as Ford functions more as an endorser. These brands can define models with ongoing uniqueness in style and features. Certainly Mustang and Crown Victoria have distinctive style associations. Some of these brands, such as Thunderbird, also have the potential to add personality and self-expressive benefits to a selection that otherwise would seem rather corporate.

Ford is a brand that has real strength in terms of quality and innovation credibility but may lack distinctiveness and personality, at least in some segments. Thus, it is unlikely that the Ford line of vehicles would be as strong without subbrands. Having said that, however, several questions arise: Could the SUV line have used a single brand instead of three? In fact, might not the Ford brand be used in the SUV space so that no subbrands would be required? Could one of the seven car brands be stretched over multiple models, thereby giving it more market presence and reducing the number of brand mouths to feed? Do the brand-building budgets appropriately reflect the extent to which each brand is playing a descriptive as opposed to a driver role?

In contrast, the BMW brand follows a rather classic branded house strategy, shown in Figure 10-2, with a master brand supported by a set of descriptor brands. The BMW brand has the 300 series (small), the 500 series (medium), the 700 series (large), the M series (high performance), the Z4 (roadster), and the X5 (SUVs). The master brand, which captures associations such as German engineering, the thrill of owning the "ultimate driving machine," the reassurance of safety features, and prestige of the BMW label, plays the driver role throughout the line. The result is the leverage and clarity associated with a pure branded house model.

There are customer-facing advantages of a branded house model, particularly in a cluttered category like automobiles. Whereas Ford supports at least ten brands in the car and SUV arena, these brands are seen by the customer in a context of well over two hundred nameplates from GM, Chrysler, Toyota, Volvo, and Honda, among others, to say nothing of the variants of each. The choice becomes for some overwhelming. The auto buyer first has to decide on whether he or she should buy a car, a minivan, a truck, or an SUV. Then comes the maker decision (Ford vs. Buick vs. Honda), and finally the model.

Compare the information and decision process suggested by the BMW brand portfolio. The BMW option is a BMW. The customer then

FIGURE 10-1
A PARTIAL FORD BRAND PORTFOLIO

Ford

Ford Cars & Minivans	Ford SUVs	Ford Focus
Subbrand	Subbrand	LX
ZX2	Escape	SE Sedan
Focus	Explorer Sport	SE Wagon
Mustang	Explorer Sport Trac	ZTS Sedan
Thunderbird	Explorer	ZX3
Taurus	Expedition	ZX5
Crown Victoria	Excursion	ZXW Wagon
Windstar		SVT

decides what level, which is usually based on a budget; which BMW can you afford? Then there are options, such as a performance 3-level or a sports car version. The analysis and decision process becomes easier, and the customer is more likely to be comfortable with the outcome.

There are also advantages of the BMW approach with respect to brand management and brand building. BMW can focus its resources on the BMW brand as long as the BMW brand identity works across models. The "ultimate driving machine" is a functional and self-expressive claim on which BMW delivers and that does apply across the line. The brand and the brand-building effort are thus focused and leveraged. The Ford brand, in contrast, will need to support many of its ten subbrands plus the Ford brand itself—a difficult prospect when resources are limited and brand building is costly.

The experience of GM is instructive. It viewed its thirty-five brands under the major nameplates (Chevrolet, Buick, Cadillac, Pontiac, Oldsmobile, Saturn, and GMC) as opportunities related to thirty-five refined segments. One problem was that potential buyers did not fit nicely into these segments. Another is that GM could not simultaneously support all

Figure 10-2
The BMW Brand Portfolio

BMW			
Core Models		**Specialty Models**	
Small	300 Series	High Performance	M Series
Medium	500 Series	SUV	X5
Large	700 Series	Convertible	Z4

of the brands with differentiated models and brand-building efforts. As a result, it shifted its policy, deciding to emphasize the major nameplates more and de-emphasize the subbrands.

GM also failed to maintain a role for each of the major nameplates and made the difficult decision to drop Oldsmobile. During the 1930s, GM beat up on Ford by introducing a well-positioned line of cars. The Chevrolet, Pontiac, Oldsmobile, Buick, and Cadillac lines provided very different styling and self-expressive benefits, which allowed GM to take over market leadership from Ford (which was offering a single model). People started with the economical Chevrolet and had the opportunity to move up to the Pontiac and the Oldsmobile. The Cadillac was the ultimate success statement, and the Buick was only slightly behind.

Over time, however, the nameplate brands blurred, in part because each was an autonomous division with incentives to create a complete line of cars. So Chevrolet offered an expensive sports car and full-size Buick-type sedans. And Cadillac had its ill-fated Cimarron, which was a thinly disguised Chevrolet subcompact with quality issues. Later, each nameplate had to have its own SUV. And there was confusing overlap; Pontiac's Firebird Trans Am and Chevy's Camaro are just one example of identical cars under two brands in the GM portfolio. As a result, the nameplate brands struggled for identity, with the possible exception of Pontiac (which had always supported associations like power and energy). Efforts to revive Oldsmobile with the Aurora subbrand failed; when it became clear that three mid-tier nameplates could not be justified, Oldsmobile was sacrificed.

• • •

This chapter continues the thrust of the last chapter—namely, moving from justifying the addition of brands and subbrands to the creation of focus and clarity by eliminating them or dialing them down. In that light, some very different questions are asked. How can you reduce the number of brands and customer offerings? How do you create a limited number of platform brands and leverage them? Instead of looking at adding and employing brands, we will consider deleting brands or reducing their roles and responsibilities. Instead of adding product variants and complicating the offering space, we will seek to develop brand-driven simplicity.

In this chapter, we address two problems. First, are there too many brands? Have brand proliferation and overlapping offerings created a lack of focus, a diffusion of brand-building efforts, and confusion in the marketplace? How many brands have significant driver roles? How can they be prioritized? Which are the strategic brands? Second, are there too many product or service variants? Have line extension programs developed so many variants, so many options, that the decision process is confusing, annoying, or worse? Is there a brand-driven solution to the resulting cluttered decision process?

TOO MANY BRANDS?

Too many firms "discover" that their portfolio contains too many brands, the consequences of which can range from inefficiency and confusion to paralysis in managing the portfolio. An overbranded portfolio can result in strategic brands losing equity and market position because marginal brands are absorbing brand-building dollars and, worse, managerial talent. Managers simply follow an instinct to solve problems rather than exploiting opportunities, and too many marginal brands create a host of problems.

An overbranded portfolio can also result in debilitating confusion. Rather than clarity, there may be brands with complex branding structures that lack logic and consistency. Some brands may reflect product types, others price or value, and still others customer types or applications. The branded offerings may even overlap. The totality simply reflects a mess; customers have a hard time understanding what is being offered and what to purchase. Even employees may be confused.

How can it happen? How does an organization become so undisciplined that brands proliferate? To provide a remedy, it is well worth looking at the causes.

The prime culprit is usually the process. There should be discipline behind the branding process, including a group within the organization with authority to approve the introduction of new or acquired brands and subbrands. The decision to add a new brand or subbrand should be based on two questions:

- Is the business associated with the new brand or subbrand substantial enough and will it have a long enough life to justify creating or maintaining a brand?
- Would the use of any existing brand inhibit or even detract from the promise of the offering of the other ones, or result in that brand being damaged or diluted?

The decision to retain an acquired or existing brand involves slightly different questions:

- Is the business associated with the acquired or existing brand or subbrand substantial enough, and does it have a long enough life to justify creating or maintaining a brand?
- Can brand equity from the acquired or existing brand or subbrand be transferred to another brand within the portfolio with a justifiable budget without putting that brand at risk?

The process to screen brand additions and deletions can fail in several ways. The most certain failure occurs when there is, in fact, no process at all. Brands and subbrands are added and/or retained in an ad hoc, uncontrolled manner with little concern for the total brand portfolio going forward. This is especially common in the decentralized organizational structure to which most firms adhere. When a business unit manager is empowered to be entrepreneurial and judged by the unit's profitability over time, it is difficult to then remove one of the strategic levers—namely, the brand strategy—from his or her arsenal. It is, of course, possible to develop brand discipline within a decentralized operation if the will is there and the brand talent is available, but too often one or both of these is lacking.

In other contexts, the process is there, but mistakes are made. The prospects for a new business are overestimated, for example, as predictions of customer demand simply turn out to be wrong. People within organizations charged with coming up with a new product or even new product modifications in order to fuel growth are inclined to exaggerate the "newness" of the product, the sales prospects, and its potential for long-term success. They recognize, often correctly, that having a new brand or subbrand may make their argument for more product introduction resources more persuasive and may help the probability of success. Further, they have a parental feeling toward the product and the ability to create a new name is very satisfying, whereas assimilation into an existing family can be tantamount to having their child taken from its home.

When brands are acquired, the decision to drop an acquired brand is often not so easy. The acquired brand may have significant customer and market equity, based on performance and tradition, that can be difficult to transfer, particularly to a corporate brand that lacks credibility in the involved product-market. Further, organizational sensitivities may cause eliminating acquired brands to create tensions in an already difficult organizational merger. An acquired brand can become a symbol of people and an organization, and its equity may become exaggerated by those already threatened by the merger. The result can be a set of brands that in combination become unwieldy or overlap.

One solution is to simply reduce the number of brands and/or prioritize brands so that the key brands can be identified and thus supported in order to achieve their assigned roles. Unfortunately, there is no natural mechanism to get rid of or dial down marginal or redundant brands after they have outlived their usefulness. In government, some laws have a sunset provision whereby the laws go away unless the legislature renews them, but there are no sunset laws for brands. All brands develop patrons, and it is unusual for anyone in the organization to suggest dumping or even withdrawing support from a brand. The reaction is to avoid using political capital in such a struggle, or, sometimes worse, attempt to turn a losing brand around.

A case can thus be made for a periodic review of the brand portfolio, supported by an in-depth analysis. Just as thinning a forest makes it healthier because the remaining trees have more access to sun and nu-trients, so can pruning the brand portfolio. A brand portfolio review can precipitate decisions that are too easily put off, and it can deal with po-litical costs of making tough decisions in the face of turf issues. Closing a defense base is virtually impossible because of powerful local politi-cians, unless a neutral, bipartisan committee with no local ties provides an analysis and recommendations. Similarly, a dispassionate review of the portfolio by brand specialists can provide the same decision struc-ture and organizational cover when it is needed.

The Strategic Brand Consolidation Process

The goal is to create a comprehensive and objective process that will systematically review the strength and utility of the brands in the port-folio. Such a process, termed the *strategic brand consolidation process,* is organized into six steps, as suggested by Figure 10-3. The first step is to determine the relevant brand set to appraise. The second, developing assessment criteria, is followed by brand evaluation, identifying the strategic status of each brand, creating a revised brand portfolio strategy, and finally designing a migration strategy.

IDENTIFY THE RELEVANT BRAND SET

The brand set will depend on the problem context. It can include all brands and subbrands, of course, but often the focus will be on a subset or grouping of comparable brands. For example, an analysis for GM could include its major nameplates (Chevrolet, Pontiac, Buick, Cadillac, Saturn, and GMC). Another analysis stage could then be subbrands at-tached to a master brand; for Pontiac, the subbrands would be Vibe, Aztek, Bonneville, Firebird, Grand Am, Grand Prix, Montana, and Sun-fire. When brands are involved that share similar roles, it becomes easier to evaluate the relative strength.

BRAND ASSESSMENT CRITERIA

If brand priorities are to be established, evaluation criteria need to be established as well. Moreover, these criteria need to have metrics so that brands can be scaled. The process of making the process highly struc-tured and quantified is to provide stimulation and guidance to the dis-cussion and the decision process. There should be no illusion that the decision will default to simply picking a higher number. The criteria will depend on the context, but in general there will be four criteria, each with several subcriteria:

Brand Equity
- **Awareness.** Is the brand well known in the marketplace?
- **Reputation.** Is the brand well regarded in the marketplace? Does it have high perceived quality?
- **Differentiation.** Does the brand have a point of differentiation? A personality?
- **Relevance.** Is it relevant for today's customers and today's applications?
- **Loyalty.** Are customers loyal to the brand?

Business Strength
- **Sales.** Is this brand driving a significant business?
- **Share/market position.** Does this brand hold a dominant or leading position in the market?
- **Profit margin.** Is this brand a margin contributor? Or is the cost position or the market conditions such that margins are unfavorable?
- **Growth.** Are the growth prospects for the brand positive within its existing markets? Is the brand likely to gain share or participate in a growing market?

Strategic Fit
- **Extendability.** Does the brand have the potential to extend to other products, either as a master brand or an endorser? Can it be a platform for growth?
- **Business fit.** Does the brand drive a business that fits strategically with the direction of the firm? Does it support a product or market that is central to the future business strategy of the firm?

Branding Options
- **Brand equity transferability.** Could the brand equity be transferred to another brand in the portfolio by reducing the brand to a subbrand or by developing a descriptor?
- **Merging with other brands.** Could the brand be aggregated with other brands in the portfolio to form one brand?

EVALUATING THE BRANDS

Brands need to be evaluated with respect to the four criteria, and each criterion score can play a role in evaluating a brand. A total score, obtained by adding up the criterion scores, can be helpful when comparing brands, but any decision will require deeper analysis. Introducing weighting is an option, although refining the analysis is usually not worthwhile given its subjectivity.

The profile of a brand across the criteria provides more detailed diagnostics. It can happen that a brand will have a place in the portfolio only if it meets some minimal level on one or two key criteria, no matter how it does overall. For example, a low score on strategic fit may be enough to signal that the brand's role needs to be assessed. Or, if the brand is a significant cash drain, then it might be a candidate for review even if it otherwise appears healthy.

The criteria scores will be based on the business and market knowledge of the brand team or perhaps some of their colleagues. If there are gaps in knowledge, it might be worthwhile to go outside the groups. Formal marketing research may be useful or even indispensable to confirming assumptions that might lead to some radical judgments about the brand portfolio.

PRIORITIZING BRANDS

The brands that are to live, be supported, and be actively managed need to be prioritized or tiered in some way. The number of tiers will depend on the context, but the logic is to categorize brands so that precious brand-building budgets are allocated wisely.

The top tier will include the strategic power brands—those with existing or potential equity that are supporting a significant business, or have the potential to do so in the future. The top tier can also contain strategic linchpin brands that can provide a point of differentiation for important business units. Identification of the strategic power and linchpin brands is the first step, because their identity indirectly makes a statement about the other brands.

One type of second-tier brands would be those with a specialized role, such as a flanker or silver bullet. Another type would involve a smaller business, perhaps a niche or local business. The third tier would be brands with even less equity or business size; these would be greater candidates for consolidation.

FIGURE 10-3
THE STRATEGIC BRAND CONSOLIDATION PROCESS

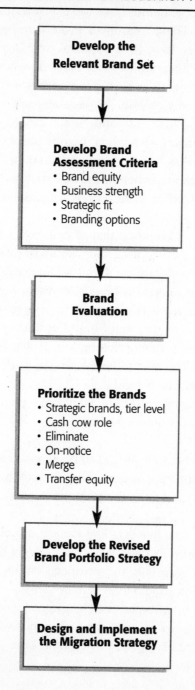

Like Unilever, Nestlé has long had brand portfolio prioritization in place. Twelve global brands are the tier-one brands on which they focus. Each of the global brands has a top executive that is designated as its brand champion. These executives make sure that all activities enhance the brand; they have final approval over any brand extensions and major brand-building efforts. Peter Brabeck, when he became CEO, elevated six of these brands as having top priority within Nestlé: Nescafé for coffee, Nestea for tea, Buitoni for pasta and sauces, Maggi for bouillon cubes, Purina for pet food, and Nestlé for ice cream and candy. Nestlé has also identified 83 regional brands that receive management attention from the Swiss headquarters. In addition, there are hundreds of local brands, which are either considered strategic (in which case the headquarters is involved) or tactical (in which case they are managed by the local teams).

Another category of brands is that of cash cows, brands that should be dialed down into a descriptive role with no resources behind them at all. Such brands are not eliminated, but no longer drain brand-building resources from more important brands. Further, they are less likely to get in the way of the total offering and create confusion in the marketplace. The dial-down or descriptor brand option works best when the brand name suggests a descriptive option. If that is not the case, the brand would need to be able to be known for its descriptive task without brand-building efforts behind it.

The remaining brands need to be eliminated, placed on notice, or restructured somehow, as outlined below:

- **Eliminate.** If a brand is judged to be ill suited for the portfolio because of performance, redundancy, or strategy fit issues, a plan to eliminate the brand from the portfolio is needed. Sell it to another firm, or simply kill it.
- **On notice.** A brand that is failing to meet its performance goals but has a plan to turn its prospects around might be put on an on-notice list. If the plan fails and prospects continue to look unfavorable, elimination should then be considered.
- **Merge.** If a group of brands can be merged into a brand group, the goal of creating fewer, more focused brands will be advanced. Microsoft combined its Word, PowerPoint, Excel, and Outlook appli-

cations into a single product called Office. The original product brands are now reduced to subbrands.

- **Transfer equity.** As described earlier, Unilever transferred the equity of Rave hair products to Suave and the Surf detergent products to All.

DEVELOP THE REVISED BRAND PORTFOLIO STRATEGY

With brand priorities set, the brand portfolio strategy will need to be revised. Toward that end, several brand portfolio structures should be created. These could include a lean structure (close to a branded house or set of branded houses) as well as a rich structure (more toward a house of brands, with several levels of subbrands) and the current brand portfolio structure. The most promising options are likely to be in between the extremes of the spectrum. The idea is to create two or three viable options, with perhaps two or three sub-options under each.

Each of the major brand portfolio structure options, together with its sub-options, needs to be evaluated with respect to whether it:

- Supports the business strategy going forward
- Provides suitable roles for the strong brands
- Leverages the strong brands
- Generates clarity both to customers and to the brand team

The most promising option still will need to be refined to make sure that the final brand portfolio structure is effective. The options that were evaluated were necessarily limited; thus, it often will be the case that none of them will represent the best final structure. Rather, it is likely that one of the options will be modified, or perhaps a combination of them will be most suitable.

TWO CASES: CENTURION AND SAFEWAY

A large manufacturing firm, which we will label here as Centurion Industries, went through a strategic brand consolidation process before selecting its portfolio strategy. The process started when the CEO observed that the existing brand portfolio in a major division was too diffused, and that future growth and market position depended on creating a simpler, more focused portfolio of powerful brands. The division had grown in part by acquisitions and now had nine product brands, only three of which were endorsed by the Centurion corporate brand. The nine brands served a variety of product-markets that could be roughly clustered into two logical groupings. One, which we will call the green business group, included five brands. The other, the blue business group, involved four brands. Competitors with less brand fragmentation and more natural brand synergy had developed stronger brands and were enjoying share growth.

In the green business group, a brand assessment supported by customer research was conducted on all five brands. One, Larson, represented the largest business, had substantial credibility in that business, and had high awareness levels. Further, it could be stretched to cover the other four areas, even though it had no current presence in any of those areas. It did have a visible quality problem, however, that was being addressed. The decision was made to migrate all of the green business brands to Larson and to make the quality issue at Larson a corporate priority. The first migration stage was to endorse three of the brands with Larson and replace the fourth brand, which drove a small business, with the Larson brand. The second stage, to occur within two years, was to convert all the brands in the green business group to the Larson name and add an endorsement by the corporate brand.

In the blue business group, the brand Pacer emerged from the brand assessment stage as the strongest, especially in terms of awareness, image, and sales. Because Pacer was in a business area closely related to that of the other three brands, using the Pacer brand for the entire blue business group was feasible. However, one of the four brands in the blue group, Cruiser, was an extremely strong niche brand with a dominant position in a relatively small market and delivered significant self-expressive benefits to a hard-core customer base. Thus, it was decided that migrating the Cruiser brand to Pacer would be too risky; the Cruiser brand would be retained, but the balance of the blue group would operate under the Pacer brand. Again, both Pacer and Cruiser going forward would be endorsed by the corporate brand.

The end result was a brand portfolio structure involving three brands rather than nine, with all three consistently endorsed by the corporate brand. The critical decision was making the tough call that in the long run the brand portfolio would be stronger if niche brands were migrated into one of two broader brands. There were emotional, political, economic, and strategic forces and arguments against each move. The fact that one exception was allowed made the overall case more difficult to argue and to implement. Critical to organizational acceptance was the use of an objective assessment template, which clearly identified the dimensions of the decision and facilitated the evaluation. It helped that much of each assessment was quantified from hard sales and market research data. Also critical was the strategic vision of the top management, because at the end of the day owners of some of the niche brands were not on board. Without a commitment from the top, nothing would have happened.

The Safeway grocery chain went through a similar process with its private-label program, which had grown to over two dozen brands. Most of these brands were very weak, given that they had few brand-building resources and had not found any way to capture any synergy. The decision was made to reduce this number to four, eliminating brands that did not have a good reason to exist. Safeway Select was the premium brand, usually positioned as equal or superior to the best brands in a category. Conversely, the "S" brands were the value brands, always priced among the lowest in each category. The other two brands, Lucerne in the dairy department and Mrs. Wright for packaged bakery items, were perceived to have significant equity and were retained. This brand rationalization decision was based on a realistic appraisal of the existing brand equities, the value proposition offered to customers, the economics of carrying extra brands, and the brand-building synergies of having the two base brands all over the store.

IMPLEMENT THE STRATEGY

The final step is to implement the portfolio strategy, which usually means a transition from the existing strategy to a target strategy. This transition can be made abruptly or gradually.

An abrupt transition can signal a shift in the overall business and brand strategy; it becomes a one-time chance to provide visibility and credibility to a major change affecting customers. When Norwest Bank acquired and changed its name to Wells Fargo, it saw the opportunity to communicate new capabilities that would enhance the offering for customers. In particular, Norwest customers could be assured that the personal relationships they expected would not change, but they could also

expect upgraded electronic banking services because of the competence of Wells Fargo in that area. The name change thus reinforced the
improved organization and the repositioning message.

An abrupt change in brands requires a positioning effort and substance behind the claims. The new brand promise will need to be communicated effectively and with credibility, otherwise the one-time
chance to make a statement will be wasted. The business strategy also
needs to be in place, or the effort will backfire. If, for example, the Wells
Fargo technology could not be delivered right away, the best course
would be to delay the name change until the substance behind the new
position was available.

The other option is to migrate customers from one brand to another
gradually. This will be preferred when the following conditions exist:

- There is no newsworthy reposition that will accompany the
  change.
- Customers who may not have high involvement in the product
  class may need time to learn about and understand the change.
- There is a risk of alienating existing customers by disrupting their
  brand relationship.

In the Centurion case, the ultimate brand name, Larson, was first
added as an endorser. Over time the endorsement was to become more
prominent and eventually become the master brand. Thus, customers
gradually associated Larson with the product without disturbing the
brand loyalty.

The transfer of the Contadina brand to Buitoni provides another illustration. Nestlé bought a pasta company in 1987 that was immediately rebranded as Contadina Pasta and Cheese. A year later, Nestlé purchased
Buitoni. As the two brands overlapped, the decision was made to make
Buitoni the global Italian brand for Nestlé. Although the Buitoni presence in the United States was weak, it had become the more authentic
Italian brand and was much stronger in Europe. Buitoni's Italian heritage
dated back to 1827 (when Mamma Giulia Buitoni first sold pasta com-
mercially), and its home and symbol, the Casa Buitoni, had established
itself as an ongoing source of new recipes and products.

The conversion stated in 1994 when Contadina was endorsed with
Della Casa Buitoni ("from the house of Buitoni"). Imagery and equity

FIGURE 10-4
THE TRANSITION FROM CONTADINA TO BUITONI

from both brands went into the package design. In 1998, the Buitoni endorsement was increased, and the visual symbol changed from a woman to the house. In 1999, the name was changed to Buitoni with a Contadina endorsement. In 2001, Nestlé sold the Contadina brand, clearing the way for the final conversion to Buitoni. Figure 10-4 shows the visual indicators of the transition.

Elevate the Corporate Brand

As was discussed in Chapter 9, the corporate brand is a candidate in some contexts to carry more responsibility in the brand portfolio when other brands need to be eliminated or dialed down. The corporate brand has several attributes that make it powerful and flexible. First, because it represents the total organization, and it has the potential to span everything connected to the firm. Second, the corporate brand is the natural home for any firmwide brand building, such as a World Cup sponsorship that would benefit all the firm's business units. Third, because it represents the organization, it lends itself to the endorsement role and thus does not need to be restricted to a product-branding role.

Recall in the last chapter the case of Schlumberger, the company that had acquired brands representing specialized oil-field services. These brands, such as Anadrill, Dowell, and GeoQuest, became endorsed brands that continued to drive customer relationships and organizational cultures. Schlumberger decided to migrate all of them to the Schlumberger corporate brand in order to reinforce the concept of delivering a systems solutions supported by a Schlumberger team and to focus the brand-building efforts behind one brand to create more impact.

Replacing Subbrands with Descriptors

One fruitful opportunity to achieve focus and clarity is to convert subbrands to descriptors. Three conditions make this option attractive: when the subbrands have little brand equity, when a descriptor that works can be found, and when the master brand can play the driver role in the resulting product brand. A descriptor is the ultimate in clarity and maximizes the leverage of the master brand.

Dell Computers analyzed its brand portfolio in 1999 and found that its business units serving market segments (such as homes, small businesses, and large enterprises) and product offerings (desktops, notebooks, servers, and so on) had succumbed to a perceived need to develop subbrands. The resulting brand proliferation had created confusion between customers and employees and greatly complicated the communication effort, from advertising to the website. At one point, there were separate brands with different logos for the same product being sold to the three major markets. There was no firmwide logic, such as having a brand that would represent value offerings throughout the line. And research showed that when customers wanted a specific item—for example, a router from Dell that would work with a particular piece of hardware—a subbrand often just got in the way.

The response was a decision to review the brand names and logos to see if they were clear and consistent and had created worthwhile equity. Figure 10-5 shows a set of eight brands in 1999 that had their own unique brand names and logos. Many of these brands, such as Giga-buys, E-Support, and Dell.net, had surprisingly low awareness levels—even with users. Further, a good percentage of those who were aware of the brands did not realize that they were part of Dell, or were confused as to what they did. Others, such as Premier Access, had a visual presentation that did not at all fit into the Dell family. By 2001, all brand names and visuals had been replaced by a simple, consistent style consisting of Dell, a vertical blue line, and a descriptor that indicated what was being offered. The result was not only clarity but a visual presentation with a family coherence that elevated and reinforced the Dell brand.

FIGURE 10-5
SIMPLIFYING THE DELL BRAND PORTFOLIO

Dell Brands—1999	Dell Logos—1999	Dell Logos—2001
E-Support	e-support DIRECT FROM DELL	Dell | Expert Services
Support.Dell.com	support.dell.com	Dell | Support Dell.com
Premier Pages	DELL PREMIER PAGES SERVICE	Dell | Premier Dell.com
Gigabuys	GIGABUYS	Dell | Software & Peripherals
Ask Dudley!	ASK DUDLEY!	Dell | Online Instant Answers
Premier Access	DELL Premier ACCESS	Dell | Premier Access
Dell Host.com	DELL HOST.COM	Dell | Hosting Services
DellNet	DELL net	Dell | Internet Access for Home

One value of a descriptor that precisely represents the offering is that it reduces the risk of overpromising. For example, when Dell competes with IBM, especially in services, it will often lack the scope of offering. A vague brand name representing the response to an industry problem (such as Dell Solutions) may imply that Dell's scope is equal to that of IBM's. The use of descriptive brands tends to manage expectations. It also reduces the communication and positioning challenge. In that spirit, by explicitly co-branding Dell/EMC, an enterprise storage offering, Dell suggested the value proposition through the name itself.

Creating a descriptor to form a product brand is not always easy. The challenge relates to the relevance issue addressed in Chapter 4: Does the descriptor represent what the customer is looking for? Sometimes the industry has created a category brand, like notebooks or servers. Some descriptors (such as Custom Factory Integration) are fairly clear. Others are not. Dell, for example, found that accessories were not as descriptive to customers as software and peripherals. Again, the answer is to identify the category that the customer is looking for in response to a problem or need.

Limits to Brand Rationalization

So fewer brands are better and the best structure is a single brand, perhaps the corporate brand (also known as the branded house). Not exactly!! It is not that simple.

To put the role of a master brand in perspective, we will review some of the reasons why it can be damaging to stretch a brand over too many products, as the discussion in Chapters 2, 4, 7, and 8 indicated. There is no free lunch. For perspective, some of the more prominent reasons include the following:

- A master brand might lack the credibility and authenticity needed. Black & Decker does not have the credibility to make power tools for the professional carpenter; a new brand DeWalt was needed to break through.
- The value of creating a brand around a segment or application requires a separate brand. Thus, P&G brands such as Head & Shoulders and Pantene have developed images with no compromises, because they are stand-alone brands.

- Similarly, when a niche brand has a tradition behind it and a loyal following, transferring that equity to a corporate brand may be difficult. Some prestige private-banking brands faded when they were acquired by a major investment house, lost their brand, and saw their customer relationships erode.

- A master brand may have connotations that make it unacceptable. The Clorox corporate brand could not be used on its food products, like Hidden Valley Dressing. Ford may be too corporate and have too much heritage for some of its target segments.

- A brand extension may diffuse a clear image and thus reduce the brand's equity, especially if some part of the brand's appeal is based on a product class association or perhaps excellence on some aspect of the product class.

The fact is, there are alternatives to using a master brand to drive the business across products and markets. As Chapter 2 discussed, a master brand can be leveraged with a subbrand or as an endorsed brand, and these options should always be on the table. In particular, one option is to leverage the master brand using linked brand names (such as the Citigroup-linked names, which include CitiMorgage and CitiBanking). In this approach, the various brands have some space, but the master brand still acts as a visible umbrella over them.

As strategists should always remember, the goal is to have strong brands in the key markets that support the business strategies going forward, reinforced by effective, efficient brand-building programs. This goal might not necessarily be enhanced by having the same brand across products. The key is what the brand stands for in the customer's mind and how that can evolve or change to take on a larger task.

TOO MANY PRODUCT VARIANTS: DECISION FATIGUE

Among the goals of a brand portfolio are leverage and clarity. Line extensions are important tools that can help to achieve both goals. A line extension is a different version of the product within the same product class and under the same brand; new features, flavors, materials, service packages, packaging, or sizes are all examples. The aggressive use of line extensions will enhance the leverage of the brand because they make the brand work in more contexts. Line extensions can also create so many options, however, that the result is confusion, frustration, and a failure to achieve the extensions' objectives.

To keep line extensions in perspective, it's useful to consider the major strategic and tactical rationales for using them, which include the following:

- *Energizing a brand.* As noted in Chapter 5, a line extension can revitalize a brand, giving it some news, something to talk about. Glade Air Fresheners began with aerosols and have since added solid forms (for continuous freshening), clip-ons (for the car), and a variety of more cosmetic packages.
- *Providing variety.* New entrees for the Healthy Choice frozen dinner line allow customers to change their daily eating routine while remaining loyal to the brand. New Club Med resorts allow patrons to enjoy a variety of vacation experiences.
- *Expanding the user base.* Cheerios was extended into a number of variants, starting with Honey Nut Cheerios, in order to reach out to buyers who prefer presweetened cereals. A convertible version of a car, a squeeze bottle for margarine, or a conveniently located mini-version of a fast food restaurant can attract new customers to the brand.
- *Blocking or inhibiting competitors.* A competitor can exploit holes in a product line where a brand chooses not to extend. Adding line extensions even if they make little financial sense can keep competitors from gaining a foothold in the customer base loyal to your brand. For consumer products, line extensions can result in more shelf space, which also tends to frustrate competitors.

While each individual line extension may be initially justified, though, sometimes the total package that emerges may be out of control. Some extensions may have sales less than expected. Others may not have been needed to retain customers. The net result is a high-cost line and the result is a profit drain on the firm that is not easily remedied by dropping the offending products, because they will have attracted loyal buyers.

Perhaps worse, the variety of options becomes overwhelming to the

FIGURE 10-6
CLUTTER IN THE SUPERMARKET

Choices in the Supermarket

	1999	1970
Crest toothpaste	45 SKUs (tubes and pumps of gel, paste, tartar control, baking soda, glitter for kids, mint or original flavor)	15 SKUs (mint or original, various sizes)
Orange juice	70 SKUs (six brands, four pulp levels, vitamin C, calcium, frozen, fresh squeezed, various containers)	21 SKUs (two or three brands, various containers)
Bagels	35 SKUs (ranging from sugar-free sesame to whole wheat cranberry)	4 SKUs (one flavor)
Philadelphia cream cheese	30 SKUs (15 flavors, various forms)	3 SKUs (one flavor)
Coca-Cola	25 SKUs (diet, cherry, caffeine-free)	6 SKUs (one flavor in different containers)

buyer. Some eye-opening statistics comparing the 1970 world with that of 1999 were compiled by Steven Cristol and Peter Sealey in their marvelous book, *Simplicity Marketing*.[4] The average supermarket contained 8,000 distinct product offerings, or stockkeeping units (SKUs), in 1970, versus more than 37,000 in 1999. Further, a shopping list containing orange juice, bagels, Philadelphia cream cheese, Crest toothpaste, and Coca-Cola could involve over 200 choices in 1999, compared to 41 in 1970. Figure 10-6 shows why.

It is not only the supermarket. The number of car models is overwhelming. In addition to some forty-five nameplates in the U.S. market involving well over two hundred brands, there are many options to select, starting with color, entertainment variations, and navigation aides. Cameras might be worse, with digital options on top of 35mm and bewildering variations in speed, focus, size, red-eye reduction, and so on. Olympus, for example, has 35mm Point & Shoot, 35mm SLR, and Advanced Photo Systems (APS). So far, so good. But then the Point & Shoot set breaks down further into Stylus, Stylus Delux, Accura, and Trip Series, with no real way to distinguish them.

Creating Clarity by Simplifying the Choice

How can the brand portfolio be reshaped to reduce the frustration and create clarity? One approach is simply to trim the options. This may seem risky and painful because sales (even if modest) are difficult to sacrifice, especially when a competitor is lurking. However, a decline in market share is not inevitable, especially over the long run, in part because efficiencies can lead to more effective brand building. In addition, excessive line extensions can adversely affect perceptions. One study of the computer industry found that market share was not positively associated with line extensions.[5]

Another approach is to bundle attributes into a limited number of options. Bundling options can reduce the confusion and customer frustration and therefore add value. They basically take the research and decision process out of the hands of the customer by recommending a set of predefined choices.

A classic example is the entry of imported cars into the U.S. market. When Japanese and German cars became factors in the United States in the late 1960s and early 1970s, one of several reasons for their success was the ease of choice. Instead of having to make dozens of option decisions and then wait for the right car to be built, the buyer of a Toyota or Honda often had two choices—standard or deluxe, and the color. Accessories and options were bundled into packages. Reducing the total number of options from thousands to less than a dozen made the process much easier and less intimidating. Further, it diverted attention from options to more basic quality and performance issues, a plus for the imports at that time. And in reality, all those options were not really so important and adversely affected delivery.

Other examples of this approach are easy to find:

- The iMac computer was introduced by Apple in 1998 into an extremely confusing complex computer space. The tagline, reflecting simplicity, was "One decision. One box. One price. $1,299." The computer contained in a single unit the CPU (usually in a box separate from the monitor for most other computers), a monitor, a keyboard, a network card, a modem, and speakers. In addition, the computer, with its famed Apple software, was ready to pick up, take home, and start using right away. The iMac brought Apple back from some bleak times.

- Colgate Total broke through Crest's long-time stranglehold on the toothpaste market. The Total subbrand combined a set of features into one brand. Toothpaste is a category that is particularly prolific with line extensions, as suggested by Figure 10-6 (or by a casual trip through the supermarket).

- The Healthy Choice brand provides a significant communication role. Most food categories could have information and products related to low sodium, low fat, low saturated fat, low sugar, and protein-fortified versions. As a result, customers would have to cope with brands with five or more subbrand descriptors. The Healthy Choice label saves all that effort. Although it doesn't communicate whether the product excels on one of the specific nutritional dimensions, it conveys that within reason and taste constraints, the product will be relatively healthy. For most consumers, that is exactly what they are looking for, and they are willing to compromise on the details.

- The name of the One-A-Day brand of vitamins says it all in an extremely complex category. Even experts who obsess about studies and theories seem confused regarding the best blend of vitamins. The One-A-Day combination may not be totally optimal, but it probably is close enough for buyers so that they do not feel compelled to do research. Of course, even One-A-Day now has several versions (such as for women, and for people over fifty), but even choosing among those seems simple compared to the task of working with individual vitamins.

- The Magellan Fund, the star of the Fidelity Fund Family, provides an alternative to sorting through Fidelity's many other variations (Fidelity Small Cap, Fidelity Large Cap Growth, and so on). Magellan has a clear philosophy and track record that save a lot of analysis and worry.

Issues in Exerting Control over Line Extensions

When it comes to line extensions, how many are too many? How many line extensions are optimal? How do you avoid getting too many? And how do you cut back? The answers are not easy, but considering the following questions and related issues will help the process.

1. What are the economics of an individual line extension? Does the marginal revenue support the marginal cost? Ultimately, line extensions that have small sales and profits should be candidates for elimination unless there are other compelling reasons for them to be retained.

The accounting system will usually provide a base answer, although the sales going forward are the key issue. Recent sales trends are relevant to predicting, but there is no substitute for understanding the underlying customer and market dynamics that could drive sales. It is also necessary to project costs and be aware of cost drivers, whether they are raw materials or technology.

2. What is adequate product line breadth? What is perceived by customers to be an extensive product line breadth? Customers may prefer a more complete product lineup, so that when the line is squeezed down the brand becomes less attractive. A frozen dinner, for example, might have more affinity to Swanson's with a wide variety available. If the scope of options was limited, the appeal of Swanson's might become less. Similarly, a buyer of industrial tools may desire a brand with a full line so he or she can go to one source for a complete solution. The absence of a product variant thus can become a reason to go to a competitor.

The issue, then, is what constitutes a complete product line. What product variant will be so valued that its absence will imply that the line is deficient? This analysis is tricky for two reasons. First, the answer is likely to be a moving target, because competitors are likely to introduce variants that can change perceptions of completeness. New dinner varieties from Banquet might change perceptions of the Swanson line. Similarly, a maker of saws and drills could come up with some sizes that might broaden the definition of a complete line of tools. Second, it may be hard for market experts or customers to define a complete line. As the line narrows, market stresses might build up, but where a brand crosses the line to become less of a complete supplier is always difficult to determine.

3. Is there a competitor threat that line extensions address? Will competitors be willing or able to exploit a gap in the product line to enter or improve their position? Is the niche represented by the line extension relevant enough to the market to support a viable market position? If, for example, a line extension represents an attribute or segment that could be the basis for a new position, the risk of foregoing the extension will be greater. If the niche is truly a small, stagnant market segment, the danger of foregoing the extension is much less.

4. Has the line extension accomplished its task of creating a burst of energy and so now should be retired? Some firms making products like athletic shoes (Nike), cereal (General Mills), ice cream (Dreyer's), Japanese beer (Kirin), and pet food (Purina) have a business strategy, termed *strategic opportunism,* that involves creating line extensions to capitalize on an emerging application or market trend. These line extensions are designed from the outset to have a limited life, then be phased out. Their goal is to create energy and news. Such a strategy can be a way to view and manage line extensions.

5. How confused or frustrated are customers with the decision process? Do they understand the options, and are they able to find their preferred choice easily with transparent information? Or do they throw up their hands in frustration and either go to another brand or become irritated?

Customer research is usually needed to address this problem. Exploring whether they understand the choice structure is one tack; is it perceived to be logical and understandable? For example, if a toothpaste has a series of clear descriptive subbrands (mint, tartar control, whitening, etc.), then at least the customer will understand the options. Another is whether the choice structure is perceived as not only clear but helpful. Still another is whether the firm is perceived as a leader and innovator because of the extensive product line, or simply greedy and/or unfocused.

6. Is there a branding solution to the product line breadth problem? Is there a brand like Colgate Total that can satisfy most of the market and therefore reduce the complexity?

STRATEGIC BRAND CONSOLIDATION

There is a natural bias toward adding brands, subbrands, and line extensions to capture niche opportunities and to build brand platforms. Unfortunately, though, it is easier to add than subtract. Brands and line extensions that have lost their purpose or will never be viable should be deleted, phased out, dialed down, or combined with other brands or offerings. Organizations, however, instinctively want to solve a brand problem by turning it around; another painless option is benign neglect. No matter how dismal the brand's future is, it is likely that some person's latitude of management is related to the brand, and he or she will resist it becoming a target for demise. There is rarely a brand killing champion willing to battle these organizational biases.

There are two implications in all this. First, new brands, subbrands, and line extensions should be added only when they are truly justified. There should be sunset rules, or an understanding as to what conditions should prompt a decision to kill or dial down the brand or line extension. The trigger point may be a failure to support a business, or the fact that its purpose is over because the trend or promotion that prompted it has ended.

A second implication is that, periodically, it is healthy to take a close look at the brands and line extensions in the brand family to evaluate their roles and their performance. Weak brands, brands that no longer fit the strategy, or disappointing line extensions should be candidates for removal from the portfolio. Perhaps they could be phased out, dialed down, sold, or put on the shelf until needed in another context. The end result can be a healthier, more focused brand portfolio.

QUESTIONS FOR DISCUSSION

1. Conduct a strategic brand consolidation exercise for a subset of brands. What criteria set should be used? How do the brands stack up? What is the interpretation of the results? What changes are implied?

2. Evaluate your brands and subbrands with respect to whether they have significant equity. Could any be replaced with descriptors?

3. Look at the product offerings from the customer perspective. Are they confusing? Why? How could they be made clearer?

Epilogue: Brand Portfolio Strategy—20 Takeaways

1. Allocate brand-building resources. Allocation should be according to the roles brands play within the portfolio, not on the basis of the sales and profits they are now generating. Future power brands, linchpin brands, and silver bullet brands should receive adequate funding.

2. Understand the roles of subbrands and endorsed brands. A subbrand will allow some distance from a master brand, an endorsed brand more, and a new brand the most. How much distance is needed? Three questions are involved. Will existing brands enhance the offering? Will the offering enhance the brand? Is there a compelling reason to generate a new brand?

3. Link brand portfolio strategy to business and brand strategy. Brand portfolio strategy cannot be conceived or modified in isolation. It is intimately connected to the business strategy and the brand strategy. The business strategy will indicate the product-market growth directions, the value proposition on which the firm will compete, and the assets that lead to advantage. The brand strategy will include the brand identity and position of the brands in the portfolio, which will affect what roles they can and should play.

4. Consider portfolio objectives. An assessment of the portfolio strategy with respect to the objectives of enhancing portfolio synergy, leverage, and clarity and creating relevant, differentiated, energized brands should be done regularly. It can be accompanied by a portfolio strategy audit, which can generate portfolio options and issues.

5. Relevance is key. A brand needs to gain and maintain relevance, or no amount of differentiation and loyalty will matter. Relevance means that the brand will be considered for a product category or subcategory, and that the product category or subcategory will be needed. If people want an SUV, it doesn't matter if they believe you make the best minivan.

6. Strategies of trend responders differ from trend drivers. Trend responders maintain relevance by detecting and evaluating trends and adapting by changing the scope of the brand, or by using subbrands, endorsed brands, or new brands. Trend detection involves separating fads and talk from real substance. Trend drivers, who create new product categories and subcategories and manage their definitions and labels, need to have the right offering at the right time and support it with the right resources.

7. Branded differentiators can create strong brand positions. Differentiation, the engine that runs the brand train, is difficult to attain and' maintain in a mature market. One route is to use a branded differentiator—an actively managed branded feature, ingredient, service, or program that creates a meaningful point of differentiation for an offering over an extended time period. The Heavenly Bed, for example, is a branded differentiator for Westin Hotels.

8. Most brands could benefit from a branded energizer. This is especially true for established brands most of which are noticeably bland and tired. A branded energizer is a branded product, promotion, sponsorship, symbol, program, or other entity that by association significantly enhances a target brand. The branded energizer can be controlled by the firm (for example, the Pillsbury Doughboy) or by another organization (World Cup). In either case, the associations of the energizer with the target brand need to be actively managed over an extended time period.

9. External brands can be part of the portfolio and so managed. The use of a brand alliance can provide an expeditious and powerful response to an emerging market trend, allow the brand to stretch with less risk, and lead to the sharing of brand-building investment. Brand alliance partners should have associations that enhance the partner's brand and organizational compatibility. A big insight is that branded alliance partners are part of the brand portfolio, and their role and relationship to other portfolio brands should be managed.

10. A brand alliance should have a long-term perspective and supporting programs. A successful brand alliance usually is surrounded by programs so that its impact is fully leveraged. Further, it will tend to involve a long-term relationship so that the equities based on the brand alliance and organizational experience can be leveraged over time. However, dialing up the alliance means that the risk of disappointing a partner will be greater.

11. Leverage strong brands. A growth option is to leverage strong brands through extensions. Extension opportunities should be sought for which the brand will fit and add value through its associations and customer base. The extension should also enhance the brand by providing visibility, associations, energy, access to growth arenas, and communication efficiencies. A brand can be leveraged as an endorser, or as a master brand. As an endorser it can add credibility to an offering and benefit from the latter's associations and visibility.

12. Develop platform brands. Rather than conducting ad hoc brand extensions, it is strategically better to develop brand platforms with a vision of the ultimate future of the brand, a set of associations that can travel, and a planned program of extensions.

13. Leverage the portfolio into super-premium arenas. Brands that attempt to move up into the super-premium market in order to access margins and product vitality often lack sufficient credibility and self-expressive benefits. These issues can be addressed by removing the brand from the low end, by repositioning the brand to work vertically, by using a subbrand, or by creating a new brand.

14. Consider accessing value markets. Brands that attempt to move down to access volume and growth channels risk both unsuccessful offerings and brand damage. The danger can be reduced if the value offering can be separated from the other offerings through a subbrand or endorsed brand, or by having it apply to different product-markets. In some situations, however, the best option is to allow the brand itself to be repositioned as a value brand, or to create a new brand.

15. Leverage the corporate brand. A corporate brand can be a powerful master brand or endorser because it is uniquely suited to capture the organization's heritage, assets and skills, people, values, citizenship, and performance. While competitive products may be similar, organizations rarely are; corporate brands are thus a potential source of differentiation. A corporate brand will be most effective when it stands for something meaningful to the customer. Being big and successful usually is not enough.

16. Actively manage the corporate brand. A corporate brand is inherently large and ponderous and is often used by many decentralized business groups. Thus, active management of the corporate brand will be needed to address such challenges as maintaining relevance, avoiding negatives, managing the brand in different contexts, and making the brand identity happen.

17. A new name may not be the answer. Do not fall for the illusions that a name change will by itself change associations, that a new globally available name with acceptable associations can be found, and/or that brand equity can be transferred to a new name with a reasonable budget.

18. Focus brand-building resources. Microsoft's goal, for example, is to invest in building the fewest number of the strongest brands needed to cover and compete in all desired markets. Resist adding new brands that are not needed, and be disciplined about removing existing brands from the portfolio if they are not needed.

19. Get rid of or dial down weak brands. If a brand or subbrand is weak even if it has had a significant life, consider treating it as a descriptor or even eliminating it. Don't manage under the illusion that a brand has developed equity and a following when it has not.

20. Create clarity of offerings. Make sure that an offering has clarity to both customers and employees. Confusion is a signal that the current portfolio strategy is not working.

NOTES

CHAPTER 1. BRAND PORTFOLIO STRATEGY

1. Katrina Brooker, "The UnCEO," *Fortune,* September 16, 2002, pp. 88–96.

2. Sam Hill and Chris Lederer, *The Infinite Asset,* Boston: Harvard Business School Press, 2001.

CHAPTER 2. THE BRAND RELATIONSHIP SPECTRUM

1. *Business Week,* August 5, 2002.

2. John Saunders and Fo Guoqun, "Dual Branding. How Corporate Names Add Value," *Journal of Product and Brand Management,* Vol. 6, No. 1, 1997, pp. 40–47.

3. Berry Khermouch, "Call It the Pepsi Blue Generation," *Business Week,* February 3, 2003, p. 96

4. Interview with Mr. Eric Kim, global marketing manager for Samsung, April 2003.

CHAPTER 3. INPUTS TO BRAND PORTFOLIO DECISIONS

1. Based on the Nikkei BP annual survey of some 1,200 brands in Japan, 2001 and 2002.

2. The Techtel tracking data documents the polarization. For a description of the Techtel database, see Techtel.com.

3. Information on this section is based on the Citigroup website and Citigroup and Citicorp annual reports from 1999 to 2002.

4. David A. Aaker, *Developing Business Strategies* (7th ed.), New York: The Free Press, 2004.

5. Scott M. Davis and Michael Dunn, *Building the Brand-Driven Business,* San Francisco: Jossey-Bass, 2002, p. 41.

6. Spenser E. Ante, "The New Blue," *Business Week,* March 17, 2003, pp. 79–88.

7. For a detailed description of brand identity and position, see David A. Aaker, *Building Strong Brands,* New York: The Free Press, 1996; David A. Aaker and Erich Joachimsthaler, *Brand Leadership,* New York: The Free Press, 2000.

CHAPTER 4. BRAND RELEVANCE

1. Sonia Reyes, "Muscling In: Clif Bar Pumps First TV; Eyes Athletes, Noshers on the Run," *Brandweek,* December 4, 2000, p. 7.

2. Stephanie Thompson, "Yoplait's Revenge Is Portable Yogurt That Kids Slurp Up," *Advertising Age,* September 12, 2000, p. 28.

3. From the Siebel website 2003.

4. Juliet E. Johansson, Chandru Krishnamurthy, and Henry E. Schlissberg, "Solving the Solutions Problem," *McKinsey Quarterly,* No. 3, 2003, pp. 117–125.

5. Andy Serwer, "Why Handheld Cereal Is So Hot," *Fortune,* October 14, 2002, p. 48.

6. Howard Schultz, *Pour Your Heart Into It,* New York: Hyperion, 1997, pp. 118–120.

7. Asahi Beer website, 2003.

8. Pallavi Gogoi and Michael Arndt, "Hamburger Hell," *Business Week,* March 3, 2003, pp. 104–108.

9. David Grainger, "Can McDonald's Cook Again?" *Fortune,* April 14, 2003, pp. 120–129.

10. Information for this section is drawn from John Gorham, "Charles Schwab, Version 4.0," *Forbes,* January 8, 2001, pp. 89–94; Schwab annual reports for 2000, 2001, and 2002; and the Schwab website.

11. Mita Sujan, "Consumer Knowledge: Effects on Evaluation Strategies Mediating Consumer Judgments," *Journal of Consumer Research,* June 1985, pp. 31–46.

12. James Daly, "Sage Advice—Interview with Peter Drucker," *Business 2.0,* August 22, 2000, pp. 134–144.

13. Louis V. Gerstner, Jr., *Who Says Elephants Can't Dance?* New York: Harper-Business, 2002, p.271.

14. For an extensive discussion of this issue, see David A. Aaker, *Developing Business Strategies* (6th ed.), New York: Wiley & Sons, 2001, Chapter 8.

Chapter 5. Energizing and Differentiating the Brand

1. Humphrey Taylor, "Sony Retains Number One Position in the Harris Poll Annual 'Best Brand' Survey for Third Year in a Row," Harris Poll, July 2002.

2. Interview with Mr. Idei conducted by David Aaker and Hotaka Katahira, March 1998.

3. Eryn Brown, "Sony's Big Bazooka," *Fortune,* December 30, 2002, p. 114.

4. Kenneth Hein, "When Is Enough Enough?" *Brandweek,* December 2, 2002, p. 27.

5. Scott M. Davis and Michael Dunn, *Building the Brand-Driven Business,* San Francisco: Jossey-Bass, 2002, p. 36.

6. Sony financial statements for the fiscal year ending March 31, 2003.

7. Stuart Agris, presentation to Stanford University, March 2001.

8. Todd Wasserman, "Canon Touts 'Digic' as Digital Camera's Best Friend," *Brandweek,* May 12, 2003, p. 12.

9. Jack Neff, "Pampers," *Advertising Age,* August 16, 2001, p. S4.

10. Gregory S. Carpenter, Rashi Glazer, and Kent Nakamoto, "Meaningful Brands from Meaningless Differentiation: The Dependence on Irrelevant Attributes," *Journal of Marketing Research,* August 1994, pp. 339–350.

11. "Tiny Targets," *Advertising Age,* January 21, 2002, p. 14.

12. Barry Khermouch, "Call It the Pepsi Blue Generation," *Business Week,* February 3, 2003, p. 96.

13. Jack Neff, "P&G Cosmetics Save Face," *Advertising Age,* April 15, 2002, pp. 1, 43.

14. Norihiko Shirouzu, "This Is Not Your Father's Toyota," *Wall Street Journal,* March 26, 2002, p. B1.

15. From Robert Hanson, "Angostura's Past Helps Revive Bitters," *Adweek's Marketing Week,* May 23, 1988, pp. 53–55.

CHAPTER 6. ACCESSING STRATEGIC ASSETS: BRAND ALLIANCES

1. Judann Pollak and Pat Sloan, "ANA: Remember Consumers," *Ad Age,* October 14, 1996, p. 20.

2. Akshay R. Rao and Robert W. Ruekert, "Brand Alliances as Signals of Product Quality," *Sloan Management Review,* Fall 1992, p. 90.

3. Paul F. Nunes, Stephen F. Dull, and Patrick D. Lynch, "When Two Brands Are Better Than One," *Outlook,* 2003, Number 1, pp. 11–23.

4. Bernard L. Simonin and Julie A. Ruth, "Is a Company Known by the Company It Keeps? Assessing the Spillover Effects of Brand Alliances on Consumer Brand Attitudes," *Journal of Marketing Research,* February 1998, pp. 30–42.

5. Kalpesh Kaushik Desai and Kevin Lane Keller, "The Effects of Ingredient Branding Strategies on Host Brand Extendability," *Journal of Marketing,* January 2002, pp. 73–93.

6. Kevin Lane Keller, *Strategic Brand Management* (2nd ed.), Saddle River, NJ: Prentice-Hall, 2003, p. 317.

7. James Crimmins and Martin Horn, "Sponsorship: From Management Ego Trip to Marketing Success," *Journal of Advertising Research,* July-August 1996, pp. 11–21.

8. Ibid.

9. Ed Garsten, "Youthful Buyers Wanting Rendezvous with Buick," Associated Press, July 23, 2002.

10. Rachel Miller, "Sales Promotion," Haymarket Publishing Services, February 3, 2000, p. 1.

11. "Lifestyle Brands Get Smarter," *Brand Strategy,* July 26, 2002, p. 26.

CHAPTER 7. LEVERAGING THE BRAND INTO NEW PRODUCT-MARKETS

1. David C. Court, Mark G. Leiter, and Mark A. Loch, "Brand Leverage," *McKinsey Quarterly,* 1999, No. 2, pp. 100–110.

2. Gillian Oakenfull, Edward Blair, Betsy Gelb, and Peter Dacin, "Measuring Brand Meaning," *Journal of Advertising Research,* September/October, 2000, p. 43–53.

3. Adapted from Figure 3 in Edward M. Tauber, "Brand Franchise Extension: New Product Benefits from Existing Brand Names," *Business Horizons, 47,* March-April 1981, pp. 36–41.

4. David A. Aaker and Kevin Lane Keller, "Consumer Evaluations of Brand Extensions," *Journal of Marketing, 54,* January 1990, pp. 27–41.

5. Paul A. Bottomley and Stephen J. S. Holden, "Do We Really Know How Consumers Evaluate Brand Extensions? Empirical Generalizations Based on Secondary Analysis of Eight Studies," *Journal of Marketing Research,* November 2001, pp. 494–500.

6. Aaker and Keller, op. cit.

7. Bottomley and Holden, op. cit.

8. Susan M. Broniarczyk and Joseph W. Alba, "The Importance of the Brand in Brand Extension," *Journal of Marketing Research,* May 1994, pp. 214–228.

9. Aaker and Keller, op. cit.

10. Sandra J. Milberg, C. Whan Park, and Michael S. McCarty, "Managing Negative Feedback Effects Associated with Brand Extensions: The Impact of Alternative Branding Strategies," *Journal of Consumer Psychology,* 6 (2), 1997, 119–140.

11. Richard R. Klink and Daniel C. Smith, "Threats to the External Validity of Brand Extension Research," *Journal of Marketing Research,* August 2001, pp. 326–335.

12. Mary Sullivan, "Measuring Image Spillovers in Umbrella Branded Products," *Journal of Business,* July 1990, pp. 309–329.

13. Al Ries and Jack Trout, *Positioning: The Battle for Your Mind,* New York: McGraw-Hill, 1985.

14. Al Ries and Laura Ries, *The 22 Immutable Laws of Branding,* New York: HarperBusiness, 1998, p. 9.

15. Peter A. Dacin and Daniel C. Smith, "The Effect of Brand Portfolio Characteristics on Consumer Evaluations of Brand Extensions," *Journal of Marketing Research,* June 1994.

CHAPTER 8. PARTICIPATING IN UPSCALE AND VALUE MARKETS

1. Information for this section was drawn from the Marriott and Holiday Inn websites.

2. Carol M. Motley and Srinivas K. Reddy, "Moving Up or Moving Down: An Investigation of Repositioning Strategies," Working Paper 93-363, College of Business Administration, University of Georgia, 1993.

3. Johan Arndt, "Role of Product Related Conversation in the Diffusion of a New Product," *Journal of Marketing Research,* 3 (August), 291–295.

4. David Aaker and Kevin Lane Keller, "The Effects of Sequential Introduction of Brand Extensions," *Journal of Marketing Research,* February 1992, pp. 35–50.

5. Barbara Loken and Deborah Roedder John, "Diluting Brand Beliefs: When Do Brand Extensions Have a Negative Impact?" *Journal of Marketing,* July 1993, pp. 71–84.

6. David A. Aaker and Stephen Markey, "The Effects of Subbrand Names on the Core Brand," Working Paper, University of California, Berkeley, 1994.

7. Gregory L. White and Shirley Leung, "Middle Market Shrinks As Americans Migrate Toward the High End," *Wall Street Journal,* March 29, 2002, p. 1.

8. Peter H. Farquhar, Julia Y. Han, Paul M. Herr, and Yuji Ijiri, "Strategies for Leveraging Master Brands," *Marketing Research,* September 1992, pp.3–10.

9. Sandra Dolbow, "Luxury Loves Company," *Brandweek,* October 8, 2001, pp. 39–40.

Chapter 9. Leveraging the Corporate Brand

1. Interview with Dell brand team, April 2003 and Dell website.

2. Private communication, 1997.

3. Information for this section was drawn from Julia Kirby, "Jim Kelly of UPS: Reinvention with Respect," *Harvard Business Review,* November 2001, pp. 116–123; UPS website, 2003.

4. David A. Aaker and Bob Jacobson, "The Strategic Role of Product Quality," *Journal of Marketing,* October 1987, pp. 31–44; David A. Aaker and Bob Jacobson, "The Financial Information Content of Perceived Quality," *Journal of Marketing Research,* May 1994, pp. 191–201; and linking attitude to stock return, David A. Aaker and Bob Jacobson, "The Value Relevance of Brand Attitude in High Technology Markets," *Journal of Marketing Research,* November 2001, pp. 485–493.

5. "Esso—Should the Tiger Change Its Stripes?" *Reputation Impact,* October 2002, p. 16.

6. The Verizon, Clorox, and General Mills programs are reported in Halo Awards, Cause Marketing Forum, Supplement to *Advertising Age,* July 28, 2003.

7. Ed Keller, "To Regain Trust, Faking Won't Do," *Advertising Age,* February 24, 2003, p. 28.

8. Pamela Kalafut, Jonathan Low, and Jonathan Robinson, *Measures That Matter,* New York: Ernst & Young, 1997.

9. Information for this section was drawn from Redwoodcc.com, the website of the publisher of *Kraft Food & Family,* 2003.

10. Presentation by Youssef A. Nasr, CEO of HSBC USA to the conference Winning Globally, at Stanford University, January 23, 2002; and the HSBC website.

Chapter 10. Toward Focus and Clarity

1. Jack Neff, "Unilever Culls Surf, Folds Brand into All," *Advertising Age,* October 14, 2002, p. 13.

2. Alan Clendenning, "Unilever to Sell 15 North American Brands, Including Mazola and Argo," Associated Press, May 31, 2001.

3. Information for this section was drawn from the Ford and BMW websites.

4. Steven Cristol and Peter Sealey, *Simplicity Marketing—End Brand Complexity, Clutter and Confusion,* New York: Simon & Schuster, 1999.

5. Barry L. Bayus and William P. Putsis, Jr., "Product Proliferation: Empirical Analysis of Product Line Determinants and Market Outcomes," *Marketing Science,* 18 (2), 1999.

INDEX

ABOUT THE AUTHOR

DAVID A. AAKER is the Vice-Chairman of Prophet, a brand strategy consultancy, Professor Emeritus of Marketing Strategy at the Haas School of Business, University of California at Berkeley, and an advisor to Dentsu, Inc. He is a recognized authority on brand equity and brand strategy. The winner of the Paul D. Converse Award for outstanding contributions to the development of the science of marketing and the Vijay Mahajan Award for Career Contributions to Marketing Strategy, he has published more than eighty articles and eleven books, including *Developing Business Strategies,* 7th ed., *Managing Brand Equity, Building Strong Brands,* and *Brand Leadership* (co-authored with Erich Joachimsthaler). His books have been translated into twelve languages. Cited as one of the most quoted authors in marketing, Professor Aaker has won awards for the best article in the *California Management Review* and in the *Journal of Marketing* (twice). He has been an active consultant and speaker throughout the world and is on the Board of Directors of California Casualty Insurance Company.

Marriott, Ritz-Carlton, Courtyard, and Fairfield Inn logos on page 229 reprinted with permission of Marriott International, Inc.

The images and text on page 261 are reprinted with permission of United Parcel Service of America, Inc. © 2003 United Parcel Service of America, Inc. All Rights Reserved.

Material on page 273 reprinted with permission of Schlumberger Limited.

Logos on page 307 reprinted with permission of Nestlé.

Logos on page 309 reprinted with permission of Dell Inc.

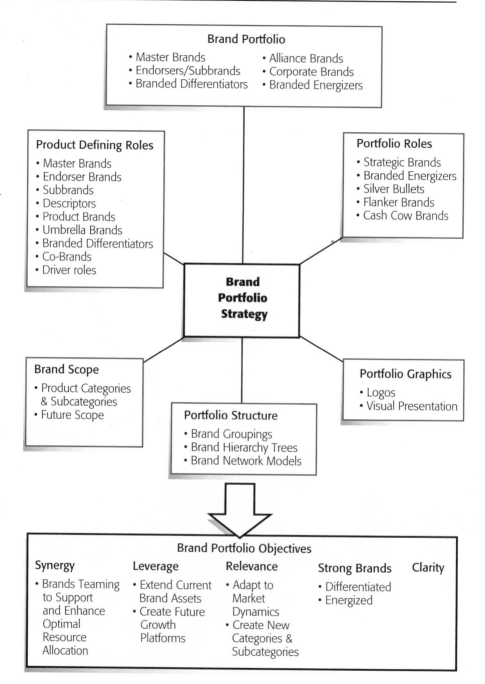

Brand Portfolio
- Master Brands
- Endorsers/Subbrands
- Branded Differentiators
- Alliance Brands
- Corporate Brands
- Branded Energizers

Product Defining Roles
- Master Brands
- Endorser Brands
- Subbrands
- Descriptors
- Product Brands
- Umbrella Brands
- Branded Differentiators
- Co-Brands
- Driver roles

Portfolio Roles
- Strategic Brands
- Branded Energizers
- Silver Bullets
- Flanker Brands
- Cash Cow Brands

Brand Portfolio Strategy

Brand Scope
- Product Categories & Subcategories
- Future Scope

Portfolio Structure
- Brand Groupings
- Brand Hierarchy Trees
- Brand Network Models

Portfolio Graphics
- Logos
- Visual Presentation

Brand Portfolio Objectives

Synergy
- Brands Teaming to Support and Enhance Optimal Resource Allocation

Leverage
- Extend Current Brand Assets
- Create Future Growth Platforms

Relevance
- Adapt to Market Dynamics
- Create New Categories & Subcategories

Strong Brands
- Differentiated
- Energized

Clarity